中國菜
CHINESE CUISINE

WEI-CHUAN'S COOK BOOK 味全食譜

Edited by Miss Huang Su-huei 黃淑惠編著

Assisted by Mr. Lee Mu-tsun 李木村協著

Translated by Miss Nina Simonds 席妮娜翻譯

封面圖片 **COLORED ENAMELWARE**
爲我國大清皇朝(1722—1735)雍正帝御
用之金胎琺瑯彩繪共蓋碗
Used by Emperor Yung Cheng
of the Ching Dynasty (1722-1735)

自從民國六十一年二月發行中國菜後；許多讀者曾要求發行中、英文對照本，但由於編排等原因，遲遲未能實現，迄今經過多次增修及創新，海內外讀者建議出版中、英文對照本的更是絡繹不絕。

為答謝讀者關愛的熱忱，並為便於參閱，乃經深入研究及考慮之後，決定在版面清晰及經濟適用的原則下，出版中、英文對照本。 在內容方面力求充實， 使宅合於讀者的要求，如有疏誤之處，敬請不吝指正。又最近市面發現有盜印本，不但由舊版翻印，且色彩模糊，請讀者購買時倍加留意，以免誤購。

Since the publication of the first English edition of "Chinese Cuisine" in February 1972, I have received overwhelming public demand for a Chinese-English bilingual edition. After repeated revisions and additions of the original edition, we have been able to meet the unending stream of requests from readers both at home and abroad.

To respond to such a warm reception by the readers, I have decided after careful research and consideration to put out a Chinese-English bilingual version to be used as a practicul cooking guide. It is hoped this volume will meet the needs of the readers in every respect. Your comments on the contents and the techniques are most welcomed and appreciated. I would also like to call to the attention of the readers the fact that recently pirated editions of this cookbook have appeared on the market. They can be detected by the inferior color printing. Your attention to this matter shall be appreciated.

黃淑惠 *Huang Su Huei* October 1976

中國菜
CHINESE CUISINE

■ 本書所用量器容量參照説明 ---------------------------- 1
■ 做中國菜・點必備調味品 ---------------------------- 2
■ 做中國菜・點必備用具 ---------------------------- 2
■ 烹飪慣用語説明 ---------------------------- 3
■ 筵席座次之排列 ---------------------------- 5
■ 筵席餐具之配置 ---------------------------- 5
■ 點菜與安排菜單之重要 ---------------------------- 6
■ 安排菜單之基本原則 ---------------------------- 7
■ 宴席菜及家常菜之份量與舉例 ---------------------------- 8
■ 常用蔬菜 ---------------------------- 12
■ 常用乾貨及罐頭 ---------------------------- 14
■ 特殊材料説明 ---------------------------- 15

Measurements and volume used in this book 1
Seasoning for Chinese cooking 2
Instruments for Chinese cooking 2
Culinary idioms 3
Arrangement of seating order at a feast 5
Arrangement of the dinner sets at a feast 5
Arrangement of food and menu 6
Basic principles of arranging of menu 7
Sample menus for banquets or ordinary meals 8
Commonly used vegetables 12
Commonly used dry materials and canned foods 14
Description of some other special ingredients 16
Helpful hints 17

● 雞　類 Chicken

雞凍　　　　Chicken in Aspic Slices 10
鹽水雞　　　Cold Salted Chicken Appetizer 29
脆皮雞　　　Crispy-Skin Chicken 32
棒棒雞　　　Bon-Bon Chicken 7
桶子油雞　　Red-Cooked Chicken Appetizer 6
葱油淋雞　　Steamed Chicken with Green Onions 28
炸八塊雞　　Deep-Fried 5-Spice Chicken 33
炸百花雞　　Stuffed Chicken Breasts 34
紙包嫩雞　　Paper Wrapped Fried Chicken 36
成都子雞　　Sauteed Chicken, Cheng Tu Style 41
核桃雞片　　Crunchy Walnut Chicken 35
宮保雞丁　　Stir-Fried Chicken with Dried Red Pepper 39
核桃雞丁　　Stir-Fried Chicken with Walnuts 40
紅油雞塊　　Cold Chicken Appetizer with Hot Sauce 30
遊龍戲鳳　　Stir-Fried Prawns and Chicken 38
栗子燒雞　　Stewed Chicken with Chestnuts 42
家鄉屈雞　　Country-Style Chicken 43
金華玉樹雞　Grilled Ham and Chicken Slices 31
蠔油扒鳳翼　Chicken Wings with Oyster Sauce 45
杏花酥雞翼　Stuffed Chicken Wings 44

● 鴿　類 Pigeon

| 炒鴿鬆 | Fried Minced Squab | 37 |
| 檸檬焗鴿 | Squab with Lemon | 46 |

● 鴨　類 Duckling

樟茶鴨	Crispy Smoked Duckling	47
香酥鴨	Crispy Pepper-Skin Duckling	48
芋泥鴨	Fried Duckling with Taro Stuffing	49
八珍扒鴨	Eight-Treasure Braised Duckling	50
酸梅子蒸鴨	Steamed Duckling with Plums	51
銀芽涼拌鴨絲	Roasted Duckling Salad	8

● 猪肉類 Pork

醬肉	Sauced Ham	13
肴肉	Tasty Chinese Ham Slices	14
回鍋肉	Double-Cooked Pork Slices	72
咕咾肉	Sweet and Sour Pork	58
蒜泥白肉	Pork Slices with Chopped Garlic	15
南乳扣肉	Steamed Pork in Preserved Bean Suace	74
梅菜扣肉	Steamed Pork with "Mei Gan Tsai"	75
京醬肉絲	Shredded Pork with Sweet Bean Paste	67
魚香肉絲	Stir-Fried Shredded Pork with Fish Flavor	68
榨菜炒肉絲	Stir-Fried Pork and Szechuan Mustard Green	70
肉絲拉皮	Tossed Pork and Egg Shreds	12
中式猪扒	Chinese-Style Pork Steak	56
葱爆里肌	Stir-Fried Pork with Green Onions	57
高麗肉條	Deep-Fried Pork Strips	59
燒金錢雞	Baked Pork Rolls	63
蜜汁火腿	Glazed Ham Slices	73
珍珠丸子	Pearl Balls	65
京都排骨	"Jing-Du" Spareribs	61
豆豉蒸排骨	Steamed Spareribs with Fermented Black Beans	60
印度煎排骨	India Fried Spareribs	62
沙茶肉串捲	Broiled Pork Slices with "Sha Cha Jiang"	64
碧綠野雞捲	Stir-Fried Pork Rolls with Broccoli	66
味全花瓜炒肉絲	Stir-Fried Pork with Pickled Cucumber	69
鹹菜花生炒肉丁	Stir-Fried Pork with Peanuts and Mustard Cabbage	71

● 牛羊肉類 Beef & Mutton

蠔油牛肉	Stir-Fried Beef with Oyster Sauce	76
紅燒牛腩	Red-Cooked Beef Slices	79
麻辣牛筋	Sliced Beef Tendons	16
青椒牛肉絲	Stir-Fried Beef with Green Peppers	77
干扁牛肉絲	Stir-Fried Beef with Vegetables	78
炒羊肉絲	Stir-Fried Lamb with Assorted Vegetables	80

● 內臟類 VISCERA

炒腰花	Stir-Fried Kidney with Assorted Vegetables	83
椒麻腰片	Kidneys in Hot Sauce	11
生炒猪肝	Stir-Fried Liver with Assorted Vegetables	82
燒焗鳳肝	Sweet and Sour Chicken Livers	53
雞腰窩渣	Pork-Brain Fritters	52
李公什碎	Li's Chop Suey	85
紅燒肥腸	Red-Cooked Tripe Sections	86
生炒雙脆	Stir-Fried Stomach and Kidney	84
菠蘿炒腎球	Stir-Fried Sweet and Sour Duck Gizzards	54
鹹菜炒肚絲	Stir-Fried Stomach and Szechuan Mustard Green	81
杏花炒雙條	Stir-Fried Chicken and Kidney Salad	55

● 魚　類 Fish

薰魚	Smoked Fish	96
糖醋魚	Sweet and Sour Fish	92
燒划水	Simmered Fish Tails	99
五柳鮮魚	Poached Fish in Sour Sauce	93
西湖醋魚	Westlake Fish	94
酥小鯽魚	Crispy Butterfish	97
紅燒黃魚	Red-Cooked Yellow Fish	98
豆瓣鯉魚	Braised Carp with Hot Bean Paste	100
清蒸海鮮	Steamed Pomfret	87
雞油海鮮	Steamed Pomfret with Ham and Mushroom Slices	89
糟溜魚片	Braised Fish Slices in Sauce	101
茄汁魚球	Fish Balls in Tomato Sauce	102
紅燒河鰻	Red-Cooked Eels with Chestnuts	124
韭黃炒鱔糊	Stir-Fried Eels with Chives	125
豆豉蒸魚	Steamed Carp with Fermented Black Beans	88
豉油王海鮮	Poached Fish with Shredded Onion and Ginger	90
麒麟蒸桂魚	Steamed Fish with Mushrooms and Ham	91
沙拉炆鯧魚	Smoked Pomfret with Mayonnaise	95
鍋貼鱸魚塊	Deep-Fried Fish Slices with Chinese Ham	104
貴妃斑魚捲	Stir-Fried Fish Rolls with Corn	103

● 蝦　類 Shrimp

鹽酥蝦	Stir-Fried Shrimp with Garlic	107
酥炸蝦	Deep-Fried Butterfly Shrimp	112
炸蝦丸	Fried Shrimp Balls	111
炸金錢蝦	Fried Golden Shrimp Balls	113
吉列明蝦	Butterfly Shrimp Slices	105
鳳尾明蝦	Prawns with Toast	106
乾燒明蝦	Spicy Stir-Fried Prawns	108
沙拉大龍蝦	Lobser Salad	5
四味龍蝦	Four-Sauce Lobster Slices	4

芥蘭蝦球	Stir-Fried Prawn Balls with Broccoli	109
玻璃蝦球	"Glassy" Shrimp Balls	110
青豆蝦仁	Stir-Fried Shrimp with Green Peas	116
腰果蝦仁	Stir-Fried Shrimp with Cashew Nuts	117
醋了蝦仁	Stir-Fried Shrimp in Sour Sauce	119
鍋粑蝦仁	Stir-Fried Shrimp over Crispy Rice	120
五彩炒蝦仁	Stir-Fried Shrimp with Assorted Vegetables	118
紙包酥蝦捲	Paper-Wrapped Fried Shrimp	114
紫菜蝦腿	Shrimp Legs with Nori	115

● 其他海產類 Sea Food

鹹蜆	Marinated Clams	20
拌蜇皮	Spicy Salted Jellyfish Salad	22
炸生蠔	Deep-Fried Oyster Rolls	131
豆豉生蠔	Sitr-Fried Oysters with Fermented Black Beans	132
鮑魚腰片	Stir-Fried Abalone with Kidney	122
鮑魚鮮菇	Stir-Fried Abalone with Straw Mushrooms	123
肉丸海參	Pork Balls and Sea Cucumbers	128
蝦子烏參	Stir-Fried Sea Cucumber and Shrimp Eggs	129
烏龍睡雪	Braised Stuffed Sea Cucumbers	130
生灼鮮貝	Fresh Scallop Slices with Oyster Sauce	17
生炒魷魚	Stir-Fried Squid with Assorted Vegetables	127
宮保魷魚捲	Stir-Fried Squid with Dried Red Peppers	126
麒麟麻鮑甫	Abalone Slices with Oyster Sauce	121
生筋田雞	Frog's Legs with Fried Gluten Balls	139
豉椒炒蟹	Stir-Fried Crab with Green Pepper	134
芙蓉炒蟹	Stir-Fried Crab Foo Yung	133
醋溜肉蟹	Stir-Fried Crab in Sweet and Sour Sauce	138
蟹肉草菇	Stir-Fried Crab Meat with Straw Mushrooms	136
蟹肉炒鮮奶	Stir-Fried Crab Meat over Fried Rice Noodles	135
蟹肉燒蹄筋	Stir-Fried Crab Meat with Pork Tendons	137

● 豆腐、蛋類 Bean Curd & Eggs

素雞	Vegetarian Chicken Loaves	147
拌干絲	Bean Curd Noodle and Celery Salad	23
鑲豆腐	Stuffed Bean Curd	143
麻婆豆腐	Ma-Po's Bean Curd	140
紅燒豆腐	Red-Cooked Bean Curd with Vegetables	141
千層豆腐	Deep-Fried Layered Bean Curd	144
鍋塌豆腐	Peking Style Fried Bean Curd	142
八寶辣醬	Eight Treasure Stir-Fried Vegetables	146
腐皮茄子	Eggplant Rolls with Chopped Pork	148
冬菇素腸	Stir-Fried Chinese Mushrooms with "Su-Tsang"	150
冬菇烤麩	Stir-Fried "Kau-fu" with Assorted Vegetables	151
冬菇扒豆腐	Braised Chinese Mushrooms and Bean Curd	145
三鮮百頁捲	Stuffed Bean Curd Rolls	149
三色蛋	Three-Color Egg Slices	154

蛋餃子	Golden Egg Dumplings	153
白油烘蛋	Golden Omelet	155
芙蓉炒蛋	Egg Foo Yung	156
洋葱炒蛋	Stir-Fried Eggs with Onion Shreds	157
土司鵪蛋	Shrimp Toast with Quail Eggs	158
虎皮鵪蛋	Wrapped Quail Eggs	159
洋菇扒鵪蛋	Braised Mushrooms with Quail Eggs	160
螞蟻上樹	Stir-Fried Bean Threads with Chopped Pork	161
東坡綉球	Shredded Egg Balls	152

● 蔬菜類 Vegetables

糖酥腰果	Crispy Cashews	18
五彩捲	Five-Color Rolls	9
麻辣黃瓜	Szechuan Gherkin Slices	21
芥末芹菜	Tossed Celery with Mustard Sauce	24
涼拌海帶	Cold Tossed Seaweed	25
廣東泡菜	Cantonese Pickled Vegetables	26
四川泡菜	Szechuan Pickled Salad	27
搶白菜	Stir-Fried Cabbage with Szechuan Peppers	164
雞油白菜	Stir-Fried Cabbage in Chicken Sauce	165
奶油焗菜胆	Baked Cabbage and Butter	166
奶油菜花	Stir-Fried Cauliflower in Milk Sauce	167
醋烹豆芽	Stir-Fried Bean Sprouts and Vinegar	168
豆芽雞絲	Stir-Fried Chicken Shreds with Bean Sprouts	169
涼拌豆芽菜	Spicy Bean Sprouts with Cucumber Shreds	19
醬燒筍	Saucy Stir-Fried Bamboo Shoots	176
季菜冬筍	Stir-Fried Bamboo Shoots	170
上湯鷺筍尖	Fresh Asparagus with Sauce	171
上湯絲瓜	Stir-Fried Cucumber	172
干扁四季豆	Dry-Cooked String Beans	175
蠔油雙冬	Stir-Fried Mushrooms & Bamboo Shoots with Oyster Sauce	177
魚香茄子	Fish-Flavored Eggplant	174
扒金銀菇	Gold and Silver Mushrooms	178
海棠百花菇	Stuffed Mushrooms with Shrimp Paste	181
鑲青椒	Stuffed Green Peppers	183
鑲萬年青	Chinese Black Mushrooms Stuffed with Chicken	180
豆豉鑲苦瓜	Stuffed Bitter Gourd with Fermented Black Beans	182
白玉藏珍	Winter Melon Surprise	173
干貝三色球	Scallops with Tri-Colored Balls	162
羅漢素菜	Stir-Fried Vegetarian Dish	179
四色蔬菜	"Four Kinds of Vegetables" Plate	163

● 什錦類 Appetizers

| 拼盤（一） | Assorted Appetizer Plate I | 2 |

拼盤 （二） Assorted Appetizer Plate II 3
柒星轉盤 Seven-Star Appetizer Plate 1

● 湯　類 Soups

三絲魚翅 Three-Flavor Shredded Soup 184
魚翅燒雞 Braised Chicken with Shark's Fin 185
燴鴨絲 Shredded Duckling and Assorted Vegetable Soup 186
羅宋湯 Beef Soup a la Lo Sung 193
酸辣湯 Hot and Sour Soup 187
黃魚羹 Yellow Fish Soup 188
肉粳 Meat Slices with Fish Paste in Broth 189
蘆筍濃湯 Fluffy Asparagus Soup 190
太極青雲 Green Peas and Corn Soup .191
當歸虱目魚 Fresh Fish and Dang Guei Broth 192
麻油雞湯 Sesame Chicken Soup 194
花瓜燉雞 Stewed Chicken with Pickled Cucumbers 195
冬菇燉雞 Stewed Chicken with Chinese Black Mushrooms 196
鳳足冬菇 Black Mushroom and Chicken-Foot Soup 197
川翼洋菇 Stuffed Chicken Wing Soup .198
洋菇鵪蛋湯 Mushroom and Quail Egg Soup 199
鮮菇蝦丸湯 Shrimp Balls in Mushroom Soup 200
清蒸粉蚌 Stuffed Clams in Broth 201
清湯合蝦 Stuffed Shrimp and Cucumber Soup 202
清湯如意捲 Egg & Shrimp Rolls in Broth 203
清湯三色捲 Three-Colored Rolls with Broth 204
如意魚捲 Steamed Fish Rolls with Broth 206
湯泡魚生 Fresh Fish and Vegetable Broth 205
原盅三味 Three-Flavor Steamed Soup .207
冬瓜火腿夾 Winter Melon Sandwiches with Chinese Ham 208
錦繡冬瓜盅 Eight-Treasure Soup in Winter Melon 209
排骨酥湯 Sparerib Soup 210
排骨黃豆芽湯 Bean Sprout and Sparerib Soup 211
蘿蔔絲鯽魚湯 Shredded Turnip and Fish Soup 212
榨菜細粉湯 Szechuan Mustard Green and Bean Thread Soup 213
菊花干貝 Stuffed Egg Flower Soup 214
豬腦蒸蛋 Steamed Pork Brain and Eggs with Broth 215
鮑魚豬肚湯 Abalone with Pork Stomach in Broth 216
砂鍋魚頭 Stewed Fish Head Casserole .217
砂鍋豆腐 Bean Curd Potage 218
砂鍋獅子頭 Lion's Head Casserole 219
什錦火鍋 Ten-Flavor Fired-Pot 220
一品燕窩 Bird's Nest Soup 221
（合計221種） (Total 221 Courses)

本書所用量器容量參照說明
Reference for the exposition on the
weights and measures used in the book

1 杯（1 飯碗）
1 Cup (1C.)
236 C.C.

1 大匙（1 湯匙）
1 Tablespoon (1T.)
15 C.C.

1 小匙（1 茶匙）
1 Teaspoon (1t.)
5 C.C.

台斤 Catty	英兩 Ounce	公分 Gram	磅 Pound
1	21	600	1⅓
	1	28.6	0.063

Seasoning for Chinese cooking

We frequently use 5 kinds of seasonings in cooking, such as salt, MSG, pepper, sugar and sesame-oil. Besides, wine, vinegar, cornstarch, fryoil etc. are also necessary.

做中國菜・點必備調味品

做菜時常用五味即鹽（或醬油）、味精、胡椒、麻油、糖，除此之外，酒、醋、太白粉、炸油，也是廚房不可缺少的必備品。

Soy sauce

Sesame oil

Vinegar

Cornstarch

Salt

MSG

Rice wine

Sugar

Black pepper

Fried oil

Instruments for Chinese cooking

Cleavers, chopping block, spatula, strainers, wok and steamers are basic instruments from which a wide variety of delicious foods can be made using roasting, frying, steaming or stewing techniques. Other tools such as a wooden bar for rolling dumplings, a sifter and hand-mixer are also employed in making Chinese snacks.

做中國菜・點必備用具

僅刀、菜板、鍋鏟、漏杓、炒鍋、蒸籠等數樣用具，足句多做炒、炸、蒸、燉、燴……等等多種美味菜餚，唯做點心得另備趕麵桿、篩子、打蛋器等。

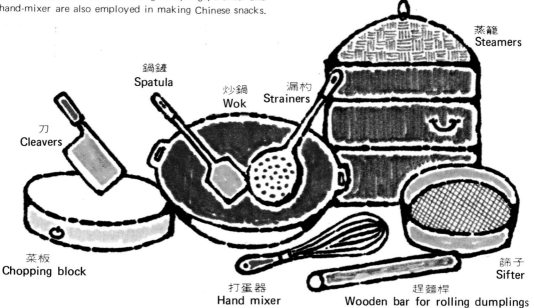

鍋鏟
Spatula

炒鍋
Wok

漏杓
Strainers

蒸籠
Steamers

刀
Cleavers

菜板
Chopping block

打蛋器
Hand mixer

趕麵桿
Wooden bar for rolling dumplings

篩子
Sifter

烹飪慣用語說明

烹調在我國向無份量之規定，亦無一定之時間，全憑經驗由己去摸索所得。本書盡其所能的把材料、佐料之份量及所需時間簡要例出，為使能更進一步了解起見，茲將調理時之工作要點及慣用詞大略說明如次：

Culinary idioms

In Chinese cuisine, cooking is a very subjective art; there are no definite quantities of any ingredient, nor any exact time limit for cooking any recipe. We encourage you to develop all of this personally, through trial and error. We have listed the basic information for the preparation of all dishes, as well as the ingredients involved, however we encourage you to revise according to your own taste. In order that you may further understand the practice, we give the significant points and explain some expressions, used often in Chinese cooking.

清洗材料
材料洗淨需漏乾水份。

CLEANING
Clean the ingredients before using, then drain and dry thoroughly.

炒
把食物置炒菜鍋內，翻攪至熟了，即曰炒。

STIR-FRYING
To put the material into a very hot pan over high heat and turn over and over. until done.

炒菜是速成之菜，故炒菜時宜將各項佐料調在碗內使用時，較方便。

Stir-frying is a very quick process. So it is advisable to prepare all of the sauces in advance, including the cornstarch and water used to thicken the final sauce.

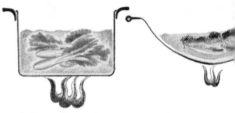

炒一盤菜，如遇使用多種材料，因其各材料性質不同，有些材料需經過泡油，煮熟或分開炒熟後再使用。

When several kinds of ingredients are used in cooking, the difference in tenderness of each ingredient will sometimes require that material to be cooked in oil, boiled or fried before mixing whichever method is used, the ingredient must be precooked till tender.

炸
把食物投入多量的沸油中炸熟謂炸。

DEEP-FRYING
To immerse the food in deep, hot oil.

先將材料調上味，並視其種類，裹上麵糊。

Prepare the material for frying, first the food must be soaked in the prescribed sauce, then it must be covered with the proper flour mixture.

油的份量要多，
注意，如果要炸
出炒鍋之六分滿

There should be p
of oil in the pan; en
to cover the mat
However if the ma
to be fried, is very

蒸
所謂蒸是把材料放蒸籠內，下放沸水，藉水蒸汽的熱力把食物蒸熟。

STEAMING
To put the material in a "steaming cage". which is then put in a pan containing boiling water inside.

先將水放入外鍋燒開。
Frist, put water in the pan and allow it to come to a boil.

宜水燒開後才把食物放入蒸熟
Then place food in cage and put into boiling water.

切材料
所配材料要切成同樣形狀，粗、細、厚、薄等均一，則燒出來的菜肴嫩度才會一致美觀。

CUTTING
All ingredients must be cut into the same size and shape, so that the cooked food will look uniform and have the same tenderness.

醃
鷄、肉、魚、蝦等要事先調上味，必要時，如能拌入蛋白及太白粉，則可增加其香嫩。

PRE-CONDITIONING
Chicken, pork, fish and shrimp must be soaked in the prescribed sauces (soy sauce, wine or cornstarch) to increase tenderness and deliciousness of food.

熱鍋
炒、煎、炸時，先空鍋燒熱，再倒進油，可防材料黏鍋。

HEATING THE PAN
The pan must be thoroughly heated before adding oil and then thoroughly lubricated with oil so that material will not stick.

以上準備妥當，將鍋燒熱後放油再入葱、薑、蒜等使其香味滲入油中，再把所要炒的材料及調好的調味料倒入鍋內炒拌，操作簡便迅速，且可防止火候過久。

When the preliminary preparation is finished, heat the pan and pour in oil. Add the onion, ginger or garlic and stir so that the oil will pick up its flavor. Then add the ingredients, with a few drops of wine, if desired, to enhance the flavor of the food. Add the sauce and stir-fry until all is mixed together. This entire process must be short and quick so that the food will not overcook.

當臨起鍋時，淋下數滴油，可增加菜肴之光澤，並有保溫之功效。

At this point, you may sprinkle a few drops of fried oil on the food. This will help to increase the brilliancy of the food and keep it warm.

浸過食物為準，但要含水份多，則以不超以免泡沫溢出危險。

contains much water, the should not occupy more n 60% of the pan, so t the oil will not splash

炸時先將油燒沸，如遇不容易炸熟者，將鍋暫時離火，以中溫或低溫，但榜出時要大火，並視其材料決定所需要的時間。

First boil the oil; remove the pan from the fire and when the oil has cooled to medium temperature, insert the material into the pan. Replace the pan over medium heat and cook until near-tender. Then turn heat to high and cook over high heat until done. This seals the flavor and ensures that the material will be completely cooked and crispy on the outside.

下鍋時如能同時下鍋，則榜出時宜一次榜起，所炸出來的東西才會一致。

All material put into the oil together, at the same time, must be removed at the same time, to maintain uniformity.

燉
所謂燉與蒸略同，外鍋內放水，內鍋放入食物及水或湯（注滿過食物）置慢火經過長時間，至食物煮軟）做出來的湯汁，非常澄清。

STEWING
Stewing is similar to steaming; put water in the outer pan and the material to be heated with water or stock to cover, in the inner pan. Cook over a moderate fire until food is tender. Soup prepared this way is very clear and clean.

溜、燴：汁或湯注入鍋中燒開，隨即加入經過、炒、炸，或煮熟之食物勾成濃稠狀，其湯汁有，糖醋汁、茄汁、醬汁、白汁、奶汁等。
燒、燜：將水淹滿食物，燒開後，加入調味料用中火或小火，將食物煮軟。
煮：將食物放入多量的水內，燒煮熟。
拌：凡不必再加熱，涼着或生着切了，拌上佐料即可吃的均是涼拌。
燻：用糖、木屑或茶葉上架鐵絲網盛放食物，四週窩蓋緊，加熱使煙與熱力慢慢把物烤熟或烤至上了茶煙之色與香味即曰燻。
烤：加熱在食物之四週，把物炙熟者即烤。

MIX-BOIL
To first put the sauce or soup into the pan by itself and allow it to boil. Then add the food. The amount of cornstarch in the sauce should be to your own taste; add more if desired. There should not be too much sauce.

MIXING
If no cooking is required, just mix together the ingredients after cutting. If ingredients have been precooked, allow to cool, then mix together; add sauce and serve.

SMOKING
To put food in an oven, or cover, on a grill over a fire. Then throw sugar, wood powder, or tea into the fire or oven so that the fumes will smoke the food and give it flavor.

ROASTING
To cook or bake food in the oven with all of the ingredients, until done.

FRYING
To cook food on each side until golden, in a little bit of oil.

筵席座次之排列

　　我國正式宴客筵席對座次之排列素為重視，向以朝向進門之一方為尊貴，靠近進門之一方（即面對尊貴之一方）則為主人座位，其座席位次因圓桌及方桌之排列不同而有所區別，但主要均為賓主聯翩，抵足而坐促膝談心，不使一人有冷落向隅之感，不似西餐多採分列方式，賓主相距較遠不足交談盡歡，茲各舉例於下而分別標示其席次：

Arrangement of Seating Order at a Feast

The seat which faces to door is always regarded as the seat of honor and the seat which is near the door (i.e. facing the seat of honor) is for the host. The seating orders vary between round tables and rectangular tables, but they are all designed to facilitate conversation between guests and the host. They are different from those of a western setting which is marked by a large distance between guests and host, limiting the possibility of their conversation. The various seating orders are illustrated and the seats marked as follows:

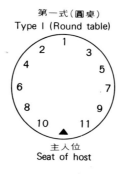

第一式（圓桌）
Type I (Round table)

主人位
Seat of host

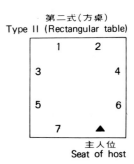

第二式（方桌）
Type II (Rectangular table)

主人位
Seat of host

（第三、第四兩式為客人與主人均為夫婦同時入席之座位）
(The type III and type IV are for the presence of both couples of guest and host)

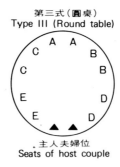

第三式（圓桌）
Type III (Round table)

主人夫婦位
Seats of host couple

第四式（方桌）
Type IV (Rectangular table)

主人夫婦位
Seats of host couple

筵席餐具之配置

　　我國筵席對餐具之配置，認為與菜餚有直接關係，故頗重視，凡杯、筷、匙、碟乃至碗、盤與酒壺、茶杯均有完整之系統配合，下列為筵席全部座客所用餐具及每一座客個人所用餐具之排列，特附圖片以供作參考。

Arrangement of the Dinner Sets at a Feast

Chinese pay much attention to the arrangement of the dinner set at a feast as they are directly related to the food and drinks. The cups, chopsticks, spoons, dishes and bowls, plates, wine pots and tea-cups are arranged according to a complete system. The arrangement of the dinner sets are shown in the following photos:

筵席全部座客所有餐具之配置圖
The arrangement of the dinner sets
for a whole table at a feast.

每一座客個人所用餐具之配置圖。
筵席進行時，可視情形撤去客人用過
之餐具而另換同樣清潔餐具代替。
The arrangement of the dinner sets
of each guest at a feast. As the
feast goes on, after using the dinner
set; it may be removed and replaced
with a clean one as required.

點菜與安排菜單之重要

　　點菜和菜單的安排，在烹飪方面是非常重要的，因此，菜餚應本着調協、融和與完整的原則，使彼此之間能有適當的調節與配合，否則，便會令人有牴牾、扞格之感，譬如我們宴客常有大宴、小酌和隨意便餐之別，即家庭之內，也因晨、午、晚餐和用餐人年齡以及時令季節之不同，於是烹調方法必須根據這些情況安排菜單，使品質的搭配腴淡適中、營養恰當，顏色優美，味道相宜，量的方面也得多少適中恰到好處。此外如用餐人的習性、嗜好以及環境和餐具等等，都與點菜和菜單安排有極度密切而重要的關係。如我們竟忽視了這一點，那麼對飲食的情趣、宴會的氣氛都會因而減色，在效果上說，這將是很大的失算了。

Arrangement of Food and Menu

　　The arrangement of food and menu is very important in cooking. Therefore, the food should be properly arranged according to the principle of harmony and completeness, otherwise it may create a conflict and be incompatible. For example, there are differences between a big party, a small gathering and a daily family dinner. There are also differences among breakfast, lunch and supper as well as the age of the guest, occasion and season. Therefore, the menu shall be arranged in accordance with these specifications in order to have a proper match, appropriate nutrition, beautiful color, fitting taste and adequate quantity. In addition, the surroundings and the dinner settings are closely and importantly related to the arrangement of food and the menu. Should we neglect this point, the atmosphere of the feast will be reduced.

安排菜單之基本原則

我國地域廣大，各處因地理環境與氣候不同，影響了飲食的味道，因此各地區的菜餚或點心，往往各具特色，儘管如此，但是宴客菜或家常菜的菜單安排，都應注意下列原則：

一、烹飪方法避免重複，應有變化：例如炒、炸、蒸、燉、溜、燴……等方式，在同一筵席或餐桌上儘可酌量調配，不僅使其外觀美麗，顏色調和，而且可因味道變化，促進食慾。

二、材料選配不可單調，應予調和：菜點材料大概不外魚、肉（包括各種肉類）、蔬果、與豆麵之類，經過烹飪便成佳餚，如選材適當，則互相襯托，各展所長，使人大快朵頤，百食不膩不厭。

三、味道清新，各具風緻：烹飪最重五味（甜、鹹、酸、苦、辣）調和，避免連續使用同一口味，才能使人味覺有清新舒暢之感，如果四樣菜餚中有了糖醋排骨，又有糖醋魚，那自然不夠理想。

四、色澤優美，配合適宜：我國菜餚向以色、香、味並重，而又以色彩列為首位，這是因為顏色配合適宜，未食之前，首先予人美感，當然這方面的條件很多，除了菜餚本身的色式應注意外，譬如夏季多用淡色系統，冬季則用濃色系統，而對盛用器皿的款式與色彩也應兼籌並顧，才能更為美化。

五、難易適中，前後有序：點菜應難易交替配合，均為難菜，則繁瑣費時，如均為易菜，則顯得單薄。同時出菜前後，應注意利用時間，以免屆時勿忙紊亂。

Basic Principles of Arranging the Menu

The food, drink and snacks of each area of China contain unique features becuase of the vastness of the region with a wide variety of tastes resulting from the difference in geographical environments.   However, the arrangement of the menu for both feast and family should pay attention to the following principles:

1. The various methods of cooking should not be repeated: for example, the many styles of cooking (i.e. sauteing, deep fat frying, steaming, stewing and braising, etc.) should be arranged not only to create a beautiful outward appearance, but also to stimulate the appetite with its varied tastes.

2. The selection of materials should be harmonious without repetition: the major ingredients should include fish, meat (beef, pork, etc.) vegetables, fruit, bean and wheat products. If properly selected, they will accent each other and provide for enjoyable eating.

3. The most important thing is the harmony of the five tastes: sweet, salty, sour, bitter and hot.   Repetition should be avoided to provide a fresh and pleasing experience to the palate.

4. Color and harmony of ingredients provides a visual effect.   Chinese food emphasizes a sense of beauty which properly matched ingredients create to stimulate the appetite.   In the summer a light colored pattern should be predominant, whereas in the winter deeper colors should prevail.   Even the style and color of the serving vessels should all be taken into consideration.

5. The dishes selected should be neither too easy nor too difficult to prepare.   When serving, the food should be arranged alternately according to the complexity of preparation. All complicated dishes would be too time-consuming to prepare, while all simple dishes would be too plain.   The menu arrangement should allow the cook time to coordinate the work comfortably.

宴席菜及家常菜之份量與舉例

中菜與西菜比較，前者在份量上的斟酌，似乎難多了，所以，應有一個標準，使它不致過多而浪費，也不致因過少而感到不足，目前餐館所用盤碗，大致分爲大、中、小三種，普通宴客筵席（十人至十二人）多用大盤（碗），菜爲十道或十二道，家常宴客如供六人進食，多用中盤（碗）四菜一湯（可視人數多寡，酌量增減）。本書所訂份量，係以十二人份和六人份爲標準，前者爲大盤（碗），後者爲中盤（碗）。茲將宴席菜與家常宴客菜各舉例如下：

Sample Menus for Banquets or Ordinary Meals

In comparing Chinese and Western cooking, the former is much more difficult to portion, therefore it is necessary to follow a model to make sure each portion is sufficient for the number of guests. Today, most restaurants divide their serving dishes and bowls into three categories: large, medium and small dishes. Usually a large size serving dish is adequate for a banquet meal of 10-12 guests. If there are 6 guests it is best to have about 4 medium-size dishes. The recipes in this book are proportioned for 10 servings, (large size dish), and 6 servings (medium size dish). Below are suggestions for banquet or ordinary meal menus:

宴席菜舉例

（例一）	（例二）	（例三）	（例四）
糖酥腰果	柒星轉盤	大　拼　盤	四　味　龍　蝦
椒麻腰片			魚　翅　燒　雞
棒　棒　雞	宮保魷魚捲	炒　鴿　鬆	醋　溜　肉　蟹
拌　蜇　皮	豆　芽　雞　絲		炸　蝦　丸
			清　蒸　粉　蚌
黃　魚　羹	三　絲　魚　翅	蘆　筍　濃　湯	奶油焗菜膽
青　豆　蝦　仁	乾　燒　明　蝦	京　都　排　骨	雞　油　海　鮮
香　酥　鴨	腐　皮　茄　子	脆　皮　雞	
原　盅　三　味	鳳　足　冬　菇	蘿蔔絲鯽魚湯	四　方　餃
鮑　魚　腰　片	四　色　素　菜	蟹　肉　草　菇	八　寶　芋　棗
西　湖　醋　魚	豆　豉　蒸　魚	糖　醋　魚	鹹　蜆
			麻辣黃瓜
雞絲炒沙河粉	蓮　子　湯	燒　賣	清粥　拌　干　絲
螺　絲　捲	八　寶　飯	糯　米　球	豆豉生蠔
冰糖芝麻糊	蝦　仁　餛　飩	雪　白　木　耳	

Sample Banquet Menus

(1)

Crispy Cashews
Kidneys in Hot Sauce
Bon-Bon Chicken
Spicy Salted Jellyfish Salad

Yellow Fish Soup
Stir-Fried Shrimp with Green Peas
Crispy Pepper-Skin Duckling
Three-Flavor Steamed Soup
Stir-Fried Abalone with Kidney
Westlake Fish

Stir-Fried Chicken and Vermicelli Shreds
Steamed Snail ("Lwo-Sz-Juan)
Sweet Sesame Soup

(2)

Seven-Star Appetizer Plate

Stir-Fried Squid with Dried Red Peppers
Stir-Fried Chicken Shreds with Bean Sprouts

Three-Flavor Shredded Soup
Spicy Stir-Fried Prawns
Eggplant Rolls with Chopped Pork
Black Mushroom and Chicken-Foot Soup
"Four Kinds of Vegetables" Plate
Steamed Carp with Fermented Black Beans

Lotus Seed Soup
8-Treasure Rice Pudding
Shrimp Won Ton

(3)

Assorted Appetizer Plate I

Fried Minced Squab

Fluffy Asparagus Soup
"Jing-Du" Spareribs
Crispy-Skin Chicken
Shredded Turnip and Fish Soup
Stir-Fried Crab Meat with Straw Mushrooms
Sweet and Sour Fish

"Shau Mai"
Glutinous Rice Balls
Sweet Fruit Soup with White Wood Ears

(4)

Four-Sauce Lobster Slices
Braised Chicken with Shark's Fin
Stir-Fried Crab in Sweet and Sour Sauce
Fried Shrimp Balls
Stuffed Clams in Broth
Baked Cabbage and Butter
Steamed Pomfret with Ham and Mushroom
  Slices
"Four-Flavor" Dumplings
8-Treasure Taro Puffs
Marinated Clams
Szechuan Gherkin Slices
Bean Curd Noodle and Celery Salad
Stir-Fried Oysters with Fermented Black
  Beans

家常菜（四菜一湯）舉例

(例一)
桶 子 油 雞
咕 咾 肉
雞 油 海 鮮
雞 油 白 菜
羅 宋 湯

(例二)
葱 油 淋 雞
中 式 猪 扒
蝦 子 烏 參
麻 婆 豆 腐
排骨黃豆芽湯

(例三)
棒 棒 雞
紅 燒 牛 腩
乾 燒 明 蝦
干 扁 四 季 豆
蘿蔔絲鯽魚湯

(例四)
八 珍 扒 鴨
青 椒 牛 肉 絲
鹽 酥 蝦
搶 白 菜
冬 瓜 火 腿 夾

(例五)
紅 油 雞 塊
炒 腰 花
豆 瓣 鯉 魚
干 貝 三 色 球
酸 辣 湯

(例六)
炸 八 塊 雞
蒜 泥 白 肉
青 豆 蝦 仁
奶 油 焗 菜 膽
黃 魚 羹

(例七)
栗 子 燒 雞
京 都 排 骨
糖 醋 魚
芥 末 芹 菜
榨 菜 細 粉 湯

(例八)
蠔 油 扒 鳳 翼
京 醬 肉 絲
酥 炸 蝦
洋 菇 扒 鶉 蛋
砂 鍋 魚 頭

Ordinary Meal Menus (Four Dishes, One Soup)

(1)

Red-Cooked Chicken Appetizer

Sweet and Sour Pork

Steamed Pomfret with Ham and Mushroom Slices

Stir-Fried Cabbage in Chicken Sauce

Beef Soup a la Lo Sung

(2)

Steamed Chicken with Green Onions

Chinese-Style Pork Steak

Stir-Fried Sea Cucumber and Shrimp Eggs

Ma-Po's Bean Curd

Bean Sprout and Sparerib Soup

(3)

Bon-Bon Chicken

Red-Cooked Beef Slices

Spicy Stir-Fried Prawns

Dry-Cooked String Beans

Shredded Turnip and Fish Soup

(4)

Eight-Treasure Braised Duckling

Stir-Fried Beef with Green Peppers

Stir-Fried Shrimp with Garlic

Stir-Fried Cabbage with Szechuan Peppers

Winter Melon Sandwiches with Chinese Ham in Broth

(5)

Cold Chicken Appetizer with Hot Sauce

Stir-Fried Kidney with Assorted Vegetables

Braised Carp with Hot Bean Paste

Scallops with Tri-Colored Balls

Hot and Sour Soup

(6)

Deep-Fried 5-Spice Chicken

Pork Slices with Chopped Garlic

Stir-Fried Shrimp with Green Peas

Baked Cabbage and Butter

Yellow Fish Soup

(7)

Stewed Chicken with Chestnuts

"Jing-Du" Spareribs

Sweet and Sour Fish

Tossed Celery with Mustard Sauce

Szechuan Mustard Green and Bean Thread Soup

(8)

Chicken Wings with Oyster Sauce

Shredded Pork with Sweet Bean Paste

Deep-Fried Butterfly Shrimp

Braised Mushrooms with Quail Eggs

Stewed Fish Head Casserole

常用蔬菜
Commonly used vegetable

① 檸檬　lemon
② 筍　bamboo shoot
③ 空心菜　"kong syin tsai"
④ 小白菜　white Chinese cabbage ("syau bai tsai")
⑤ 青江菜　bok choy
⑥ 葱　green onion
⑦ 油菜　rape ("you tsai")
⑧ 西洋菜　water cress ("syi yang tsai")
⑨ 黃豆芽　yellow soybean sprouts
⑩ 綠豆芽　small mung bean sprouts
⑪ 菠蘿　pineapple
⑫ 雪裡紅　salted cabbage or "red in snow" ("sye li hung")
⑬ 鹹菜　pickled mustard green
⑭ 荸薺　water chestnut
⑮ 絲瓜　Chinese okra
⑯ 茄子　Chinese eggplant
⑰ 小黃瓜　gherkin cucumber
⑱ 巴西利　parsley
⑲ 芹菜　celery
⑳ 白蘿蔔　Chinese turnip
㉑ 九層塔　"jiou tseng ta"
㉒ 洋菇　button mushroom
㉓ 草菇　straw mushroom
㉔ 嫩薑　ginger root
㉕ 生菜　lettuce
㉖ 榨菜　Szechuan pickled mustard green
㉗ 芥菜　mustard cabbage
㉘ 韭菜　Chinese chives
㉙ 韭黃　yellow Chinese chives
㉚ 紅蘿蔔　carrot
㉛ 大黃瓜　cucumber
㉜ 大白菜　Chinese celery cabbage
㉝ 節瓜　hairy melon
㉞ 洋葱　onion
㉟ 馬鈴薯　potato
㊱ 苦瓜　bitter gourd
㊲ 青椒　green pepper
㊳ 毛豆　green peas
㊴ 四季豆　string beans
㊵ 鮑魚菇　fresh Chinese black mushroom
㊶ 番茄　tomato
㊷ 芋頭　taro root
㊸ 包心菜　cabbage
㊹ 辣椒　hot peppers
㊺ 香菜　coriander
㊻ 芥蘭菜　Chinese broccoli
㊼ 蕃薯　sweet potato
㊽ 莧菜　kale ("sien tsai")
㊾ 冬瓜　winter melon

常用乾貨及罐頭
Commonly used dry materials and canned foods

①	魚皮	dried fish skin
②	魚翅	shark's fin
③	海參	sea cucumber ("bêche-de-mer)
④	猪蹄筋	pork tendon
⑤	炸猪皮	dried fish maw
⑥	麵筋泡	fried gluten balls ("mien jin pau
⑦	火腿	Chinese ham
⑧	香腸	Chinese sausage
⑨	扎腿	boneless, smoked pork shank
⑩	乾魷魚	dried squid
⑪	米粉	rice noodles
⑫	酒釀	fermented rice wine ("jou niang"
⑬	酸梅	pickled plums ("umeboshi")
⑭	蕗蕎	"lu chiau"
⑮	酸薑	pickled ginger
⑯	梅乾菜	"mei gan tsai"
⑰	冬粉（粉絲）	bean threads
⑱	洋菜	agar-agar
⑲	榨菜	Szechuan pickled mustard green
⑳	花椒粒	Szechuan peppercorns
㉑	八角	star anise
㉒	乾辣椒	dried red pepper
㉓	金針	dried tiger lily
㉔	木耳	dried wood ear
㉕	白木耳	white cloud ear
㉖	冬菇	dried Chinese black mushroom
㉗	紅葱頭	shallot
㉘	蝦米	dried shrimp
㉙	蓮子	lotus seed
㉚	扁魚乾	dried brill fish ("bien yu gan")
㉛	蝦片	shrimp chip
㉜	糯米紙	glutinous rice paper
㉝	紫菜	nori (purple laver sheet)
㉞	玻璃紙	heavy duty cellophane
㉟	豆腐皮	bean curd skin
㊱	營養豆腐	bean curd roll
㊲	豆腐干	pressed bean curd cake
㊳	粉皮	bean thread skin
㊴	烤麩	"kau fu"
㊵	百頁	bean curd wrapper
㊶	素腸	vegetarian gluten roll ("mien jin"
㊷	干絲	dried bean curd noodles
㊸	豆豉	fermented black beans
㊹	腐竹	bean curd stick ("fu dzu")
㊺	海蜇皮	dried jellyfish
㊻	味素	monosodium glutamate
㊼	醬油	soy sauce
㊽	筍罐	canned bamboo shoot
㊾	荸薺罐	canned water chestnut
㊿	花瓜罐	pickled cucumbers
51	洋菇罐	canned button mushroom
52	玉米筍罐	canned baby corn shoot
53	草菇罐	canned straw mushroom
54	金銀菇罐	canned golden mushroom
55	蘆筍罐	canned asparagus
56	荔枝罐	canned lichees

14

特殊材料說明

1 辣豆瓣醬‥（辣椒醬）以紅辣椒及蠶豆爲原料加工製成，色紅、味辣。

2 甜麵醬‥饅頭醱酵製成（黑色）。

3 豆瓣醬‥黃豆醱酵製成（黑色）。

4 芝麻醬‥芝麻磨製而成（茶色）。

5 粟米粉‥即玉米粉。

6 澄　麵‥小麥之澱粉（無筋）。

7 魚　漿‥魚肉攪碎後加以調味，用機械甩打製成。

8 豆　豉‥即陰豉（烏豆）。

9 網　油‥猪肚外面一層油膜呈網狀。

10 豆　乳‥即豆腐乳（SOFU 或 CHINESE CHEESE）是以豆腐醱酵製成，浙江、江蘇兩省製造最有名，市售之豆腐乳，種類甚多，隨使用之調味香料不同而分紅、白、五香、酒槽腐乳等。

11 糯米紙‥利用馬鈴薯（POTATO）、甘薯（蕃薯）（SWEET POTATO）之澱粉加工製造而成。

12 粉　絲‥即冬粉，細粉，原料爲綠豆。

13 蝦　子‥即蝦卵，深咖啡色，呈微小粒狀。

14 辣　油‥麻油燒熱，葱、花椒粒炒香，隨即冲入辣椒粉，待冷即可。

15 蠔　油‥以生蠔爲原料，加工製成之調味料。

16 熟　油‥已經開滾或使用過之油，通常於炒菜後淋上少許熟油，可保持食物之光澤及保溫作用。

17 沙茶醬‥是以花生油、花生粉、油葱、香菜子、蒜頭粉、辣椒粉、花椒、八角、蝦米磨碎製成，在雜貨店購買。

18 五香粉‥是以八角、桂皮、小茴、花椒、三奈，炒香後磨成的粉。

19 花椒粉‥花椒粒炒香後磨成的粉。

20 花椒鹽‥是以乾鍋將鹽 2 大匙炒熱，呈微黃時，加 1 小匙花椒粉（或五香粉）拌匀而成，是供油炸食物沾食用的。

21 油　條‥參照中國餐點。

22 薑酒汁‥薑拍破，加酒所擠出的汁。

● 糖　粉‥將糖磨成粉狀，使用時易於溶化。

● 芥茉粉‥芥菜籽磨成的粉。

● 洋　菜‥即菜燕。

● 發泡粉（BAKING POWDER）‥發泡粉其成份隨種類而異，通常含有碳酸氫鈉、酒石酸氫鈉、酒石酸等，主要作用係此等物質加熱後會產生二氧化碳（CO_2）氣體，故將適當之發泡粉及水拌入麵粉內後再加熱，將會使麵塊發漲。

● 小蘇打（SODIUM BICARBONATE）：小蘇打即碳酸氫鈉（$NaHCO_3$）在水溶液中呈弱鹼性反應，可防止葉綠素之消失，故燒煮青綠色之蔬菜或豆類，可加入少許小蘇打粉；又因其爲鹼性之關係，使蛋白質保水性增加，亦可使肉之組織軟化。

● 嫩精（TENDERIZER）‥市售之嫩精包含蛋白質分解酵素、鹽、蔗糖等，由於蛋白分解酵素之作用，使肉之組織變軟，而達到嫩化效果。

● 鹼塊（SODIUM CARBONATE）‥主要成份係碳酸鈉（$NaCO_3$），在水溶液中鹼性比小蘇打強，如本書36頁拌干絲內所用之鹼塊係用來泡軟干絲用。

● 洋　菇‥即毛菇。

● 麥芽糖（MALTOSE）‥甜味不如蔗糖，黏稠性大，多係由精白糯米製成。

● 炸　油‥備多量油，以供油炸用，沙拉油，花生油均可。

● 沙拉醬‥參照中國餐點。

● 太白粉‥是以樹薯或馬鈴薯做成的，可用玉米粉代替。

● 叉燒肉‥參照中國餐點。

● 麵包粉‥土司麵包烘乾，壓碎而成。

● 糖　色‥糖 4 大匙加水 2 大匙以小火煮 5 分鐘至呈褐色時，再加水半杯大火煮 3 分鐘，至糖有黏性時（約½杯）即成。

● 炸猪皮‥猪皮去毛並刮除垢穢洗淨，晒乾，「炸油」燒熱放入葱 4 枝及猪皮，以小火炸 5 分鐘至猪皮膨脹呈金黃色時撈起即成。

Description of some other special ingredients:

1. **Hot bean paste ("la do ban jiang"):**
   A thick, spicy paste made from ground hot red peppers and soy beans.
2. **Sweet bean paste ("tien mien jiang"):**
   A thick flavorful black paste made from ground, fermented steamed bread and spices.
3. **Soy bean paste ("do ban jiang"):**
   A thick black paste similar in taste to sweet bean paste, but made from fermented soybeans.
4. **Sesame paste:**
   A thick brown paste made from crushed sesame seeds.
5. **Cornstarch:**
   A white powder made from ground corn and primarily used to thicken sauces and soups and to coat foods before deep-frying.
6. **"Cheng mien" (non-gluten flour):**
   A type of high-grade no-stick flour which has the gluten removed. It is used primarily in making Chinese pastries. Potato flour may be substituted.
7. **Fish paste (fish timbale):**
   A fine mixture of fish meat and spices chopped to a smooth paste. It is used to make fish balls and for coating various meats in soups and snacks.
8. **Fermented black beans:**
   Small black beans which have been marinated in soy sauce and salt and are used to flavor steamed fish and meat or in stir-fried dishes.
9. **Pork net oil or caul fat:**
   The lacy, outside layer of fat from a pig's stomach which is used to lend flavor to steamed fish and to wrap various foods before deep-frying.
10. **Pickled bean curd or Chinese cheese ("do fu ru"):**
    Bean curd cubes which are first dried and then mixed with wine, spices and salt and allowed to ferment. It is used to season braised pork and duckling.
11. **Glutinous rice paper:**
    A type of thin, edible paper-like sheet made from potato or sweet potato flour.
12. **Bean threads:**
    A type of thin, clear noodle made from the mung bean.
13. **Shrimp eggs:**
    The tiny, grainy eggs of the shrimp, which have been dried. They are used to add extra flavoring to chopped fillings. If it is unavailable, substitute dried brill fish.
14. **Hot pepper oil ("la you")**
    A spicy, hot oil made from hot pepper powder, water and boiling oil.
15. **Oyster sauce:**
    A rich, brown sauce made from oysters and somewhat similar to soy sauce in flavor.
16. **Fried oil:**
    Oil that has already been used or boiled and usually used to sprinkle over dishes before serving to improve the appearance of the food and keep it hot.
17. **"Sha chia jiang":**
    A spicy sauce made from a mixture of peanut oil, peanuts, green onion oil, coriander seed, garlic powder, hot pepper powder, star of anise, Szechuan peppercorns and dried shrimp. If unavailable, substitute hoisin sauce.
18. **Five spice powder:**
    A combination of anise, cinnamon, fennel, clove and Szechuan peppercorns which has first been stir-fried until fragrant and then ground to a fine powder.
19. **Szechuan peppercorn powder:**
    A powder made from the spicy Szechuan peppercorn, which has first been stir-fried until fragrant and then ground finely.
20. **Szechuan Peppercorn Salt and Five-Spice Salt:**
    A mixture of 2 tablespoons of salt, which has been stir-fried in an oil-less pan until it changes color and added to 1 teaspoon Szechuan peppercorn powder or 5-spice powder. It is usually served with fried chicken, fish or shrimp balls for extra flavoring.
21. **"You tiau":**
    A deep-fried crispy Chinese cruller. Detailed directions may be found in "Chinese Snacks—Wei-Chuan Cooking Book II". It may be eaten plain or served shredded in hot soups. If unavailable, substitute toasted croutons.
22. **Ginger wine:**
    A mixture of rice wine and the juices of smashed ginger root.
- **"dang guei":**
    A type of dry, pungent herb used for flavoring in soups or braised dishes, which is very beneficial nutritionally to the body. It may be purchased at any Chinese herbal drug store.
- **"Kau fu":**
    A spongy type of vegetarian ingredient made from wheat gluten, primarily used in stir-fried dishes. It may be stored for a long period of time.
- **Fried gluten ball ("mien jin pau"):**
    A type of light, round, deep-fried ball made from wheat gluten and water. It may be stored indefinitely and is used primarily in stir-fried vegetarian dishes.
- **"Su tsang":**
    A type of long, thin roll made of wheat gluten and water. It may be stored indefinitely and is used primarily in stir-fried vegetarian dishes.
- **Glutinous rice:**
    A type of short-grained rice which becomes sticky after cooking and is used in stuffings, dumplings, puddings and as a coating for meat balls.
- **"Mei gan tsai":**
    The stalk of the mustard cabbage plant, which has been dried and salted. It is used for flavoring in braising pork and chicken and may be purchased at a Chinese grocery store.

Helpful Hints

If rice wine is unavailable, you may substitute medium-dry or pale-dry sherry.
All turnips used in recipes are Chinese turnips. If they are unavailable, substitute icicle radishes.
Straw mushrooms are available in cans, however you may substitute button mushrooms.
If Chinese ham is unavailable, you may substitute Smithfield or a high-quality smoked variety of ham.
For all recipes using green onion sections, use the white part of stalk unless otherwise specified.
All stocks are made with chicken, beef or pork bones.

To make a simple stock:
1. Place bones in pan with water to cover.
2. Boil briefly and remove scum from surface of water.
3. Add 2 stalks green onion, 2 slices ginger root and 1T. rice wine.
4. Simmer over low heat for 30 minutes and use as directed.

To prepare 1T. ginger wine, mix 2 slices smashed ginger root with 1T. rice wine; let soak briefly and remove ginger slices. Use as directed.

To precook pork tendons:
1. Soak tendons for 1 hour in 5C. warm vegetable oil.
2. Heat oil for deep-frying and drop tendons into hot oil.
3. Sprinkle ½T. water into hot oil a few times until tendons have expanded. Remove tendons, drain and use as directed.

To precook vegetables:
1. Cook in boiling water as directed or until tender.
2. Remove vegetables from boiling water and plunge immediately into cold water until cool. (This keeps colors bright and prevents further cooking).
3. Drain and use as directed.

To pre-soak Chinese black mushrooms:
1. Rinse black mushrooms lightly and place in warm water to cover until soft. (about 15 minutes)
2. Remove stems (discard) and use caps as directed. (Soaking liquid may also be added to recipe to provide added flavor and vitamins.)

To pre-soften shark's fin or fish skin:
1. Place material in a pan with water to cover and heat until just below boiling point; turn heat to low and let simmer uncovered 1-2 hours.
2. Remove pan from heat and let material cool to room temperature; rinse material lightly and place in fresh, cold water to cover. Let soak in refrigerator overnight.
3. Repeat complete process 2–3 times until material is very soft and tender.

棒棒雞⋯⋯⋯⋯適量	椒麻腰片⋯⋯⋯適量	拌蜇皮⋯⋯⋯⋯⋯適量
滷牛肉⋯⋯⋯⋯適量	鴨肫⋯⋯⋯⋯⋯3個	素雞⋯⋯⋯⋯⋯⋯適量
		糖酥核桃⋯⋯⋯3兩

❶ 棒棒雞：請參照本書第７頁棒棒雞做法。

❷ 滷牛肉：牛腱子在熱水內川燙撈起，放入滷汁內，用小火煮爛（請參照第６頁滷汁）。

❸ 椒麻腰片：請參照本書第１１頁椒麻腰片做法。

❹ 鴨肫：切去皮筋，劃刀在開水內川燙撈出。

❺ 拌蜇皮：請參照本書第２２頁拌蜇皮做法。

❻ 素雞：請參照本書第１４７頁素雞做法。

❼ 糖酥核桃：請參照本書第１８頁糖酥腰果做法。

柒星轉盤 Seven-Star Appetizer Plate

四川菜　Szechuan
12人份　12 servings

4 oz. "Bon-Bon Chicken"
4 oz. braised beef chuck
4 oz. "Kidneys in Pepper Sauce"
3 duckling gizzards
4 oz. salted jellyfish
4 oz. "Vegetarian Chicken"
3 oz. walnuts or cashews

Arrange the above ingredients on serving plate as illustrated:

❶ "Bon-Bon Chicken": See "Bon-Bon Chicken" on P. 7 and follow steps as directed; slice chicken and use as instructed above.

❷ Beef: See "braised beef" directions in "Assorted Appetizer Plate-I" on P. 2 and follow steps as directed; slice and use as instructed above.

❸ Kidneys: Follow directions as detailed in "Kidneys in Hot Sauce" on P. 11; slice and arrange on plate as directed above.

❹ Gizzard: Remove white outer membranes from gizzards; score lengthwise and crosswise; cut into bite-size pieces; blanch in boiling water for 30 seconds; remove and use as directed.

❺ Salted jellyfish: Prepare as directed in "Salted Jellyfish" on P. 22 Arrange on serving plate.

❻ Vegetarian Chicken": See "Vegetarian Chicken Loaves" on P. 147 and follow steps as directed; place on serving plate.

❼ Walnuts: See "Crispy Cashews" on P. 18 and follow steps as directed; place on serving plate.

鮑　魚、洋火腿 ⎫
滷牛肉、滷豬肝 ⎬ 各１２片　　番茄片‥‥‥‥‥‥‥‥‥‥‥‥１２片
墨　魚、叉燒肉 ⎭　　　　　　　扎腿‥‥‥‥‥‥‥‥‥‥‥‥２４片
　　　　　　　　　　　　　　　海蜇皮（３兩）‥‥‥‥‥‥１杯

❶ 鮑魚：使用鮑魚罐頭。
❷ 滷牛肉：牛腱子在熱水內川燙撈起，放入滷汁內，用小火煮爛（請參照桶子油雞的滷汁）。
❸ 墨魚：墨魚放入剛燒滾的水內，以小火煮熟切片。
❹ 滷豬肝：豬肝１斤整塊浸在醬油汁內（醬油１杯、葱２枝、薑２片、酒２大匙、蒜頭拍碎¼杯
　　　、八角１朵）小火煮１５分鐘，使滷汁保持高溫，而不滾的程度，即可熄火，蓋鍋蓋
　　　浸約２０分鐘，待冷取出切片。
❺ 叉燒肉：請參照本公司出版姊妹食譜中國餐點內叉燒肉之做法。
❻ 海蜇皮：請參照本書第２２頁拌蜇皮做法。
■ 豬肚、豬舌、鴨肫、燒鴨、燒雞、素雞‥‥等都可任意拿來做拼盤，以上用料可向燒臘店購買。

拼盤（一）　Assorted Appetizer Plate I　　　　　１２人份 **12 servings**

4　oz. abalone ⎫
4　oz. braised beef chuck ⎪
4　oz. precooked squid meat ⎬ cut each into
4　oz. ham ⎪ 12 paper-thin slices
4　oz. precooked pork or chicken liver ⎪
4　oz. barbecued pork ⎭

24 paper-thin slices salami
12 slices tomato
1　C. shredded salted jellyfish

Arrange the above ingredients in a circular pattern on serving plate as illustrated.
❶ Abalone: Use canned abalone meat; slice and use as directed.
❷ Beef: Clean beef briefly in hot water; remove and cook in "braising sauce" (see step ❶ "Red-Cooked Chicken Appetizer") covered for about 1 hour over medium heat until tender; cut and use as directed.
❸ Squid: Clean squid; cook meat in boiling water for 3 minutes over low heat; remove; slice and use as directed.
❹ Liver: Place liver in sauce made of 1C. soy sauce, 2 stalks green onion, 2 slices ginger root, 2T. rice wine, ¼C. smashed garlic and 1 star of anise; let simmer 15 minutes over low heat; turn off heat and let sit 20 minutes covered until room temperature; remove, And slice livers. Use as directed.
❺ Barbecued pork: Prepare pork as directed in "Chinese Roasted Pork" from "Chinese Snacks", if unavailable use ordinary pork roast or omit.
❻ Salted jellyfish: Follow directions for "Salted Jellyfish and Cucumber Salad" on P. 22; prepare as directed.
■ Pork stomach, tongue, duckling gizzard, roast duckling, chicken and vegetarian chicken may be substituted for any of the above ingredients.

鮑魚
滷牛肉
墨魚　　　各14片
滷豬肝
洋火腿

❶ 各料做法，請參照拼盤（一）。

■ 圍邊用材料：泡菜、紅蘿蔔、番茄、香菜

拼盤(二) Assorted Appetizer Plate II

12人份 12 servings

4 oz. abalone meat
4 oz. precooked beef chuck
4 oz. precooked squid meat   Cut each into 14 paper-thin slices
4 oz. ham
4 oz. precooked pork, chicken or beef liver

❶ Arrange the above ingredients in a circular pattern on serving plate as illustrated.
　See P. 2 "Assorted Appetizer Plate I" for directions on preparation of ingredients.

■ Garnish with pickled salad (See "Pickled Vegetables, Cantonese-style") carrot, tomato and coriander..

3

龍蝦‧‧‧‧‧‧‧‧‧‧‧‧‧ 1隻1斤4兩　　椒麻汁‧‧‧‧‧‧‧‧‧‧‧‧‧‧

粉皮‧‧‧‧‧‧‧‧‧‧‧‧‧‧‧‧‧‧‧ 10張　　　　紅油汁‧‧‧‧‧‧‧‧‧‧‧‧‧

　　　　　　　　　　　　　　棒棒汁‧‧‧‧‧‧‧‧‧‧‧‧‧ ｝各半小碗

　　　　　　　　　　　　　　薑醋汁‧‧‧‧‧‧‧‧‧‧‧‧‧

❶ 用串針或筷子，從龍蝦口部貫穿直至尾部（以免彎曲），大火蒸15分鐘，蒸熟取龍蝦頭，然後把蝦身從腹部兩旁用剪刀剪開，取蝦肉抽除腸泥切薄片，蝦殼留用。

❷ 粉皮切條，在開水內川燙撈出墊底，舖上蝦肉片，龍蝦頭、尾擺在盤兩端。

❸ 備椒麻汁、紅油汁、棒棒汁（參照本書第11頁椒麻腰片、第30頁紅油雞塊、第7頁棒棒雞）及薑醋汁（醋半小碗、薑末1大匙），各盛小碗，供龍蝦吃時沾用。

■ 圍邊用材料：黃瓜、香菜、紅蘿蔔。

四味龍蝦 Four-Sauce Lobster Slices

1 lobster (about 1⅔ lbs.)
10 bean thread or vermicelli sheets ("fen pi")

½ C. each {
"pepper sauce" ("jiau ma jr")
"hot pepper sauce" ("hon you jr")
"bon-bon sauce" ("bon-bon jr")
"ginger-vinegar sauce" ("jiang tsu jr")
}

❶ Using a chopstick or skewer, spear the lobster through the mouth, into the body. (This will keep the lobster from curling while cooking.) Steam or cook in boiling water over high heat for 15 minutes; remove and drain. Separate the head from the tail end of the lobster; remove meat from the tail end of the lobster, leaving the shell intact. Remove any veins from the meat and cut meat into paper-thin slices.

❷ Cut bean thread sheets into ½-inch strips; blanch in boiling water; remove and drain; place on serving plate. Arrange lobster meat slices on top of bean thread strips; position lobster head and tail shell on each side of meat as illustrated.

❸ "pepper sauce": Prepare as directed in "Kidneys in Hot Sauce" on P. 11.
  "hot pepper sauce": Prepare as directed in "Cold Chicken Appetizer with Hot Sauce" on P. 30.
  "bon-bon sauce": Prepare as directed in "Bon-Bon Chicken" on P. 7.
  "ginger-vinegar sauce": Chop 1T. ginger root and add to ½C. worcestershire sauce.

■ Pour sauces into small bowls and serve with lobster slices. Each person dips meat or bean thread strips into sauce of his individual choice.

■ Garnish with cucumber, coriander and carrot.

龍蝦…1 隻 1 斤

① 沙拉醬……4 兩
鹽………半小匙
味精……¼小匙

② 馬鈴薯……1 個
紅蘿蔔……半條
青豆仁……2 兩
雞蛋………2 個
番茄………1 個

沙拉醬……4 兩

❶ 用串針或筷子，從龍蝦口部貫穿直至尾部（以免彎曲），大火蒸１５分鐘，蒸熟取龍蝦頭，然後把蝦身從腹部兩旁用剪刀剪開，取蝦肉抽除腸泥切薄片，蝦殼留用。

❷ 馬鈴薯、紅蘿蔔、青豆仁、雞蛋先煮熟撈起後，把番茄在開水內川燙撈出，去皮除籽，各切小丁（青豆仁除外），加①料攪勻，放在盤中，鋪上蝦肉片，以沙拉醬擠花在上面，龍蝦頭、尾擺盤兩端即成。

■ 圍邊用材料：生菜、紅蘿蔔。

沙拉大龍蝦 Lobster Salad

廣東菜 Cantonese
12人份 12 servings

1 lobster (about 1⅓ lbs.)

① ½ C. mayonnaise
½ t. salt
¼ t. MSG

② 1 medium-sized potato
½ medium-sized carrot
⅓ C. green peas
2 eggs
1 medium-sized tomato

½ C. mayonnaise

❶ Using a chopstick or skewer, spear the lobster through the mouth into the body. (This will keep the lobster from curling while cooking.) Cook covered in boiling water over high heat for 15 minutes; remove and drain. Separate the head from the tail end of the lobster; remove meat from the tail, leaving shell intact. Remove any veins from the meat and cut meat into paper-thin bite-size pieces.

❷ Precook potato, carrot and peas until tender; remove and drain. Cook eggs until hard-boiled and remove; shell. Blanch tomato in boiling water; remove seeds and skin. Dice vegetables and eggs and mix with ① ; place on serving plate and arrange lobster slices on top of salad. Using a pastry bag, add remaining mayonnaise on top of salad in a decorative pattern. Position lobster head and tail shell on each side of salad as illustrated; serve.

■ Garnish with lettuce leaves and carrots.

<table>
<tr><td>雞⋯⋯⋯1隻2斤</td></tr>
</table>

①
水⋯⋯⋯⋯⋯6杯
紹興酒⋯⋯⋯6大匙
鹽⋯⋯⋯⋯⋯2大匙
冰糖(或糖)⋯4兩

②
花椒、丁香
八角、草菓
陳皮、甘草
桂皮
} 共1兩

醬油⋯⋯⋯3杯

❶ 將①、②料盛鍋燒開後隨加3杯醬油，以小火燒約20分鐘成滷汁，把雞放入，用滷汁多次的淋在雞身上及雞腹內，蓋鍋，小火燒10分鐘後，將雞身翻轉，再以小火燒約10分鐘，即可熄火，蓋着鍋蓋再浸約20分鐘取起待冷，塗上麻油少許，即可剁塊，排列在菜盤上，澆上少許滷汁即成。

■ 圍邊用材料：葱、紅辣椒。

■ ②料可到中藥店購買，並用小布袋裝妥備用。

■ 依此法滷 豬肝、蛋、豬舌、豆腐干等一切滷味，非常方便。

■ 滷汁所用次數愈多愈香，如果滷汁漸減少，可按上項材料比例酌量加入，爲避免滷汁變質，二、三天需燒沸一次。

桶子油雞 Red-Cooked Chicken Appetizer

廣東菜 Cantonese
12人份 12 servings

	1 chicken (about 3lbs.)	Szechuan peppercorns 花 椒	3 C. soy sauce
①	6 C. water	star anise 八 角	
	6 T. rice wine	orange peel 陳 皮	
	2 T. salt	② cinnamon 桂 皮	Combined ingredients equal to 1 oz.*
	4 oz. rock sugar (granulated may be substitured)	whole cloves 丁 香	
		fennel 草 菓	
		liquorice powder 甘 草	

❶ Place mixtures ① and ② together in a pan; heat until boiling and add soy sauce; cook covered over low heat for 20 minutes (braising sauce). Place chicken in sauce and spoon braising sauce over outside of chicken and into cavity; simmer covered for 10 minutes over low heat. Turn chicken to other side, cover and cook an additional 10 minutes. Turn off heat and let sit covered 20 minutes until chicken has cooled to room temperature; remove from pan and brush chicken exterior lightly with sesame oil; cut into bite-size pieces and arrange on serving plater; pour a little braising sauce over chicken pieces and serve.

* All listed Chinese ingredients in ② may be purchased at any Chinese herbal store. If unavailable, substitute 5-spice powder. Place ingredients of ② in a cheesecloth bag (as a bouquet garni) and use as directed.

■ Garnish with shredded green onion and red pepper.

■ Use the above braising suace to cook liver, hard-boiled eggs, tongue, pressed bean curd, etc.

■ The flavor of the braising sauce will improve after each use. Add more of ② ingredients as needed after additional braisings. To keep sauce from spoiling over a very long period of time, heat to boiling point every 3 days; cool and refrigerate until next use.

雞…１隻２斤
粉皮…１０張

① 芝麻醬……………………１½大匙
　　醬油………………………２大匙
　　糖…………………………１小匙
　　麻油………………………１小匙
　　黑醋………………………１小匙
　　味精………………………半小匙
　　葱、薑、蒜末……各半小匙

辣油…１大匙

❶ 粉皮切粗條，在開水內川燙，用筷子攪散撈起，擺於盤底。

❷ 將雞煮熟，去骨，切成粗條，擺在粉皮上，以①料均勻澆在雞肉上面，再淋上辣油即成。

■ 煮雞時，請參考第２９頁鹽水雞做法❶。

■ 圍邊用材料：白蘿蔔、香菜。

棒棒雞 Bon-Bon Chicken

四川菜　Szechuan
12人份　12 servings

1　chicken (about 2⅔lbs.)
10 bean thread or vermicelli sheets
　　　　　　　　　　("fen pi")

① 1½ T. sesame paste
2　T. soy sauce
1　t. sugar
1　t. sesame oil
1　t. worcestershire sauce
½　t. MSG
½　t. chopped green onion
½　t. chopped ginger root
½　t. chopped garlic

1　T. hot pepper oil ("la you")

❶ Cut bean thread sheets into ½-inch wide strips; blanch in boiling water; (stir to separate strips); remove, drain and place in center of serving plate.

❷ Heat 10C. water until boiling; add chicken and turn heat to low and cook 10 minutes; turn chicken to other side and cook an additional 10 minutes; remove chicken and let cool. Remove bones and cut meat into matchstick-size pieces; arrange over bean thread strips. Mix ingredients of ① and pour over meat; pour hot pepper oil on top and serve.

■ Garnish with turnip and coriander.

燒鴨……¼隻半斤		白醋………2大匙
海蜇皮………2兩		芝麻醬………2大匙
青椒………1個		糖…………半大匙
綠豆芽………1杯		鹽………1½小匙
蛋…………1個	①	味精………1小匙
		麻油………半大匙
		醬油………1大匙
		番茄醬………2大匙
		清水………2大匙

❶ 燒鴨去骨後切成細絲（約1杯），海蜇皮用溫水浸泡亦切絲。

❷ 青椒切絲，綠豆芽摘芽除根，各分別入開水內燙熟撈起。

❸ 蛋1個打勻，用少許油煎成薄皮後，亦切細絲，①料燒開備用。

❹ 上面各料盛大盤，倒入燒開①料拌勻即成。

■ 圍邊用材料：番茄、小黃瓜、巴西利。

銀芽凉拌鴨絲 Roasted Duckling Salad

廣東菜 Cantonese
12人份 12 servings

¼ pre-roasted duckling* (about ⅔ lb.)		2 T. vinegar	• ½ T. sesame oil
2 oz. salted jellyfish		2 T. sesame paste	• 1 T. soy sauce
1 medium-sized green pepper (6 oz.)	①	½ T. sugar	• 2 T. tomato ketchup
1 C. bean sprouts		1½ t. salt	• 2 T. water
1 egg		1 t. MSG	

❶ Remove bones from duck; shred meat into matchstick-size pieces (about 1C.). Soak salted jellyfish about 20 minutes; rinse, dry and shred.

❷ Remove seeds from green pepper; shred. Remove any discolored ends from bean sprouts; separately blanch green pepper and bean sprouts in boiling water for ½ minute; remove and plunge into cold water. Remove and drain.

❸ Beat eggs lightly; heat a lightly greased pan and add beaten eggs, while rotating pan so that eggs spread evenly and form a thin pancake; cook until golden and flip over to uncooked side; remove and shred. Bring ingredients of ① to a boil; remove from heat.

❹ Combine shredded duckling; egg, jellyfish, green pepper, and bean sprouts; place on serving plate. Pour ① mixture over shreds; toss lightly and serve.

* For cooking instructions, substitute duck and follow directions for "Crispy-Skin Chicken" on P. 32

■ Garnish with tomato, cucumber and parsley.

①{	白蘿蔔……1 條 鹽………2 大匙 水………1 杯 紫菜………2 張	熟雞胸肉（1公分×1公分×12公分）4條 熟火腿…（ 〃 〃 〃 〃 〃 〃 ）4條 鹹菜…（ 〃 〃 〃 〃 〃 〃 ）4條 小黃瓜…（ 〃 〃 〃 〃 〃 〃 ）4條	②{ 糖…………3 大匙 醋…………3 大匙 味精………¼ 小匙 麻油………半小匙

❶ 白蘿蔔以①料醃約6小時，用刀、片成12公分×12公分四方薄片（4張）以冷開水輕輕沖洗，拭乾水份，紫菜每張切半備用。

❷ 將白蘿蔔鹹菜與小黃瓜調入②料醃20分鐘。

❸ 白蘿蔔片攤開，舖上紫菜，中間直放鹹菜、小黃瓜、熟雞胸肉、熟火腿，再捲成圓筒形如此可做4捲，每條切6塊計24塊。

■ 圍邊用材料：小黃瓜。

五彩捲 Five-Color Rolls

台灣菜　Taiwanese
12人份　12 servings

①{	1　medium-sized turnip 2　T. salt 1　C. water	2　sheets nori* 4　⅓ -inch x ⅓-inch x 4-inch sticks precooked chicken meat 4　⅓ -inch x ⅓-inch x 4-inch sticks precooked ham 4　⅓ -inch x ⅓-inch x 4-inch sticks pickled cabbage stalk 4　⅓ -inch x ⅓-inch x 4-inch sticks cucumber	②{ 3　T. sugar 3　T. vinegar ¼　t. MSG ½　t. sesame oil

❶ Remove skin from turnip; place in ① and soak 6 hours; remove and drain. With a paring knife, start on one side of turnip and peel away a paper-thin 4-inch square; repeat 3 more times to make 4 turnip "skins"; rinse skins lightly and drain; cut nori sheets in half.

❷ Place turnip skins, pickled cabbage and cucumber sticks in ② and soak 20 minutes; drain.

❸ Place a turnip skin flat on counter; place a nori sheet directly on top; lay 1 stick pickled cabbage, cucumber, chicken and ham lengthwise across nori. Starting at nearest horizontal edge, roll up tightly to form a compact roll; repeat for other skins to make 4 rolls; cut each roll into 6 sections; place on serving plate and serve.

■ Garnish with cucumber slices.

* Nori is a thin type of seaweed also called laver. It may be purchased at any Chinese or Japanese grocery store.

雞⋯⋯⋯⋯⋯半隻1斤		清水⋯⋯⋯⋯⋯8杯
豬肉皮⋯⋯⋯⋯⋯1斤		葱⋯⋯⋯⋯⋯2枝
		薑⋯⋯⋯⋯⋯2片
	①	酒⋯⋯⋯⋯⋯2大匙
		醬油⋯⋯⋯⋯⋯半杯
		鹽⋯⋯⋯⋯⋯1小匙
		糖⋯⋯⋯⋯⋯2小匙
		八角⋯⋯⋯⋯⋯半朵

❶ 豬皮刮淨切除肥油，切約6公分四方塊，與雞同在開水內川燙撈起。

❷ ①料燒開，將雞及豬皮用中火燒煮２０分鐘，將雞身翻轉，再燒煮１０分鐘即可把雞撈起，餘汁及豬皮繼續燒煮３０分鐘至湯汁剩約３杯時，撈出豬皮。

❸ 雞除骨取肉切小丁，分別放在二只便當盒內(或一只３０公分長，２０公分寬的模型內)倒入燒雞原汁(宜以淨布過濾)待冷，置冰箱，食用時反扣出來，切長方塊盛盤即可供食。

■ 圍邊用材料：白蘿蔔、葱、香菜。

雞凍 Chicken in Aspic Slices

上海菜 Shanghai
12人份 12 servings

½ chicken (about 1⅓lbs.)
1⅓ lbs. pork skin*

	8	C. water
	2	stalks green onion
	2	slices ginger root
①	2	T. rice wine
	½	C. soy sauce
	1	t. salt
	2	t. sugar
	½	star anise

❶ Clean pork skin, removing any hairs or foreign material. Using a cleaver, scrape away any fat; cut into 2 inch squares. Blanch chicken and pork skin in boiling water to clean exterior; remove and drain.

❷ Bring ingredients of ① to a boil; add chicken and pork skin; cook covered over medium heat for 20 minutes; turn over chicken and cook an additional 10 minutes; remove chicken and drain. Continue to cook pork skin for 30 minutes until liquid is reduced to 3C.; remove pork skin and discard; retain liquid.

❸ Remove bones from chicken; dice meat and line a 10 in. by 7 in. square pan or mold with chicken; add 3C. retained liquid* and place in refrigerator to cool. When jell has set, invert square onto serving plate and cut into slices; serve.

■ Garnish with turnip, green onion and coriander.

* Before adding retained liquid to mold, use a strainer to remove onion, ginger and anise.

猪腰（大）……1只　①{花椒粒……半大匙　②{味精……1小匙、麻油……2小匙
粉皮…………5张　　葱薑末…各1大匙　　　醋……2小匙、醬油……2大匙
或小黄瓜絲…1杯　　　　　　　　　　　糖………1小匙、鹽………¼小匙

❶ 猪腰横切開去白筋，在正面劃四～五條正直線紋，再横切成斜薄片（菜刀與菜板成４５度所切之斜薄片，越斜顯得片越大）用冷水浸泡去血水。

❷ 粉皮切約１公分寬條，放入熱水内用筷子攪開撈出。

❸ 泡淨的腰片瀝乾水份，用剛燒滾的水燙熟（約２０秒）見腰片變白色即刻撈出，再用冷水浸涼。

❹ 將①料用刀剁碎（越碎越好）後，與②料攪拌混合盛於碗内。

❺ 菜盤先鋪上粉皮，再把腰片（瀝乾）放在粉皮上，最後澆上拌好的佐料，即可上桌。

■ 如喜食辣味者，可斟酌加入辣油。

■ 圍邊用材料：香菜。

椒麻腰片 Kidneys in Hot Sauce

四川菜　Szechuan
6人份　6 servings

1 pork kidney (about 6oz.)
5 bean thread sheets ("fen pi")
   or 1 C. shredded gherkin
   cucumber

①{½ T. Szechuan peppercorns
   1 T. chopped green onion
   1 T. chopped ginger root

②{1 t. MSG
   2 t. worcestershire sauce
   1 t. sugar
   2 t. sesame oil
   2 T. soy sauce
   ¼ t. salt

❶ Slice kidney horizontally, into half; remove any white membrane from center and score surface vertically; slice diagonally into very thin slices; place slices in cold water.

❷ Cut bean thread sheets into ⅓-inch strips; place in simmering water 20 seconds (stir with chopsticks to separate strips); remove and drain.

❸ Drain kidney slices; cook in simmering water 20 seconds until color changes; remove and drain. Place slices in cold water.

❹ Mix ingredients of ① and chop very finely; mix with ② and place in a bowl.

❺ Arrange bean thread strips on serving plate; drain kidney slices and place on top of bean thread slices; pour sauce on top and serve.

■ Note: Add hot pepper oil ("la you") to sauce for extra spiciness.

■ Garnish with coriander.

	里肌肉⋯⋯⋯⋯⋯2兩		香菜（切碎）⋯⋯⋯3大匙	
①	太白粉⋯⋯⋯⋯半小匙		醋⋯⋯⋯⋯⋯⋯1大匙	
	鹽⋯⋯⋯⋯⋯¼小匙		醬油⋯⋯⋯⋯⋯1大匙	
	水⋯⋯⋯⋯⋯⋯1大匙		鹽⋯⋯⋯⋯⋯⋯1小匙	
	蛋⋯⋯⋯⋯⋯⋯1個	③	糖⋯⋯⋯⋯⋯⋯1小匙	
②	太白粉⋯⋯⋯⋯1小匙		胡椒⋯⋯⋯⋯⋯¼小匙	
	水⋯⋯⋯⋯⋯⋯1小匙		麻油⋯⋯⋯⋯⋯半小匙	
	粉皮⋯⋯⋯⋯⋯10張		芥末醬⋯⋯⋯⋯1大匙	
			開水⋯⋯⋯⋯⋯2大匙	

❶ 里肌肉切細絲，調①料醃約20分鐘。蛋加②料調勻，煎成薄皮後切細絲備用。

❷ 粉皮切絲，以溫開水泡洗後撈乾盛盤。

❸ 油4大匙將肉絲炒熟置粉皮絲上，蛋皮絲、香菜末置兩旁，澆上調勻③料，即可供食。

■ 香菜可用香椿芽代替（香椿芽半兩洗淨，切碎，加鹽醃過後沖入開水，使其發出香味，撈乾，即可用）。

■ 芥末醬做法：芥末粉1大匙加溫水1大匙調勻後蓋緊，置10分鐘，即成。

肉絲拉皮 Tossed Pork and Egg Shreds

北平菜　Peking
12人份　12 servings

	2 oz. pork loin		3 T. chopped coriander	
①	½ t. cornstarch		1 T. vinegar	
	¼ t. salt		1 T. soy sauce	
	1 T. water		1 t. salt	
	1 egg	③	1 t. sugar	
②	1 t. cornstarch		¼ t. black pepper	
	1 t. water		½ t. sesame oil	
	10 bean thread sheets ("fen pi")		1 T. hot mustard*	
			2 T. water	

❶ Shred pork loin and mix with ① ; let sit 20 minutes. Mix egg with ② ; heat a lightly oiled pan; add egg mixture and tilt pan so that egg spreads to a thin, round sheet; cook until lightly browned ; flip over to uncooked side and cook a few more seconds; remove and shred.

❷ Shred bean thread sheets; rinse in hot water and drain; place on serving plate.

❸ Heat pan and 4T. oil; stir-fry pork shreds until changed in color; remove and drain. Arrange alternately pork shreds, shredded egg sheets and coriander over bean thread sections as illustrated. Mix ingredients of ③ together and pour over shredded ingredients; toss lightly and serve.

* White horseradish can be substituted.

猪前腿肉(或蹄膀)…1 斤
甜麵醬……………2 大匙

① 酒………1 大匙、糖……1 大匙
葱…………2 枝、八角……1 朵
薑…………2 片、桂皮……1 片
醬油……4 大匙、水………4 杯
味精……半小匙

❶ 猪肉洗淨拭乾水份後，用甜麵醬揉擦四週醃約 2 小時，加①料，以快鍋中火燒煮 3 0 分鐘至肉熟透，汁剩半杯即可撈出。

❷ 俟醬肉冷透後切片排盤（原汁澆在上面供食）。

■ 如無快鍋可用深底小鍋燒煮約 1 小時。

■ 也可選用較瘦的前腿肉，需切成四方塊。

醬 肉 Sauced Ham

1⅓ lbs. fresh ham
2 T. sweet bean paste

① 1 T. rice wine   • 1 T. sugar
2 stalks green onion • 1 star anise
2 slices ginger root • 1 cinnamon
4 T. soy sauce   • 4 C. water
½ t. MSG

❶ Clean fresh ham and drain off water, use sweet bean paste to rub around it and let soak 2 hours; mix with ① and cook 30 minutes in the pressure cooker over medium heat until well-cooked; retain ½C. of the juice; remove.

❷ After the ham is cool, slice and arrange it serving plate, pour the left juice over it.

■ If pressure cooker is unavailable, place ingredients in covered pan or casserole and cook 1 hour.

①		②		③	
猪蹄蹄	2 斤	葱	2 枝	醬油	半大匙
硝	1 小匙	薑	2 片	糖	1 小匙
鹽	2 大匙	酒	1 大匙	醋	半大匙
花椒	1 小匙	水	8 杯	葱末、薑末各 1 小匙	

❶ 猪蹄蹄去毛洗淨，擦乾水份，先將硝在肉的部份擦勻，再把炒好的①料塗勻肉內外醃 3 天備用。

❷ 醃好的蹄蹄略洗，放入②料內燒煮 1 小時，至肉熟取出趁熱用布包緊，用磚或石頭等重物，壓緊待冷，取出切片，食時可沾③料。

■ 做好肴肉置於氷箱，可保持三、四天不壞。

■ 圍邊用材料：紅蘿蔔、巴西利。

肴肉 Tasty Chinese Ham Slices

上海菜　Shanghai
12人份　12 servings

①		②		③	
2⅔ lbs. fresh ham		2	stalks green onion	½	T. soy sauce
1 t. niter or saltpeter*		2	slices ginger root	1	t. sugar
2 T. salt		1	T. rice wine	½	T. vinegar
1 t. Szechuan peppercorns		8	C. water	1	t. chopped green onion
				1	t. chopped ginger root

❶ Clean outside of ham; drain until dry; rub niter into surface of ham. Heat pan (no oil) and stir-fry ① until fragrant; remove and rub into surface of ham; let meat sit 3 days in refrigerator.

❷ Rinse meat lightly and place in ② ; cook 1 hour covered, over low heat. Remove ham and wrap tightly in a towel. Wrap up tightly with string or place a heavy weight on top to compress ham; let cool. Unwrap ham and cut into paper-thin slices and arrange on serving plate; pour ③ mixture into a bowl and serve with slices for dipping.

* Niter is an ingredient which aids in preservation; if unavailable, omit.

■ Ham will keep in refrigerator for 3-4 days, after cooking.

■ Garnish with carrot and parsley.

猪後腿肉…半斤

① 酒……… 1 大匙
　葱……… 2 枝
　薑……… 2 片
蒜頭……… 3 粒

② 糖……… 1 小匙
　醋……… 1 小匙
　醬油露（或醬油）2 大匙
　味精……… 半小匙
　辣椒油……… 1 大匙

❶ 猪肉洗淨放鍋内，倒入清水（水需滿過肉為宜），加入①料蓋鍋煮開後，改小火再煮約３０分鐘，撈出切大薄片，食用時在開水内川燙過，排列在菜盤内。

❷ 蒜去皮，打爛成泥，盛小碗内，調入②料攪匀，淋在排好肉片上即成。

■ 圍邊用材料：香菜。

蒜泥白肉 Pork Slices with Chopped Garlic

四川菜　Szechuan
6人份　6 servings

⅔ lb. fresh ham

① 　1　T.　rice wine
　2　stalks green onion
　2　slices ginger root
　3　cloves garlic

② 　1　t.　sugar
　1　t.　vinegar
　2　T.　soy sauce
　½　t.　MSG
　1　T.　hot pepper oil ("la you")

❶ Place pork in a pan with water to cover; add ① and let liquid come to a boil; turn heat to low and simmer covered for 30 minutes; remove. Cut into paper-thin bite-size pieces. Before serving, dip pieces in boiling water until heated through; remove, drain and arrange on serving plate.

❷ Smash garlic and mince finely; mix with ② and pour over pork slices.

■ Garnish with coriander.

牛筋	12兩		鹽	1小匙
水	6杯		味精	½小匙
香菜	少許		醬油	3大匙
葱	2支	①	醋	1小匙
			糖	2小匙
			辣油	1大匙
			麻油	1大匙

❶ 牛筋加水用快鍋煮約1小時後，撈起待涼，切薄片放於盤內。

❷ 香菜切碎，葱切斜片放在牛筋上拌入①料即可。

■ 牛筋中之皮下筋以快鍋燒煮需30分鐘，腱子牛筋與腳蹄筋時間較長，需1小時才會爛。

麻辣牛筋 Sliced Beef Tendons

四川菜　Szechuan
12人份　12 servings

- 1 lb. beef tendons*[1]
- 6 C. water
- ⅓ C. coriander
- 2 stalks green onion

①
- 1 t. salt
- ½ t. MSG
- 3 T. soy sauce
- 1 t. vinegar
- 2 t. sugar
- 1 T. hot pepper oil ("la you")
- 1 T. sesame oil

❶ Place beef tendons and water in a pressure cooker and cook 1 hour over medium heat*[2]; drain and allow beef tendons to cool; cut into paper-thin slices and arrange on serving plate.

❷ Chop coriander; diagonally cross-cut green onion into thin slices; sprinkle onion and coriander on top of sliced beef tendons; prepare ① mixture and pour on top of coriander and onions; toss lightly and serve.

*[1] All tendons except those of the flank require 30 minutes. Cook flank tendons 1 hour.

*[2] If no pressure cooker is available, place mixture in a covered pot and cook 2-3 hours over medium heat until tendons are very tender; remove and use as directed.

<table>
<tr><td>新鮮干貝 １０ 兩</td><td>葱（３公分長）６枝</td><td>蠔油……４大匙</td></tr>
</table>

新鮮干貝 １０ 兩

① 薑酒……１大匙
小蘇打…１小匙
水…………半杯

② 葱（３公分長）６枝
薑…………６片
芹頭（拍破）３粒

③ 嫩薑絲……半杯
葱絲………¼杯
紅辣椒絲１大匙

④ 蠔油……４大匙
醬油……２大匙
味精……半小匙
麻油……１小匙
水………２大匙
太白粉…半小匙

❶ 干貝切薄片，調入①料，醃約１小時半後，用清水漂洗淨備用。

❷ ３大匙油燒熱，將②料炒香加入酒１大匙，水５杯燒開煮２分鐘，再將②料撈起，將鮮干貝燙約２０秒撈出，③料置於盤底，上舖干貝。

❸ ④料煮開，做爲沾食用。

■ 圍邊用材料：紅辣椒。

生灼鮮貝   Fresh Scallop Slices with Oyster Sauce

廣東菜   Cantonese
12人份   12 servings

10 oz. fresh scallops

① 1 T. ginger wine*
1 t. baking soda
½ C. water

② 6 1-inch sections green onion
6 slices ginger root
3 cloves garlic, smashed

③ ½ C. shredded ginger root
¼ C. shredded green onion
1 T. shredded hot red pepper

④ 4 T. oyster sauce
2 T. soy sauce
½ t. MSG
1 t. sesame oil
2 T. water
½ t. cornstarch

❶ Cut scallops into paper-thin slices; mix with ① and soak 1½ hours; drain and rinse scallops lightly; drain again.

❷ Heat pan and 3T. oil; stir-fry ② until fragrant; add 1T. rice wine and 5C. water; let cook 2 minutes over high heat. Remove ② with a strainer and add scallop slices; let cook 20 seconds and remove. Arrange ③ on serving plate and place scallop slices on top.

❸ Bring ingredients of ④ to a boil; pour into a bowl and serve with scallops as a dipping sauce.

■ Garnish with hot red pepper shreds.

* See "Helpful Hints" for directions on preparation of ginger wine.

腰果(或核桃、松子)……3兩　　①{ 水……………………1杯 / 糖、麥芽糖…………各3大匙 }
「炸油」………………3杯

❶ 腰果以①料用中火燒煮5分鐘撈出，瀝乾水份。

❷ 乾淨「炸油」燒熱，以小火將腰果炸酥（約8分鐘，炸時需常常攪動），注意顏色呈淡茶色時，撈出攤開在舖有紙之盤上（便於吸油），待涼、酥脆後即可盛盤供食。

糖酥腰果 Crispy Cashews

廣東菜　Cantonese
6人份　6 servings

3　oz. raw cashews or walnuts
3　C. oil for frying

①{ 1　C. water / 3　T. sugar / 3　T. honey }

❶ Place cashews in pan with ① ; bring to a boil and cook medium heat for 5 minutes; drain.

❷ Heat oil for deep-frying; deep-fry cashews over low heat for 8 minutes (stirring occasionally) until golden brown; remove and drain on paper. Cashews will become crunchy when cool. Serve.

<table>
<tr><td>綠豆芽⋯⋯⋯半斤</td><td>萵筍⋯⋯⋯⋯1 條</td><td rowspan="6">①</td><td>醬油⋯⋯⋯⋯1 小匙</td></tr>
<tr><td>蝦米⋯⋯⋯⋯半兩</td><td></td><td>鹽⋯⋯⋯⋯⋯1 小匙</td></tr>
<tr><td></td><td></td><td>味精⋯⋯⋯⋯1 小匙</td></tr>
<tr><td></td><td></td><td>糖⋯⋯⋯⋯⋯半小匙</td></tr>
<tr><td></td><td></td><td>麻油⋯⋯⋯⋯1 小匙</td></tr>
<tr><td></td><td></td><td>醋⋯⋯⋯⋯⋯1 小匙</td></tr>
</table>

❶ 綠豆芽、蝦米用開水燙過；萵筍切絲。

❷ 菜盤先舖上萵筍，再舖上綠豆芽，最後把蝦米放在上面，淋上①料即成。

■ 如無萵筍，以菜心、小黃瓜或其他蔬菜代替。綠豆芽最好摘芽除根。

涼拌豆芽菜 Spicy Bean Sprouts with Cucumber Shreds

北平菜　　Peking
6人份　　6 servings

⅔ lb. bean sprouts
1 T. dried shrimp

1 C. shredded cucumber

① 1 t. soy sauce
1 t. salt
1 t. MSG
½ t. sugar
1 t. sesame oil
1 t. vinegar

❶ Rinse bean sprouts and remove bitter ends; rinse dried shrimp and separately blanch bean sprouts and dried shrimp in boiling water; remove and drain.

❷ Place cucumber shreds on serving plate; portion bean sprouts on top with dried shrimp in the center; pour ① over all and toss lightly; serve.

鮮蜆⋯⋯⋯⋯⋯半斤

① 醬油⋯⋯⋯⋯⋯⋯半杯
蒜頭(拍破)⋯⋯⋯⋯5粒
紅辣椒(切細)⋯⋯⋯1條
醋⋯⋯⋯⋯⋯⋯1小匙
糖⋯⋯⋯⋯⋯⋯1小匙
酒⋯⋯⋯⋯⋯⋯3大匙

❶ 鮮蜆買回後先用大碗泡清水(吐沙),數小時後將蜆洗淨,盛於鋁鍋內加清水1杯擱置約10分鐘,輕輕放於爐上用小火燒至蜆口開約0、5公分大小即可離火,瀝乾水份,盛於深碗內加①料浸泡,然後放進冰箱,約泡24小時即可食用。

■ 醃泡蜆的①料如不能醃過蜆面時,依照上項比率增加醃泡。

■ 食用過後剩餘的醃泡醬油可利用燒魚。

鹹蜆 Marinated Clams

台灣菜　Taiwanese
6人份　6 servings

⅔ lb. small clams

① ½ C. soy sauce
5 cloves garlic, smashed
1 hot red pepper, shredded
1 t. vinegar
1 t. sugar
3 T. rice wine

❶ Place clams in a bowl with water to cover and let stand 6 hours (clams will rid themselves of sand); drain and add 1C. fresh water; let stand 10 minutes and carefully move to heat. Simmer over low heat until clams open about ⅙ of an inch; remove and drain. Mix with ① and refrigerate 24 hours; serve.

■ When marinating clams, ① should cover clams; if not, increase ① or stir clams every few hours, to marinate all of the clams.

■ The marinade may be retained and used as a sauce for cooking other varieties of fish.

小黃瓜……1 斤　　薑………10片切絲　　　　醋…………2 大匙
鹽………1 大匙　　紅辣椒1 條去籽切絲　①{ 糖…………2 大匙
　　　　　　　　　麻油……………半杯
　　　　　　　　　干辣椒……5 條切段
　　　　　　　　　花椒粒………1 小匙

❶ 小黃瓜去頭尾，視其大小對剖成４或６條，加鹽醃約２０分鐘，以冷開水輕輕洗淨後，用潔巾擠乾水份置大碗內，洒上薑絲、紅椒絲。

❷ 麻油半杯燒開，以中火將干辣椒炸香，隨加花椒粒略炸，前後約３０秒，即可淋在紅椒絲、薑絲等上面，調上①料，醃約６小時，吃時取酌量切段盛盤供食。

麻辣黃瓜 Szechuan Gherkin Slices

1⅓ lbs. gherkin cucumbers
1　T. salt

10 slices ginger root, shredded
1　hot red pepper, shredded
½　C. sesame oil
5　dried hot red peppers, cut into 1-inch sections
1　t. Szechuan peppercorns

①{ 2　T. vinegar
2　T. sugar

❶ Cut off tips of cucumbers and cut each into 4 or 6 sections; mix with salt and let sit 20 minutes. Rinse lightly in cold water cucumber sections and drain; place in a bowl and sprinkle shredded ginger and hot red pepper on top.

❷ Heat pan and ½C. sesame oil; stir-fry Szechuan peppercorns over medium heat until fragrant; add dried pepper sections and stir-fry 30 seconds, remove. Pour mixture over shredded ginger and hot red pepper, add ① and mix with cucumber. Refrigerate 6 hours and before eating, cut each cucumber into 2-inch sections and place on serving plate; serve.

海蜇皮……3兩　　小黃瓜絲……半杯　　　　醬油………1大匙
　　　　　　　　　白蘿蔔絲……半杯　　　　鹽…………半小匙
　　　　　　　　　　　　　　　　　　　　　糖…………半小匙
　　　　　　　　　　　　　　　　　①｛　胡椒………¼小匙
　　　　　　　　　　　　　　　　　　　　　麻油………1小匙
　　　　　　　　　　　　　　　　　　　　　醋…………1小匙

❶ 海蜇皮切細絲加温開水1杯泡過後，用冷水3杯泡1小時，漏乾水份。
❷ 小黃瓜、白蘿蔔絲，用冷開水漂洗，備用。
❸ 備盤一只，將黃瓜絲與白蘿蔔絲先置盤，再將海蜇絲放在上面，食時淋上①料即成。
■ 配料可用西洋芹菜、紅蘿蔔、菜心等代替。喜食辣椒或大蒜，可酌量加入。

拌蜇皮 Spicy Salted Jellyfish Salad

北平菜　　Peking
6人份　 6 servings

3　oz. salted jellyfish　　　½　C. shredded cucumber
　　　　　　　　　　　　　½　C. shredded turnip*

①｛
1　T.　soy sauce
½　t.　salt
½　t.　sugar
¼　t.　black pepper
1　t.　sesame oil
1　t.　vinegar

❶ Rinse jellyfish and shred; place in warm water to cover for 3 minutes and drain: place in fresh, cold water to cover for 1 hour; remove and drain.
❷ Rinse cucumber and turnip shreds lightly in coldwater; drain.
❸ Place the cucumber and turnip shreds on serving plate; portion softened, shredded jellyfish on top; pour ① over ingredients and toss lightly; serve.
* 　Shredded celery, carrots, or vegetable hearts may be substituted for the above vegetables. If turnips are unavailable, substitute icicle radishes. Chopped garlic may be added to ① for extra flavor.

干絲⋯⋯⋯4兩　①{ 碱塊⋯⋯⋯¼個　②{ 鹽⋯⋯⋯⋯1小匙
芹菜⋯⋯⋯2兩　　　開水⋯⋯⋯6杯　　　味精⋯⋯⋯半小匙
　　　　　　　　　　　　　　　　　　　　麻油⋯⋯⋯半小匙

❶ 芹菜切成小段，用滾開水略燙後，泡冷水撈出。

❷ ①料燒開，待碱塊溶化時熄火，把干絲放入用筷子攪散泡約１０分鐘，見干絲呈白色軟化時，
　撈起用冷水多洗數次，以去碱味。

❸ 干絲、芹菜同置碗內，加②料合拌，即可盛盤。

■ 干絲因乾度不同，泡碱時間隨之不定，可於泡碱時，隨個人喜好軟度撈起即可。

■ 圍邊用材料：紅辣椒。

拌干絲 Bean Curd Noodle and Celery Salad

四川菜　Szechuan
6人份　6 servings

4　oz. bean curd noodles　①{ 2　t.　baking soda　②{ 1　t.　salt
2　oz. celery　　　　　　　 6　C.　boiling water　　½　t.　MSG
　　　　　　　　　　　　　　　　　　　　　　　　　　　½　t.　sesame oil

❶ Wash and trim celery of leaves; cut into 1-inch sections; blanch sections in boiling water; remove and place in cold water to cool; remove and drain.

❷ Dissolve baking soda in boiling water and add bean curd noodles; stir noodles lightly to separate. Soak about 10 minutes until noodles are soft and have turned white; drain and rinse repeatedly in cold water until noodles are rid of baking soda mixture; drain.

❸ Place noodles and celery sections in a mixing bowl and add ② ; toss lightly to mix ingredients and place on serving plate; serve.

■ The texture of bean curd noodles often varies and so the soaking time required may vary too. Test noodles for tenderness and revise soaking time if necessary.

■ Garnish with hot red pepper.

	西洋芹菜‥‥‥‥‥‥1斤		鹽‥‥‥‥‥‥1⅓小匙	
①	芥末‥‥‥‥‥‥3大匙	②	味精‥‥‥‥‥‥半小匙	
	温開水‥‥‥‥‥1½大匙		糖‥‥‥‥‥‥半小匙	
			水‥‥‥‥‥‥1杯	
			太白粉‥‥‥‥‥1½小匙	

❶ 芹菜洗淨切4公分長段，粗的部份開兩半，用滾水燙1分鐘，再以冷開水漂涼，瀝乾水份。

❷ ①料調勻蓋嚴置約10分鐘（使味道香辣即成芥末醬），燒開②料拌入①料，待冷澆在芹菜上面即可。

芥末芹菜 Tossed Celery with Mustard Sauce

北平菜 　 Peking
12人份 12 servings

	1⅓ lbs. celery hearts		1⅓ t. salt
①	3 T. hot mustard	②	½ t. MSG
	1½ T. warm water		½ t. sugar
			1 C. water
			1½ t. cornstarch

❶ Rinse celery; cut stalks into 1½-inch sections. (If end is very thick, cut in half). Cook 1 minutes in boiling water; remove and place in cold water; when cool, remove and drain.

❷ Mix ① cover and set for 10 minutes; boiling ② ; add in ① ; let cool and pour over celery; toss lightly and serve.

■ You can also substitute broccoli or cauliflower for celery and follow recipe as directed above.

<table>
<tr><td>海帶絲…………4兩</td><td>薑絲…………1 大匙</td></tr>
</table>

①
鹽…………半大匙
水…………3 杯

②
薑絲…………1 大匙
葱絲…………半大匙
紅辣椒絲……半大匙
鹽…………半小匙
味精…………⅓小匙
麻油…………⅔大匙
醋…………1 小匙

❶ 海帶絲略切，放入①料內燒開撈出，隨即調入②料，拌勻置於菜盤即可。

凉拌海带 Cold Tossed Seaweed

四川菜　Szechuan
6人份　6 servings

4 oz. seaweed strips

①
½ T. salt
3 C. water

②
1 T. shredded ginger root
½ T. shredded green onion
½ T. shredded hot red pepper
½ t. salt
⅓ t. MSG
⅔ T. sesame oil
1 t. worcestershire sauce

❶ Cut seaweed into 3-inch strips; place in ① and heat until liquid boils; remove and drain. Mix with ② and place on serving plate; serve.

①{
白蘿蔔…………半條
小黃瓜…………１條
紅蘿蔔…………半條
} 淨重爲半斤
（２杯）

薑………………１０片

紅辣椒(切小段)…半條

②{
鹽…………半大匙
糖…………３大匙
醋…………３大匙
}

❶ ①料切滾刀塊，與薑、紅辣椒加鹽半大匙醃約６小時。

❷ 醃好①料等以冷開水輕輕沖洗，瀝乾，用潔巾擠乾水份，加②料拌勻，再醃約６小時即可供食。

■ ①料可切丁、切絲、或菱形，依所切大小來決定醃料所需時間長短。

廣東泡菜 Cantonese Pickled Vegetables

廣東菜　Cantonese
6人份　6 servings

①{
½ turnip
1 cucumber
½ carrot
} Combined ingredients equal ⅔ lb.

10 slices ginger root
½ hot red pepper, diced

②{
½ T. salt
3 T. sugar
3 T. vinegar
}

❶ Cut ingredients in ① into bite-size pieces (equal to about 2 cups); add ginger root slices, hot red pepper and salt. Mix and let stand 6 hours.

❷ Lightly rinse vegetables; drain and add ② ; mix ingredients and let mixture stand 6 hours in refrigerator; serve.

■ Ingredients of ① may be diced, shredded, or diagonally cross-cut into big or little pieces according to your preference and the soaking time should be revised accordingly.

包心菜 ⎫
白蘿蔔 ⎬ 計2斤
紅蘿蔔 ⎭

① ⎧ 紅辣椒（切丁）⋯⋯⋯¼杯
　 ⎩ 嫩薑（切丁）⋯⋯⋯⋯¼杯

② ⎧ 酒⋯⋯⋯⋯⋯⋯2大匙
　 ⎪ 鹽⋯⋯⋯⋯⋯⋯3大匙
　 ⎨ 花椒粒⋯⋯⋯⋯半大匙
　 ⎩ 冷開水⋯⋯⋯⋯6杯

❶ 包心菜去老葉洗淨，撕成約5公分四方片，紅蘿蔔、白蘿蔔洗淨連皮切丁，全部晾乾水份約半天時間。

❷ 將泡菜罈或玻璃罐洗淨，擦乾水份，放入①料、晾乾的各種材料及拌勻的②料倒入浸泡，並將容器口密封，泡3～4天即可。

■❶ 第一次泡出來的泡菜，味道較差，如第二次再泡時，酌量再加鹽及酒泡約2天。但泡數次以上後，味道變酸，便應按照②料比例斟酌加入混合使用。

　❷ 泡菜材料所切形狀、大小可依個人喜愛而定。

　❸ 切記夾泡菜時所使用之筷子、湯匙之類要保持清潔乾燥，以免滷汁發霉變味。

四川泡菜　Szechuan Pickled Salad

四川菜　Szechuan
6人份　6 servings

Chinese cabbage ⎫
carrot　　　　 ⎬ Combined weight
turnip*　　　　⎭ should equal about 2⅔ lbs.

① ⎧ ¼ C. diced hot red pepper
　 ⎩ ¼ C. diced ginger root

② ⎧ 2　T. rice wine
　 ⎪ 3　T. salt
　 ⎨ ½　T. Szechuan peppercorns
　 ⎩ 6　C. water

❶ Rinse cabbage and tear into 2-inch squares. Rinse carrot and turnip, with skin and dice; drain vegetables thoroughly. (Let dry about ½ day.)

❷ Place ① in a clean glass container or bowl; add all vegetables. (② should cover vegetables) Cover and let soak 3-4 days in refrigerator; serve.

■ 1. The marinade ② may be used again and again to soak new vegetables and will improve with age. The second time, add salt and rice wine and soak vegetables 2 days. If necessary, add more water to marinade after each use, so that vegetables are covered while soaking.

　2. Vegetables may be cut to different sizes and shapes, according to your preference.

　3. When removing vegetables from marinade, use clean chopsticks to prevent any foreign matter from getting into marinade.

* If unavailable, substitute icicle radish.

<table>
<tr><td>雞‧‧‧‧‧‧1隻2斤</td><td rowspan="5">①</td><td>鹽‧‧‧‧‧‧‧‧‧‧‧1大匙</td><td rowspan="2">②</td><td>太白粉‧‧‧‧‧1小匙</td></tr>
<tr><td>蔥絲‧‧‧‧‧4大匙</td><td>味精‧‧‧‧‧‧‧‧1小匙</td><td>水‧‧‧‧‧‧‧‧‧‧1小匙</td></tr>
<tr><td>嫩薑絲‧‧‧2大匙</td><td>酒‧‧‧‧‧‧‧‧‧‧1大匙</td></tr>
<tr><td></td><td>蔥‧‧‧‧‧‧‧‧‧‧‧2枝</td></tr>
<tr><td></td><td>薑‧‧‧‧‧‧‧‧‧‧‧2片</td></tr>
</table>

❶ 將①料抹勻雞身內外，醃約２０分鐘後，雞胸朝上大火蒸約２５分鐘，把雞切塊擺在盤內，再將蔥薑絲散蓋於雞塊上面並洒上胡椒，油４大匙燒開，澆於蔥薑絲上，蒸雞餘汁以②料勾汁，淋在雞上即成。

蔥油淋雞 Steamed Chicken with Green Onions

廣東菜　Cantonese
12人份　12 servings

1　whole chicken (about 2⅔lbs.)
4　T.　green onions, cut into 2-inch shreds
2　T.　ginger root, cut into 2-inch shreds

①
1　T.　salt
1　t.　MSG
1　T.　rice wine
2　stalks green onion
2　slices ginger root

②
1　t.　cornstarch
1　t.　water

❶ Rub ① mixture over exterior and interior of chicken; let sit 20 minutes. Place chicken in steamer, breast-side up and steam over high heat for 25 minutes; remove chicken (retain steaming liquid) and cut into bite-size pieces; place pieces on serving plate. Sprinkle green onion and ginger shreds over chicken pieces. Heat 4T. oil until smoking and spoon over onion and ginger shreds; heat retained, steaming liquid until boiling and add ② to thicken; portion over chicken pieces and serve.

雞……1隻2斤

① 鹽………1½大匙
味精………1小匙
酒………1大匙
葱………2枝
薑………2片

② 雞湯…………1杯
鹽…………¼小匙
味精………¼小匙
麻油………1小匙

❶ 將①料抹勻雞身內外，醃約３０分鐘，鍋放入１０杯水及雞(水需淹至雞之半身以上爲宜)大火燒開後，改小火煮約１０分鐘，把雞身翻轉，續煮１０分鐘，取出待冷。

❷ 將雞斬塊，順序擺在中碗內，淋上②料，放入冰箱，吃時，倒扣在盤內即成。

■ 圍邊用材料：番茄、生菜。

盐水雞 Cold Salted Chicken Appetizer

1 chicken (about 2⅔ lbs.)

① 1½ T. salt
1 t. MSG
1 T. rice wine
2 stalks green onion
2 slices ginger root

② 1 C. chicken stock
¼ t. salt
¼ t. MSG
1 t. sesame oil

❶ Spoon ① mixture over outside and inside cavity of chicken; let stand 30 minutes. Place chicken in 10C. water (water should reach halfway up chicken's side) and cook over high heat until water reaches a boil; turn heat to low and cook covered 10 minutes. Turn chicken over to other side and cook an additional 10 minutes; remove chicken and let cool.

❷ Cut chicken into bite-size pieces and place skin-side down in a medium-sized soup bowl (pack pieces tightly as to fill a mold); add ② mixture and place in refrigerator to cool and become firm. Before serving invert onto serving plate to form illustrated shape; serve.

■ Garnish with tomato and lettuce.

雞⋯⋯⋯⋯1隻2斤		
	薑末⋯⋯⋯⋯2小匙	
	葱末⋯⋯⋯⋯2小匙	
	醬油⋯⋯⋯⋯3大匙	
①	味精⋯⋯⋯⋯半小匙	
	麻油⋯⋯⋯⋯2小匙	
	鎮江醋⋯⋯⋯1大匙	
	糖⋯⋯⋯⋯2小匙	
	辣椒油⋯⋯⋯2大匙	

❶ 鍋放入１０杯水及雞(水需淹過雞身一半以上爲宜)，燒開後改用小火煮１０分鐘，將雞身翻轉續煮１０分鐘，取出待冷。

❷ 將雞斬塊，排好在菜盤，把①料攪勻淋在雞塊上，以香菜圍邊即可供食。

■ 宴客時，斬好雞塊順序擺在中碗內，然後倒扣在盤內，增加美觀。

■ 圍邊用材料：香菜。

紅油雞塊 Cold Chicken Appetizer with Hot Sauce

四川菜 Szechuan
12人份 12 servings

1 chicken (about 1⅔ lbs.)

① 2 t. chopped ginger root
2 t. chopped green onion
3 T. soy sauce
½ t. MSG
2 t. sesame oil
1 T. worcestershire sauce
2 t. sugar
2 T. hot pepper oil ("la you")

❶ Place chicken in 10C. water; (water should reach halfway up chicken's side) and cook over high heat until water reaches a boil; turn heat to low and cook 10 minutes; turn chicken to other side and cook an additional 10 minutes; remove chicken and let cool.

❷ Cut chicken into bite-size pieces and arrange on serving plate; pour ① over chicken pieces and serve.

■ Note: You may also use method of lining a bowl with chicken pieces as explained on P. 29 step ❷ to create a pretty design on serving plate.

■ Garnish with coriander.

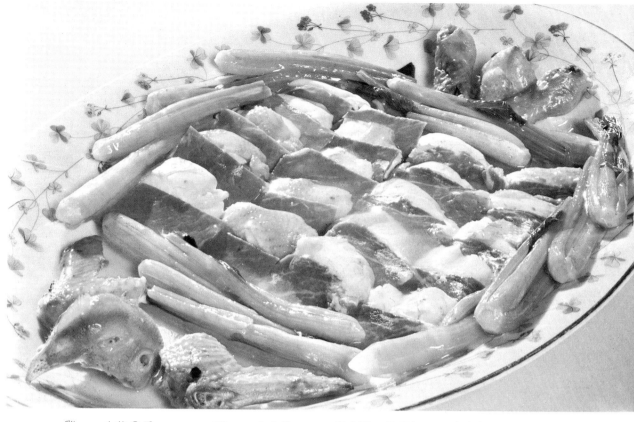

雞……1隻2斤

$①$
鹽……1大匙
味精…1小匙
酒……1大匙
糖……半小匙
葱………2枝
薑………2片

$②$
瘦火腿…3兩
糖……1大匙
酒……1大匙
葱………2枝
薑………2片

$③$
太白粉…1小匙
水………2小匙
油菜………1斤

❶ 雞調入①料，醃泡３０分鐘後，將醃汁倒入雞肚內，置於蒸盤，雞胸朝上，用大火蒸約２０分鐘，蒸熟倒出雞汁，候冷取出全骨，雞肉切塊，排好置於菜盤。

❷ 火腿加②料預先蒸熟，切薄片（與雞肉塊同大小），然後取火腿一片，夾入雞塊內（如圖）。

❸ 鍋內入雞汁１杯，燒開以③料勾汁，澆於雞肉上，以油菜炒熟圍邊。

金華玉樹雞 Grilled Ham and Chicken Slices

廣東菜　Cantonese
12人份　12 servings

$①$
1　chicken (about 2⅔lbs.)
1　T. salt
1　t. MSG
1　T. rice wine
½　t. sugar
2　stalks green onion
2　slices ginger root

$②$
3　oz. Chinese ham
1　T. sugar
1　T. rice wine
2　stalks green onion
2　slices ginger root

$③$
1　t. cornstarch
2　t. water
1⅓lbs. precooked rape sections*

❶ Rub outside surface of chicken with ① ; let stand 30 minutes; Spoon ① into cavity of chicken and place in steamer, breast side up; steam over high heat for 20 minutes; remove chicken and let cool (retain liquid); remove bones and cut chicken meat into 2-inch paper-thin slices.

❷ Rub ② mixture over surface of ham; place in steamer and steam over medium heat for 20 minutes; remove and cut into slices the same size as chicken. Arrange ham and chicken slices alternately on serving plate as illustrated in picture.

❸ Heat 1C. retained liquid until boiling; add ③ to thicken and pour over chicken and ham slices; place precooked vegetable around meat slices; serve.

* Rape ("you tsai") may be purchased at a Chinese grocery store. Rape sections should be 3-inches long and ½-inch thick. You may substitute brocolli or celery cabbage.

雞……1隻2斤　　　　　┌ 麥芽糖(或蜜)1大匙、熱水……3大匙　　　「炸油」…1〇杯
五香鹽…1大匙　　　①｛ 白醋…………1大匙、酒………1大匙
　　　　　　　　　　　└ 太白粉………1小匙

❶ 雞以熱水洗淨，擦乾水份備用。

❷ ①料置盆攪勻(麥芽糖和熱水先溶化)多次的淋在雞身上，至雞皮完全沾勻後把五香鹽半大匙在
雞肚內抹勻，以牙籤縫合，然後吊起吹乾(約需7、8小時)。

❸ 「炸油」1〇杯燒開，將雞(眼球弄破以免油爆)下鍋，炸時以慢火炸熟(約需2〇分鐘)見雞整隻
熟了就開大火，炸成雞肉嫩，外皮脆，即成脆皮雞做好剁塊，排列大盤內，用半只檸檬汁澆在
雞塊上，此道菜最好熱食。

■ 做此菜時宜天氣晴朗，晾在有陽光通風處。

■ 五香鹽做法：乾鍋將2大匙鹽炒熱後盛起，加半小匙五香粉，或半小匙花椒粉拌勻即成。

■ 圍邊用材料：檸檬、櫻桃、蔥、紅辣椒。

脆皮雞 Crispy-Skin Chicken

1　chicken (about 2⅔ lbs.)
1　T. five-spice salt or Szechuan
　peppercorn salt*1

①┌1　T. light corn syrup or honey
　│3　T. hot water
　┤1　T. vinegar
　│1　T. rice wine
　└1　t. cornstarch

10 C. oil for frying

❶ Clean chicken ih boiling water to remove any foreign matter; drain.
❷ Mix ingredients of ① in a pan over low heat until corn syrup or honey dissolves; pour over chicken and continue basting until chicken is completely coated. Rub ½T. 5-spice salt into cavity of chicken and use a toothpick to close cavity opening; hang outside to dry for about 8 hours.*2
❸ Heat oil for deep-frying; using a chopstick, punch out chicken's eyes if still remaining to prevent their exploding during frying. Deep-fry chicken over low heat for 20 minutes ; before removing turn heat to high and cook an additional minute until golden brown; remove and drain. Cut into bite-size pieces and arrange on serving plate as illustrated; sprinkle with lemon juice and serve with remaining 5-spice salt.
■ Garnish with lemon, cherries, shredded green onion and hot red pepper.
*1 Heat a pan (no oil) and stir-fry 2T. salt over low heat until very hot; remove and mix with ½ t. 5-spice powder or Szechuan peppercorn powder and use as directed in recipe.
*2 It's best to make this chicken on a sunny and breezy day to aid the drying out; however, you may also use an electric fan and hang inside the house.

雞……1 隻 2 斤

①
鹽 …………… 1 小匙
味精 ………… 1/4 小匙
糖 …………… 1 小匙
醬油 ………… 1 大匙
麻油 ………… 1/2 小匙
五香粉 ……… 1/4 小匙
酒 …………… 1 大匙
薑 …………… 2 片
葱 …………… 2 枝

②
蛋黃 ………… 1 個
太白粉 ……… 4 大匙
「炸油」……… 6 杯

❶ 雞切粗塊，調①料拌勻，醃 2 0 分鐘後將葱、薑拿掉，先攪入蛋黃再拌入太白粉，備用。

❷ 「炸油」燒開，放入雞塊中火炸約 4 分鐘撈出，續將油燒至沸滾，重將雞塊投入，炸至雞皮酥脆（二次計約 5 分鐘）撈出，置於菜盤中，另擺椒鹽。

炸八塊雞 Deep-Fried 5-Spice Chicken

1 whole chicken (2⅔ lbs.)

①
1　t.　salt
¼　t.　MSG
1　t.　sugar
1　T.　soy sauce
½　t.　sesame oil
¼　t.　5-spice powder
1　T.　rice wine
2　slices ginger root
2　stalks green onion

②
1　egg yolk
4　T.　cornstarch
6　C.　oil for frying

❶ Cut chicken into bite-size pieces; mix with ① and let stand 30 minutes; remove onion stalks and ginger slices and dip each piece of chicken into egg yolk; coat each piece with cornstarch.

❷ Heat oil for deep-frying; deep-fry chicken pieces over medium heat for 4 minutes; remove and heat oil until very hot; add chicken pieces and deep-fry an additional minute; remove, drain and place on serving plate; serve with salt.

雞胸肉⋯⋯⋯2個(12兩)		蝦仁⋯⋯⋯⋯⋯4兩

①{
薑酒⋯⋯⋯⋯⋯⋯1大匙
鹽⋯⋯⋯⋯⋯⋯⋯1小匙
味精⋯⋯⋯⋯⋯半小匙
胡椒⋯⋯⋯⋯⋯¼小匙
麻油⋯⋯⋯⋯⋯半小匙
蛋白⋯⋯⋯⋯⋯⋯1個
太白粉⋯⋯⋯⋯⋯2大匙
}

②{
荸薺
紅蘿蔔
冬菇
葱
}切絲計半杯

「炸油」⋯⋯⋯⋯6杯

❶ 將每個雞胸肉，切成二大薄片，修成一樣厚薄之四方片（6公分×10公分）調入¾的①料醃約20分鐘。

❷ 蝦仁剁爛調剩餘①料後，與②料拌勻成餡，分成4份。

❸ 雞肉攤開（雞皮朝下）洒少許太白粉，將餡抹上。

❹ 「炸油」燒熱，將鑲好雞肉入鍋炸熟(約4分鐘)撈起切塊即成。

■ 圍邊用材料：小黃瓜。

炸百花雞 Stuffed Chicken Breasts

台灣菜 Taiwanese
12人份 12 servings

2 deboned chicken breasts (about 1lb.)

①{
1 T. ginger wine*
1 t. salt
½ t. MSG
¼ t. black pepper
½ t. sesame oil
1 egg white
2 T. cornstarch
}

4 oz. raw, shelled shrimp

②{
shredded water chestnuts
shredded carrot
shredded mushroom
shredded green onion
} Combined ingredients equal to ½C.

6 C. oil for frying

❶ Slice each chicken breast through thickness in half; lightly pound with blunt edge of cleaver to form 4 thin rectangles 2 inches by 3 inches; mix meat pieces with ¾ of ① mixture; let sit 20 minutes.

❷ Chop shrimp finely; add remaining ¼ of ① mixture and mix well; add ② and mix vigorously to thoroughly combine ingredients (filling); separate into 4 portions.

❸ Lay each chicken rectangle flat on counter (skin side down); sprinkle surface lightly with cornstarch and spread filling evenly over surface (use a spoon dipped in water to smooth surface of filling.)

❹ Heat oil for deep-frying; deep-fry stuffed chicken pieces for 4 minutes over medium heat until golden; remove and drain. Slice and place on serving plate; serve.

■ Garnish with cucumber slices.

* A mixture of rice wine and the juice of smashed ginger root.

雞胸⋯⋯⋯2個
（雞肉半斤）

① 酒⋯⋯⋯半大匙
鹽⋯⋯⋯¾小匙
味精⋯⋯半小匙
胡椒⋯⋯¼小匙
蛋⋯⋯⋯1個
太白粉⋯3大匙

核桃⋯⋯1½杯
「炸油」⋯⋯6杯

❶ 雞肉去皮切成0.3公分大薄片，調①料醃約20分鐘。
❷ 水4杯燒開，把核桃燒煮2分鐘，剝去薄膜，切碎，將雞片拌入太白粉3大匙並兩面沾上核桃。
❸ 「炸油」燒熱，中火將雞肉炸約3分鐘撈起，置於盤上即成。
■ 圍邊用材料：番茄、生菜。
■ 核桃可用腰果、花生取代，如用熟的，油炸時可縮短爲2分鐘。

核桃雞片 Crunchy Walnut Chicken

廣東菜 Cantonese
12人份 12 servings

⅔ lb. chicken meat

① ½ T. rice wine
¾ t. salt
½ t. MSG
¼ t. black pepper
1 egg
3 T. cornstarch

1½ C. walnuts*
6 C. oil for frying

❶ Remove skin from chicken and cut meat into paper-thin slices; add ① and let soak 20 minutes.
❷ Boil 4C. water and cook walnuts 2 minutes; remove, drain and peel away dark outer skin and chop finely. Dust chicken slices with 3T. cornstarch and coat with chopped walnuts.
❸ Heat oil for deep-frying; deep-fry chicken pieces over medium heat for 1 minute until golden brown; remove, drain and serve with Szechuan peppercorn salt.
■ Garnish with cucumber slices
* You may substitute roasted cashews or peanuts.

雞肉…半斤

① 鹽……1小匙　　香菜………………………16片
　糖……半小匙　　紅辣椒絲………………16條
　酒……1小匙　　玻璃紙（10公分四方）16張
　味精…¼小匙　　「炸油」………………6杯

❶ 雞肉切16塊，拌上①料，醃約20分鐘。

❷ 每張玻璃紙包上1塊雞肉、紅辣椒絲1條及香菜1片。

❸ 「炸油」6杯燒開，投包好之雞塊下炸（小火），炸約1.5分鐘，即成。

■ 主要材料除雞肉外，可用牛肉、魚肉、蝦仁等任意選用，配料使用香菜、紅辣椒以外，也可用香腸、火腿、香菇、青豆仁、芹菜、洋葱、紅蘿蔔等任意選用。

紙包嫩雞 Paper-Wrapped Fried Chicken

廣東菜　Cantonese
12人份　12 servings

⅔ lb. chicken meat

① 1 t. salt
　½ t. sugar
　1 t. rice wine
　¼ t. MSG

16 sprigs coriander
16 shreds hot red pepper
16 pieces heavy-duty cellophane, cut into 4-inch squares
6 C. oil for frying

❶ Slice chicken meat into 16 paper-thin pieces; mix with ① and let soak 20 minutes.

❷ On each square of cellophane, place 1 shred hot red pepper, 1 sprig coriander and 1 piece chicken meat; wrap securely to form little packages.

❸ Heat oil for deep-frying; deep-fry chicken packages over low heat for 1½ minutes; remove and drain. Place packages on serving plate and serve.

■ You may substitute beef tenderloin, fish fillets or shrimp for the chicken meat and add Chinese sausage, ham, green peas, celery, onion or carrot slices as desired.

乳鴿⋯⋯⋯1 隻　　熟筍（切碎）⋯⋯½杯　　鹽⋯⋯⋯⋯1 小匙
里肌肉⋯⋯6 兩　　荸薺（切碎）⋯⋯½杯　　味精⋯⋯⋯1 小匙
雞肝⋯⋯⋯3 只　　冬菇（切碎）⋯1 大匙　　糖⋯⋯⋯⋯半小匙
雞油⋯⋯⋯1 兩　　葱末⋯⋯⋯⋯⋯1 大匙　②醬油⋯⋯⋯1 大匙
①胡椒⋯⋯¼小匙　薑末⋯⋯⋯⋯⋯1 大匙　　麻油⋯⋯⋯1 小匙
　蛋黃⋯⋯⋯1 個　　　　　　　　　　　　太白粉⋯⋯1 小匙
　　　　　　　　　　　　　　　　　　　　水⋯⋯⋯⋯2 大匙
　　　　　　　　　　　　　　　　　　　　炸米粉⋯⋯⋯1 兩
　　　　　　　　　　　　　　　　　　　　生菜⋯⋯⋯24 张

❶ 乳鴿去骨取肉、里肌肉去白筋，雞肝、雞油全部各切小粒，入①料拌勻。筍用潔巾擠乾水份。

❷ 油4 大匙，將調好味的鴿肉等爆炒至乾後，鏟於一邊，再把葱、薑末炒香即可下筍等各料大火
　 炒鬆，並加酒1 大匙及②料拌炒盛起。

❸ 炸米粉盛盤內，炒好鴿鬆置其上，食時以生菜包着吃。

■ 如無鴿子，可用里肌肉代理。

炒鴿鬆 Fried Minced Squab

廣東菜　Cantonese
12人份　12 servings

1　squab (about 5 oz.)	½　C. chopped precooked bamboo shoot	⎧ 1　t.　salt
6　oz. pork loin	½　C. chopped water chestnuts	⎪ 1　t.　MSG
3　chicken livers	1　T. chopped, pre-softened Chinese black mushroom	½　t.　sugar
1　oz. chicken fat	1　T. chopped green onion	②⎨ 1　T.　soy sauce
①⎧ ¼　t.　black pepper	1　T. chopped ginger root	⎪ 1　t.　sesame oil
⎩ 1　egg yolk		⎪ 1　t.　cornstarch
		⎩ 2　T.　water
		1　oz. fried rice noodles*
		24　leaves of lettuce

❶ Remove any fat or tough membrane from pork and debone squab; minced squab meat, pork loin, chicken liver and chicken fat finely. Mix all of minced ingredients with ① ; stir vigorously to combine ingredients; drain bamboo shoot of any excess water.

❷ Heat pan and 4T. oil; stir-fry meat mixture and chopped vegetables until dry; push mixture to side of pan (add more oil if necessary) and stir-fry green onion and ginger until fragrant; mix together all ingredients and stir-fry over high heat; add 1T. rice wine and ② ; stir-fry together and remove.

❸ Place fried rice noodles in center of serving plate; portion stir-fried squab and vegetables on top; serve. When eating, wrap a portion of stir-fried squab and vegetables with fried noodles in a leaf of lettuce.

■ If squab is unavailable, omit and increase pork loin.

* To fry rice noodles: heat oil for deep-frying; deep-fry noodles over medium heat until golden brown and expanded (turn over to fry on both sides); remove, drain and use as directed.

大明蝦…3條6兩
雞肉……6兩
① 鹽………半小匙
酒………1小匙
蛋白………1個
太白粉……半大匙

生魷魚…………半斤
筍……………1枝
② 紅蘿蔔……半條
豌豆角(半杯)…2兩
葱(3公分長)…6枝
薑…………6片
「炸油」………3杯

酒…………半大匙
鹽………1小匙
味精……半小匙
③ 糖……半小匙
胡椒……¼小匙
麻油……半小匙
水……3大匙
太白粉…1½小匙

❶ 明蝦去殼用鹽洗淨切片，雞肉亦切薄片同入①料攪勻。

❷ 生魷魚去皮切薄片備用。

❸ 筍、紅蘿蔔煮熟切片，豌豆角燙熟。

❹ 「炸油」燒熱，將明蝦片、雞肉片、魷魚片下鍋以中火泡熟撈起留油3大匙，將葱、薑炒香，即倒入②料略炒，隨加入蝦、雞肉、魷魚、酒半大匙，及③料拌炒，再加熟油1大匙即成。

遊龍戲鳳 Stir-Fried Prawns and Chicken

廣東菜　Cantonese
12人份　12 servings

3　prawns (⅓lb.)
½　lb. chicken meat
① ½　t.　salt
1　t.　rice wine
1　egg white
½　T.　cornstarch

⅔ lb. squid meat
② 1　medium-sized bamboo shoot
½　medium-sized carrot
½　C.　snow peas
6　1-inch sections green onion
6　slices ginger root
3　C.　oil for frying

½　T.　rice wine
1　t.　salt
½　t.　MSG
½　t.　sugar
③ ¼　t.　black pepper
½　t.　sesame oil
3　T.　water
1½ t.　cornstarch

❶ Remove shells from prawns; clean and devein; cut into thin slices. Cut chicken meat into thin bite-size slices; mix shrimp and chicken slices with ① ; let sit 20 minutes.

❷ Clean squid meat and cut into thin bite-size slices.

❸ Precook bamboo shoot and carrot in boiling water for 20 minutes; cut into thin bite-size slices. Remove stem and any veiny strings from snow peas; blanch in boiling water 30 seconds; place in cold water to cool and drain.

❹ Heat oil for deep-frying; deep-fry prawns, chicken and squid slices over medium heat until changed in color; remove and drain. Reheat pan and 3T. oil; stir-fry green onion and ginger until fragrant; add ② and stir-fry briefly; add prawn, chicken and squid slices, ½T. rice wine and ③ ; stir-fry to mix ingredients and add 1T. oil; remove and serve.

	雞肉⋯⋯⋯⋯⋯半斤		干辣椒（斜段）⋯⋯¾杯		酒⋯⋯⋯⋯⋯1 小匙
	醬油⋯⋯⋯⋯1 大匙		油⋯⋯⋯⋯⋯⋯半杯		醬油⋯⋯⋯⋯1 大匙
①	酒⋯⋯⋯⋯⋯1 小匙				味精⋯⋯⋯⋯¼小匙
	水⋯⋯⋯⋯⋯2 大匙			②	糖⋯⋯⋯⋯⋯2 小匙
	太白粉⋯⋯⋯2 小匙				麻油⋯⋯⋯⋯半小匙
					黑醋⋯⋯⋯⋯1 小匙
					水⋯⋯⋯⋯1½大匙
					太白粉⋯⋯⋯1 小匙

❶ 雞肉用刀輕輕拍鬆，切成二公分四方塊，調入①料拌和醃約２０分鐘。

❷ 油半杯燒熱，中火將干辣椒下鍋炒香，隨即將雞丁也下去炒熟，見顏色轉白就可倒入②料拌炒盛於盤上。

■ 醬油顏色如不夠紅，可放約半小匙醬色，加入②料內。醬色做法請參照特殊材料說明。

宮保雞丁 Stir-Fried Chicken with Dried Red Pepper

四川菜　Szechuan
6人份　6 servings

	⅔ lb. chicken meat	¾ C. dried red pepper, cut diagonally			1 t. rice wine *[2]
	1 T. soy sauce	into 1-inch sections*[1]			1 T. soy sauce
	1 t. rice wine	½ C. oil			¼ t. MSG
①	2 T. water			②	2 t. sugar
	2 t. cornstarch				½ t. sesame oil
					1 t. worcestershire sauce
					1½ T. water
					1 t. cornstarch

❶ Using blunt edge of cleaver, lightly pound chicken meat; cut into bite-size pieces; mix with ① and let sit 20 minutes.

❷ Heat pan and oil; stir-fry dried red pepper sections over medium heat 30 seconds; add chicken pieces and stir-fry until chicken changes color. Add ② and stir-fry until ingredients are mixed and sauce has thickened; remove to serving plate and serve.

*[1] Red peppers may differ, from one area to the next, in various degrees of hotness; revise the amount of peppers accordingly.

*[2] A dark, heavy soy sauce will add to the flavor and appearance of this dish.

①	雞肉⋯⋯⋯⋯１２兩	核桃⋯⋯⋯⋯⋯２杯	②	鹽⋯⋯⋯⋯⋯１小匙、麻油⋯⋯⋯⋯半小匙
	薑酒⋯⋯⋯⋯１大匙	「炸油」⋯⋯⋯⋯３杯		味精⋯⋯⋯⋯半小匙、水⋯⋯⋯⋯⋯２大匙
	鹽⋯⋯⋯⋯⋯１小匙	葱（３公分長）⋯⋯６枝		糖⋯⋯⋯⋯半小匙、太白粉⋯⋯１½小匙
	蛋白⋯⋯⋯⋯１個	薑⋯⋯⋯⋯⋯⋯６片		胡椒⋯⋯⋯⋯¼小匙
	太白粉⋯⋯⋯１大匙	酒⋯⋯⋯⋯⋯１小匙		

❶ 雞肉拍鬆，切粗丁調①料，醃２０分鐘，加太白粉１大匙攪勻。

❷ 核桃加水４杯，鹽１小匙，小火燒煮８分鐘撈出瀝乾，以乾淨油，小火炸８分鐘，呈淡茶色撈出。

❸ 「炸油」燒熱，將雞肉泡油３０秒鐘（需用鍋鏟攪散），見顏色轉白即可撈起，留油２大匙，將葱薑炒香，隨下雞丁、酒、②料及核桃，炒拌均勻即可。

■ 除主要材料雞肉外，其他配料也可用青豆仁、筍、紅蘿蔔、青椒、香菇、紅辣椒、腰菓等，依個人喜好變化，但需視其材料之不同，先煮熟或炸熟後再與雞丁同炒。

核桃雞丁 Stir-Fried Chicken with Walnuts

①	1 lb. chicken meat	2 C. walnuts	②	1 t. ricewine
	1 T. ginger wine	3 C. oil for frying		1 t. salt • ½ t. sesame oil
	1 t. salt	6 1 inch sections of		½ t. MSG • 2 T. water
	1 egg white	green onion		½ t. sugar • 1½ t. cornstarch
	1 T. cornstarch	6 slices ginger root		¼ t. black pepper

❶ Pound chicken meat; cut into bite-size pieces; mix with ① and let sit 20 minutes; add 1T. cornstarch and mix evenly.

❷ Add 4 cups water and 1t. salt to walnuts; simmer over low heat 8 minutes; remove walnuts and let water drain off. When dry, deep-fry walnuts over a low flame for 8 minutes until golden; remove and drain.

❸ Heat pan and oil; deep-fry chicken for 30 seconds; when chicken changes color, remove. Remove all but 2T. oil from pan; stir-fry green onion and ginger until fragrant; add chicken, rice wine, ② and walnuts; stir-fry until ingredients are mixed. Serve.

■ Variations: Green peas, bamboo shoots, carrots, green peppers, mushrooms, hot red peppers, or cashews may be substituted for walnuts.

| ① | 雞肉‧‧‧‧‧‧‧‧‧‧‧‧‧‧‧半斤
醬油‧‧‧‧‧‧‧‧‧‧‧‧‧1 大匙
酒‧‧‧‧‧‧‧‧‧‧‧‧‧‧‧1 小匙
水‧‧‧‧‧‧‧‧‧‧‧‧‧‧‧2 大匙
太白粉‧‧‧‧‧‧‧‧‧‧‧2 小匙
「炸油」‧‧‧‧‧‧‧‧‧‧‧3 杯 | ② | 葱、薑、蒜末‧‧‧‧‧各 1 大匙
辣豆瓣醬‧‧‧‧‧‧‧‧‧1 大匙
豆苗或菠菜‧‧‧‧‧‧‧‧‧半斤 | ③ | 酒‧‧‧‧‧‧‧‧‧‧‧‧‧‧‧1 小匙
醬油‧‧‧‧‧‧‧‧‧‧‧‧‧1 大匙
味精‧‧‧‧‧‧‧‧‧‧‧‧‧¼ 小匙
糖‧‧‧‧‧‧‧‧‧‧‧‧‧‧‧2 小匙
麻油‧‧‧‧‧‧‧‧‧‧‧‧半小匙
醋‧‧‧‧‧‧‧‧‧‧‧‧‧‧‧1 小匙
水‧‧‧‧‧‧‧‧‧‧‧1 ½ 大匙
太白粉‧‧‧‧‧‧‧‧‧‧‧1 小匙
花椒粉‧‧‧‧‧‧‧‧‧‧‧⅓ 小匙 |

❶ 雞肉切約4公分長條狀，拌上①料醃２０分鐘。

❷ 「炸油」燒熱，用中火將雞肉泡熟，撈起；留油３大匙，投入②料炒香，再下雞肉及③料，並加熱油１大匙炒勻盛起，盤兩邊置上炒熟豆苗即成。

成都子雞 Sauteed Chicken, Cheng-Tu Style
四川菜　Szechuan
12人份　12 servings

| ① | ⅔ lb. chicken meat
1 T. soy sauce
1 t. rice wine
2 T. water
2 t. cornstarch
3 C. oil for frying | ② | 1 T. chopped green onion
1 T. chopped ginger root
1 T. chopped garlic
1 T. hot bean paste ("la do ban jiang")
⅔ lb. precooked spinach | ③ | 1 t. rice wine
1 T. soy sauce
¼ t. MSG
2 t. sugar
½ t. sesame oil
1 t. vinegar
1½ T water
1 t. cornstarch
⅓ t. Szechuan peppercorn powder |

❶ Cut chicken meat into 1½-inch long matchstick-sized pieces; mix with ① and let soak 20 minutes.

❷ Heat oil for deep-frying; deep-fry chicken pieces over medium heat until changed in color; remove and drain. Remove all but 3T. oil from pan; reheat and add ② ; stir-fry until fragrant and add chicken pieces and ③ . Continue to stir-fry and add 1T. oil; mix and remove to serving plate. Portion precooked vegetable on both sides of chicken and serve.

① 雞……半隻1斤　　　酒………1大匙　　③ 太白粉…半小匙
　醬油………¼杯　　　水………1杯　　　　　水………1小匙
　栗子(罐頭)‥半杯　②糖………半大匙　　　　麻油……1小匙
　「炸油」……3杯　　　味精……半小匙
　葱薑末…1小匙　　　胡椒……¼小匙

❶ 雞切成約4公分四方塊，用醬油醃漬備用。

❷ 「炸油」燒開，分別將雞塊及栗子下炸約2分鐘，各撈起備用。

❸ 油2大匙燒熱，中火炒香葱薑，將雞塊倒入調上酒1大匙，隨即調入②料連同醃雞醬油汁燒開
　改小火煮約１０分鐘，即可把栗子倒入再煮約3分鐘餘汁剩一半時，以③料調成薄糊狀，再淋
　下麻油即可起鍋。

栗子燒雞 Stewed Chicken with Chestnuts

四川菜　　Szechuan
12人份　 12 servings

① ½ chicken (about 1⅓ lbs.)　　1 T. rice wine　　③ ½ t. cornstarch
　¼ C. soy sauce　　　　　　　1 C. water　　　　　1 t. water
　½ C. chestnuts*　　　　　②½ T. sugar　　　　　1 t. sesame oil
　3 C. oil for frying　　　　　½ t. MSG
　1 t. chopped green onion　　¼ t. black pepper
　1 t. chopped ginger root

❶ Cut chicken (through bones) into bite-size pieces; coat with soy sauce and let sit 20 minutes; drain and retain soy sauce.

❷ Heat oil for deep frying; deep-fry chicken pieces and chestnuts about 2 minutes until golden; remove and drain.

❸ Heat pan and 2T. oil; stir-fry green onion and ginger root over medium heat until fragrant; add chicken, rice wine and ② ; add retained soy sauce and simmer covered 10 minutes. Add chestnuts and cook an additional 3 minutes or until sauce has reduced to about half of original quantity; add ③ to thicken and sesame oil; mix together and remove to serving plate; serve.

* Chestnuts may be purchased in 2 forms: canned or dried. If using dried, place in warm water and let soak until soft (about 8-10 minutes); drain and use as directed. If using canned, drain, rinse and use as directed.

<table>
<tr><td>雞…1隻2斤</td><td>金針菜………1兩</td><td rowspan="6">①</td><td>鹽……２小匙</td><td rowspan="2">②</td><td>太白粉…1大匙</td></tr>
</table>

雞…1隻2斤　　金針菜………1兩　　　　　鹽……２小匙　　　太白粉…1大匙
「炸油」…6杯　木耳…………半兩　　　　　味精…1小匙　②　水………1大匙
　　　　　　　冬菇…………3朵　　①　糖……1小匙
　　　　　　　筍……………1枝　　　　胡椒…¼小匙
　　　　　　　葱(3公分長)6枝　　　　酒……半大匙
　　　　　　　薑……………6片　　　　水………5杯

❶ 雞以醬油２大匙抹勻雞身，醃約２０分鐘。醬油餘汁加入①料。

❷ 金針菜用水泡軟去梗打結，木耳、冬菇泡軟均切大塊，筍煮熟泡涼切薄片(配料)。

❸ 「炸油」燒開，用大火將雞炸1分鐘，呈金黃色取出，留油1大匙，炒香葱薑，隨下配料、雞及①料，以大火燒開，改小火燜煮約２０分鐘取出。

❹ 將配料置盤底，雞斬塊置於上，餘汁用②料勾汁，並澆上麻油半小匙、熟油1小匙，淋於雞肉上即成。

■圍邊用材料：龍蝦片。

家鄉屈雞 Country-Style Chicken

1 chicken (2⅔lbs.)　　1　oz. dried tiger lily buds　　　　2　t.　salt　　　　②{1　T. cornstarch
6 C. oil for frying　　½　oz. dried wood ears　　　　　1　t.　MSG　　　　　1　T. water
　　　　　　　　　　3　Chinese black mushrooms　　1　t.　sugar
　　　　　　　　　　1　medium-sized bamboo shoot　①{¼　t.　black pepper
　　　　　　　　　　6　1-inch sections green onion　　½　T. rice wine
　　　　　　　　　　6　slices ginger root　　　　　　5　C. water

❶ Rub chicken exterior and interior with 2T. soy sauce; add any left-over soy sauce to ① ; let chicken stand 20 minutes.

❷ Soak tiger lily buds in warm water until soft; drain and tie each into a knot; soak wood ears and black mushrooms in warm water until expanded and soft; cut into bite-size pieces. Precook bamboo shoot in boiling water about 20 minutes; remove, drain and cut into thin bite-size slices.

❸ Heat oil for deep-frying; deep fry chicken 1 minute over high heat until golden brown; remove chicken and all but 1T. oil; stir-fry green onion and ginger root; add all other vegetables, chicken and ① . Bring liquid to a boil and simmer covered 20 minutes. Remove from fire and take out chicken; drain.

❹ Remove vegetables and arrange in center of serving plate; cut chicken into bite-size pieces and place pieces over vegetables. Heat soup left from steaming, until boiling; add ② to thicken and 1T. sesame oil; mix together and spoon sauce over chicken; serve.

■ Garnish with shrimp chips.

雞翼………１２隻	蝦仁…………半斤	酒…………半小匙、麻油……¼小匙
太白粉……１大匙	肥肉………１兩	鹽…………半小匙、蛋白………１個
炸杏仁………半兩	「炸油」………６杯	味精………¼小匙、太白粉…１大匙
		胡椒………¼小匙

① 將雞翼去大骨、洒太白粉，炸杏仁切碎。

② 蝦仁拭乾水份與肥肉剁爛，調①料拌勻，做成１２個蝦球每個蝦球糊在每隻雞翼一端並抹平洒上杏仁。

③ 「炸油」燒熱中火將雞翼炸約５分鐘撈起，盛盤上即成。

■ 如無炸杏仁，可用花生或腰果代替。

■ 圍邊用材料：生菜、番茄。

杏花酥雞翼 Stuffed Chicken Wings

廣東菜　Cantonese
12人份　12 servings

12 chicken wings	⅔ lb. raw, shelled shrimp		½ t. rice wine
1 T. cornstarch	1 oz. pork fat		½ t. salt
3 T. roasted almonds*	6 C. oil for frying		¼ t. MSG
		①	¼ t. black pepper
			¼ t. sesame oil
			1 egg white
			1 T. cornstarch

❶ Remove central bone from chicken wing; sprinkle each wing with cornstarch; crush roasted almonds.

❷ Rinse and devein shrimp; drain. Chop pork fat and shrimp very finely; add ① and mix vigorously to combine ingredients; divide into 12 portions and roll each portion to a ball. Place each ball on deboned portion of chicken wing. Use a spoon dipped in water to smooth filling surface; sprinkle crushed almonds on top and press lightly so almonds won't fall off during deep-frying.

❸ Heat oil for deep-frying; deep-fry stuffed wings over medium heat for 3 minutes; remove, drain and serve.

■ Garnish with coriander and tomato.

* Roasted peanuts or cashews may be substituted for almonds.

雞翼⋯⋯⋯⋯１２隻
油菜⋯⋯⋯⋯⋯８棵
葱（３公分長）6枝
薑⋯⋯⋯⋯⋯⋯6片

① 蠔油⋯⋯⋯１大匙
鹽⋯⋯⋯⋯半小匙
味精⋯⋯⋯¼小匙
糖⋯⋯⋯⋯半小匙
胡椒⋯⋯⋯¼小匙
水⋯⋯⋯⋯⋯１杯

② 太白粉⋯⋯⋯半大匙
水⋯⋯⋯⋯⋯半大匙

❶ 雞翼切成二節，加醬油１大匙拌勻，炸至金黃色撈起。

❷ 油菜去老菜，切１０公分長用開水燙熟撈起，加鹽¼小匙炒勻，排於菜盤上。

❸ 油３大匙燒熱，葱薑下鍋炒香，將炸好雞翼，酒半大匙及①料放入鍋內，蓋鍋，中火煮約１５
分鐘後，以②料勾汁並加麻油半大匙即可盛盤。

蠔油扒鳳翼 Chicken Wings with Oyster Sauce

12 chicken wings
8 stalks green vegetable heart*
6 1-inch sections green onion
6 slices ginger root

① 1 T. oyster sauce
½ t. salt
¼ t. MSG
½ t. sugar
¼ t. black pepper
1 C. water

② ½ T. cornstarch
½ T. water

❶ Cut each chicken wing at the elbow into two parts; coat with 1T. soy sauce. Heat oil for deep-frying; deep-fry chicken wings until golden brown; remove and drain.

❷ Clean vegetable and cut into 4-inch sections; precook in boiling water 1 minute; remove and plunge into cold water to cool; remove and drain. Heat pan and 3T. oil; stir-fry green vegetable and ¼t. salt; remove and arrange on serving plate as illustrated.

❸ Heat pan and 3T. oil; stir-fry green onion and ginger until fragrant; add chicken wings, rice wine and ① ; cover and cook 15 minutes over medium heat; add ② to thicken and ½T. sesame oil. Mix ingredients together and remove to serving plate; serve.

* Any kind of green vegetable hearts, cut to sections 3 inches thick.

①		②		③	
乳鴿·4隻1斤4兩		檸檬（去皮）半個		黑醋……2大匙	
醬油……2大匙		洋葱（切塊）半杯		番茄醬……2大匙	
酒………1大匙		葱………2枝		糖………1大匙	
葱………2枝		薑………2片		鹽……1½小匙	
薑………2片		酒………半大匙		味精……半小匙	
				水…………1杯	

❶ 乳鴿洗淨剁去脚，調入①料醃約半小時後，炸呈金黃色取出。

❷ 油2大匙燒熱，將②料炒香，隨下乳鴿、酒半大匙及③料中火燒煮（需翻拌）至汁快乾，淋油1
大匙拌勻，將乳鴿取起切塊，盛盤，澆上燒鴿餘汁即成。

■ 圍邊用材料：炸龍蝦片。

■ 鴿子可用雞取代，但先剁塊再調入①料，其他用料、做法相同。

檸檬焗鴿 Squab with Lemon

①		②		③	
4 squab (about 1⅔lbs.)		½ lemon (peeled)		2 T, worcestershire sauce	
2 T. soy sauce		½ C. onion, diced		2 T. tomato ketchup	
1 T. rice wine		2 stalks green onion		1 T. sugar	
2 stalks green onion		2 slices ginger root		1½ t. salt	
2 slices ginger root		½ T. rice wine		½ t. MSG	
				1 C. water	

❶ Clean squab and cut off feet; discard. Rub squab exteriors with ① and let soak 30 minutes. Heat
oil for deep-frying and deep-fry squab until golden brown; remove and drain.

❷ Heat pan and 2T. oil; stir-fry ② until fragrant and add squab, ½T. rice wine and ③ . Cook squab, turning
occasionally, over medium heat until sauce is reduced to ½C.; add 1T. oil and remove squab. Cut each
squab into 6 pieces and arrange on serving plate; pour sauce on top and serve.

■ Garnish with shrimp chips.

鴨⋯⋯⋯１隻

鹽⋯⋯⋯３大匙

①{花椒⋯１小匙
八角⋯⋯１朵
硝⋯⋯１小匙

②{樟木屑¼杯
茶葉２大匙 或 {茶葉¼杯
糖２大匙

「炸油」⋯⋯⋯⋯⋯⋯⋯８杯

葱（６公分長）２４枝

③{甜麵醬⋯⋯⋯２大匙
糖⋯⋯⋯⋯２大匙
水⋯⋯⋯⋯２大匙

❶ 鹽用小火炒至淡黃色加入①料拌勻起鍋。

❷ 將炒好花椒鹽，擦勻鴨全身內外，醃２～６小時後洗淨，水燒開大火蒸４０分鐘至熟。

❸ 烤箱燒至４５０度，鴨放在烤箱中層，把②料盛在烤盤置於烤箱下層，燻５分鐘至外皮呈金黃色取出。

❹ 「炸油」燒熱，中火把燻好的鴨炸８分鐘，至皮脆，取出斬塊盛盤。

❺ 麻油４大匙燒熱，把調好的③料拌炒均勻盛起，此為沾鴨用料，與葱段一併食之。

樟茶鴨 Crispy Smoked Duckling

四川菜　Szechuan
12人份 12 servings

1 duckling (about 4lbs.)

3 T. salt

①{1 t. Szechuan peppercorns
1 star anise
1 t. saltpeter or niter*

②{¼ C. wood scraps
2 T. tea leaves
or
¼ C. tea leaves
2 T. sugar

8 C. oil for frying

24 2-inch sections green onion

③{2 T. sweet bean paste ("tien mien jiang")
2 T. sugar
2 T. water

❶ Heat pan and stir-fry salt (no oil) over medium heat until it becomes lightly brown; add ① and stir-fry until fragrant; remove.

❷ Rub interior and exterior of duckling thoroughly with salt mixture; let sit 6 hours. Rinse duckling lightly and drain. Place in a heatproof pan and steam 40 minutes over high heat.

❸ Preheat oven to 450°; place ② mixture in a pan on lower shelf of oven; place duckling on rack directly above tea mixture and bake 5 minutes until outside is golden brown; remove.

❹ Heat oil for deep-frying; deep-fry duckling 8 minutes until skin is crispy; remove, drain and cut into bite-size pieces. Place on serving plate.

❺ Heat pan and 4T. oil; stir-fry ③ until boiling; pour into a small bowl and serve as a dipping sauce with duckling and green onion sections.

* Saltpeter and niter aid in preservation; however, may be omitted.

鴨⋯⋯⋯⋯ 1 隻 2 斤半　　　葱⋯⋯⋯⋯⋯⋯ 5 枝
「炸油」⋯⋯⋯⋯ 1 0 杯　　　薑⋯⋯⋯⋯⋯⋯ 6 片
　　　　　　　　　　　　酒⋯⋯⋯⋯⋯⋯ 1 大匙
　　　　　　　　① 鹽⋯⋯⋯⋯⋯⋯ 3 大匙
　　　　　　　　　　　　花椒粒⋯⋯⋯⋯ 1 小匙
　　　　　　　　　　　　八角⋯⋯⋯⋯⋯⋯半朶

❶ 鴨以①料全身內外抹勻，醃約 3 0 分鐘後，蒸爛，取出趁熱以 1 大匙醬油在鴨身上抹勻。

❷ 「炸油」燒開，將鴨入鍋大火炸約 1 0 分鐘，至呈金黃色撈起，切塊，排在盤上即成。

❸ 吃香酥鴨時可沾花椒鹽，上桌時也可整隻不切端出，且可用小花捲排在周圍配着吃。

■ 圍邊用材料：香菜。

香酥鴨 Crispy Pepper-Skin Duckling

湖南菜　Hunan
12人份 **12** servings

1 duckling (about 3⅓lbs.)　　　5 stalks green onion
10 C. oil for frying　　　　　　6 slices ginger root
　　　　　　　　　　　① 1 T. rice wine
　　　　　　　　　　　　3 T. salt
　　　　　　　　　　　　1 t. Szechuan peppercorn
　　　　　　　　　　　　½ star anise

❶ Rub duckling interior and exterior with ① ; let sit about 30 minutes . Place duckling in a steamer and steam about 2½ hours over medium heat; remove and rub surface of duckling with 1T. soy sauce.

❷ Heat oil for deep-frying; deep-fry duckling over high heat until golden brown (about 10 minutes); remove and drain; cut into bite-size pieces and place on serving plate; serve.

■ Garnish with coriander.

■ Note: Duckling pieces may be served with 5-spice salt for dipping see directions for preparation of 5-spice salt on P. 32. Duckling may be served whole and accompanied by lotus (mandarin) pancakes or rolls.

鴨⋯1隻2斤
葱⋯⋯⋯2枝
薑⋯⋯⋯2片
酒⋯⋯⋯1大匙
①醬油⋯⋯2大匙
鹽⋯⋯⋯1小匙
花椒⋯半小匙
八角⋯⋯1朵

蒸熟芋茸⋯⋯⋯⋯⋯⋯1½杯
鹽⋯⋯1小匙、五香粉⋯¼小匙
味精⋯半小匙、麻油⋯⋯1小匙
②糖⋯⋯半小匙、猪油⋯⋯1大匙
胡椒⋯¼小匙、太白粉1½大匙

香菜(切碎)⋯¼杯
③蛋黃⋯⋯⋯⋯1個
太白粉⋯⋯1大匙
「炸油」⋯⋯6杯
④鴨汁⋯⋯⋯半杯
葱末⋯⋯1大匙
薑末⋯⋯半大匙
太白粉⋯⋯1小匙

❶ 將①料抹勻鴨身內外醃２０分鐘，以快鍋蒸爛（約４０分鐘）除去鴨骨，平擺在盤上（肉厚部份切丁留用），修整成四方形，肉面塗勻攪勻之③料。

❷ 芋茸與②料調勻再拌入鴨肉丁及香菜，鴨皮朝下，抹在鴨肉面上（總厚２公分），兩面均抹多量太白粉待炸。

❸ 「炸油」燒熱，用中火炸芋泥鴨８分鐘，外皮呈金黃色，撈出切塊盛盤，吃時沾上燒開④料。

■ 圍邊用材料：生菜、番茄。

芋泥鴨 Fried Duckling with Taro Stuffing

廣東菜 Cantonese
12人份 12 servings

①	②	③ ④
1 duckling (about 2⅔lbs.) 2 stalks green onion 2 slices ginger root 1 T. rice wine 2 T. soy sauce 1 t. salt ½ t. Szechuan peppercorns 1 star anise	1½ C. precooked taro root*¹ 1 t. salt ½ t. MSG ½ t. sugar ¼ t. black pepper ¼ t. five-spice powder 1 t. sesame oil 1 T. lard or vegetable shortening 1½ T. cornstarch	¼ C. chopped coriander 1 egg yolk 1 T. cornstarch 6 C. oil for frying ½ C. duckling stock*² 1 T. chopped green onion ½ T. chopped ginger root 1 t. cornstarch

❶ Rub duckling exterior and interior with ① mixture; let sit 20 minutes; place duckling in pressure cooker*² and cook 40 minutes over minutes over medium heat (retain liquid from steaming for ④). Remove duckling from pressure cooker and place on a serving plate dusted with cornstarch; remove bones and flatten duckling with fingertips. (Remove meat in thick places, dice and set aside.) Pat sides of duckling to even and form a large square. Spread ③ mixture evenly on surface.

❷ Mix mashed taro, ② , diced duckling meat and coriander into a smooth dough; with skin-side facing downward, spread evenly over meat of duckling and smooth with palm. (Combined duckling meat and filling should be ⅔ of an inch thick.) Remove stuffed duckling from plate and sprinkle both sides heavily with cornstarch; cut into sections 2 inches wide.

❸ Heat oil for deep frying; deep-fry duckling sections 8 minutes over medium heat until golden brown; remove and drain; cut into thick slices and place on serving plate. Boil ingredients of ④ and serve with duckling for dipping.

■ Garnish with lettuce and tomato slices

*¹ To prepare taro: remove outer skin and cut into slices; steam over medium heat until tender (about 20 minutes); remove and mash finely. If taro is unavailable, substitute sweet potato.

*² You may use a covered casserole and increase cooking time to 3 hours over medium heat (duckling should be very tender).

鴨……1隻3斤 、 冬菇………3朵
醬油……1大匙 、 筍………半枝
「炸油」……6杯 、 紅蘿蔔…¼條
葱(3公分長)6枝 、 青江菜…2棵
薑………6片

① {
葱………2枝 、 醬油……3大匙
薑………2片 、 八角……1朵
酒………1大匙 、 花椒粒半小匙
鹽………1小匙 、 水………5杯
糖………2小匙
}

② {
海參………2條
蹄筋………2兩
洋菇……¼杯
豬腰………1個
}

③ {
雞肉………2兩
鴨肫………2個
}

④ {
煮鴨湯汁1½杯
味精……半小匙
麻油……半小匙
}

⑤ {
太白粉……2大匙
水………1大匙
}

❶ 鴨從背剖開，以1大匙醬油抹勻鴨身，用大火炸至金黃色（約2分鐘）撈出，加①料用快鍋煮爛（約40分鐘）取出盛盤即為紅鴨。

❷ 海參、蹄筋均切塊，豬腰對剖二開、切除白筋切花、泡清水備用。

❸ 雞肉切片、調太白粉¼小匙拌勻，鴨肫去皮切花。

❹ 冬菇泡軟去蒂，筍、紅蘿蔔煮熟切片，青江菜去老葉煮熟對剖四開。

❺ 油半大匙燒熱，葱薑炒香入酒半大匙，水2杯燒開，將②料分別燙熟，撈出。

❻ 油3杯燒熱將③料泡油半分鐘撈出，留油1大匙，入上項各料（豬腰除外）及酒半大匙，並加④料燒開，最後下豬腰並用⑤料勾汁，淋上2大匙熱油倒在鴨肉上即可供食。

八珍扒鴨 Eight-Treasure Braised Duckling

廣東菜　Cantonese
12人份　12 servings

1 duckling (about 4lbs.)
1 T. soy sauce
6 C. oil for frying
6 1-inch sections green onion
6 slices ginger root
3 Chinese black mushrooms
½ medium-sized bamboo shoot
  (approx ¾C.)
¼ carrot
2 stalks green cabbage*¹

① {
2 stalks green onion
2 slices ginger root
1 T. rice wine
1 t. salt
2 t. sugar
3 T. soy sauce
1 star anise
½ t. Szechuan peppercorns
5 C. water
}

② {
2 sea cucumbers(bêche-de-mer)
2 oz. pork tendons
¼ C. button mushrooms
1 pork kidney
}

③ {
3 oz. chicken meat
2 duck gizzards
}

④ {
1½ C. duckling stock
  (retained from steaming)
½ t. MSG
½ t. sesame oil
}

⑤ {
2 T. cornstarch
1 T. water
}

❶ Make a deep vertical cut down the backside of duckling; rub duckling interior and exterior with 1T. soy sauce. Heat oil for deep-frying; deep-fry duckling over high heat for 2 minutes until golden brown; remove and drain. Place duckling in pressure cooker*² with ① and cook 40 minutes over medium heat, until meat is very tender. Remove and place on serving plate. (retain soup from steaming)

❷ Cut sea cucumber and pork tendons into bite-size pieces; cut pork kidney in half and remove any white membrane; score lengthwise and crosswise; cut into bite-size pieces and place in cold water to keep fresh.

❸ Cut chicken meat into thin bite-size slices; mix with ¼t. cornstarch. Remove any white membrane from duck. Remove lengthwise and crosswise and cut into bite-size pieces.

❹ Soften black mushrooms in warm water; remove stem and discard. Precook bamboo shoot and carrot 20 minutes; remove and cool; cut into thin bite-size slices. Precook green cabbage until tender; remove and cut into 4-inch sections.

❺ Heat pan and 1T. oil; stir-fry onion and ginger until fragrant; add ½T. rice wine and 2C. water; let liquid boil and add ② (except kidney pieces); cook 2 minutes; add kidney and cook an additional 20 seconds; remove and drain. (discard liquid)

❻ Heat 3C. oil for deep-frying; add ③ and cook ½ minute; remove and drain. Heat pan and 1T. oil; add all meat pieces and vegetables (except kidney) and ½T. rice wine, ④ and mix together; add kidney pieces. Let liquid boil and add ⑤ to thicken; mix together and add 2T. oil; toss lightly and portion on top of duckling; serve.

*¹ Green cabbage may be purchased at a Chinese grocery store. If unavailable, substitute broccoli.
*² If no pressure cooker is available, place duckling and① in a steamer and steam 3 hours over medium heat.

鴨…………1隻　　氷糖(或糖)3大匙　　┌鹽………1大匙　┌酒………1大匙　┌太白粉‥半大匙
醬油……2大匙　　豆瓣醬……2大匙　①┤醬油……1大匙　②┤葱………2枝　③┤水………1大匙
蒜頭………2個　　　　　　　　　　　└味精……半小匙　└薑………2片　└「炸油」…‥6杯
酸梅………¼杯

❶ 鴨以2大匙醬油抹勻全身，燒開「炸油」炸至呈金黃色撈起。

❷ 蒜頭拍碎，酸梅去子打爛，氷糖壓碎，豆瓣醬調入①料。

❸ 油3大匙燒熱，將蒜頭炒香，即倒入酸梅、氷糖、豆瓣醬炒勻，煮至氷糖溶化即可倒入鴨腹內
，上撒②料，入蒸鍋蒸約2小時。

❹ 蒸爛鴨子，將肚內餘汁倒入碗內，即將鴨切塊排在盤上蒸鴨餘汁以③料勾汁加麻油1小匙，熟
油半大匙，淋在切好鴨塊上即成。

■ 圍邊用材料：香菜。

酸梅子蒸鴨 Steamed Duckling with Plums

廣東菜　Cantonese
12人份　12 servings

1　duckling (about 4lbs.)
2　T. soy sauce
2　cloves garlic
¼　C. pickled plums ("umeboshi")
3　T. rock or granulated sugar
2　T. soy bean paste ("do ban jiang")

① { 1　T. salt
1　T. soy sauce
½　t. MSG

② { 1　T. rice wine
2　stalks green onion
2　slices ginger root
1　T. sesame oil

③ { ½　T. cornstarch
1　T. water
6　C. oil for frying

❶ Rub duckling exterior and interior with 2T. soy sauce; heat oil for deep-frying; deep-fry duckling until golden brown; remove and drain.

❷ Smash garlic cloves; remove pits from plums and chop plums finely; crush rock sugar. Mix soy bean paste with ① .

❸ Heat pan and 3T. oil; stir-fry smashed garlic until fragrant; add chopped plums, sugar and soy bean paste mixture; stir-fry over medium heat until sugar dissolves; remove and spoon mixture into cavity of duckling. Sprinkle ② on top of duckling and place in steamer; steam 2 hours over high heat until meat is very tender.

❹ Remove duckling from steamer (retain liquid) and cut duckling into bite-size pieces; arrange pieces on serving plate. Heat retained sauce until boiling; add ③ to thicken and 1t. sesame oil; mix well and pour liquid over duckling pieces; serve.

■ Garnish with coriander.

猪腦⋯⋯⋯1只	粟米粉⋯⋯半杯	湯⋯⋯⋯2½杯
葱⋯⋯⋯1枝	② 蛋黃⋯⋯⋯3個	③ 鹽⋯⋯⋯1小匙
① 薑⋯⋯⋯1片	水⋯⋯⋯5大匙	味精⋯⋯半小匙
酒⋯⋯⋯1小匙	酒⋯⋯⋯1大匙	太白粉⋯1大匙
	猪油⋯⋯1大匙	「炸油」⋯⋯6杯

❶ 猪腦用火柴棒捲去上面一層薄膜，洗淨，加①料蒸約4〜5分鐘取出，用刀壓爛成泥狀。

❷ ②料調成麵糊，加入壓爛猪腦備用。

❸ 將油1大匙燒熱，加入酒1大匙及③料燒開，並將麵糊徐徐放入用力攪拌約2〜3分鐘，全部攪勻再放入猪油1大匙，取出置盤上，待冷切塊，沾上太白粉分兩次油炸，用大火炸約4分鐘，呈金黃色即成。

■ 因猪腦較易買到，故用猪腦代替雞腰6只。食時，可沾些糖粉或蠔油。

雞腰窩渣 Pork-Brain Fritters

廣東菜　Cantonese
12人份　12 servings

1 pork brain	½ C. cornstarch	2½ C. stock
1 stalk green onion	② 3 egg yolks	③ 1 t. salt
① 1 slice ginger root	5 T. water	½ t. MSG
1 t. rice wine	1 T. rice wine	1 T. cornstarch
	1 T. lard	6 C. oil for frying

❶ Using the wooden end of a matchstick, pull off the thin outer skin of the pork brain; rinse brain lightly and mix with ① . Place in a bowl in steamer and steam 5 minutes over medium heat; remove brain and mash brain finely.

❷ Mix ingredients of ② to a smooth paste; add mashed pork brain and mix ingredients together.

❸ Heat pan and 1T. oil; add 1T. rice wine and ③ . When mixture begins to boil, slowly add ② mixture in a thin stream while beating mixture continuously to keep smooth. Cook 3 minutes over low heat; add 1T. lard and pour into a deep serving plate; let cool (mixture will solidify to one piece). Cut into diamond-shaped bite-size sections; coat pieces with cornstarch. Heat oil for deep-frying; deep-fry fritters 4 minutes over medium heat; remove, drain and serve.

■ Fritter may be served with super-fine sugar or oyster sauce.

雞肝……… 1 斤
① { 薑酒…… 1 大匙
鹽……… 半小匙

② { 番茄醬… 3 大匙
辣醬油… 1 大匙
鹽……… ⅓ 小匙
糖……… 1 大匙
清水…… 2 大匙

「炸油」…… 6 杯

❶ 雞肝洗淨切塊，輕輕劃刀，調①料醃約２０分鐘備用。

❷ 「炸油」燒開，將醃好的雞肝，下鍋中火炸約４分鐘，呈金黃色撈起。

❸ 麻油 1 大匙燒熱，下雞肝及②料燒煮約２分鐘，至汁收乾即可裝盤。

■ 圍邊用材料：小黃瓜。薑酒請參照特殊材料說明。

燒焗鳳肝 Sweet and Sour Chicken Livers

廣東菜　Cantonese
12人份　12 servings

1⅓ lbs. chicken livers
① { 1　T.　ginger wine *
½　t.　salt

② { 3　T.　tomato ketchup
1　T.　worcestershire sauce
⅓　t.　salt
1　T.　sugar
2　T.　water

6　C. oil for frying

❶ Cut livers into bite-size pieces; lightly score pieces lengthwise and crosswise; mix with ① and let soak 20 minutes.

❷ Heat oil for deep-frying; deep-fry chicken livers over medium heat for 4 minutes until golden; remove and drain.

❸ Reheat pan and 1T. sesame oil; add chicken livers and ② ; cook 2 minutes or until sauce is near-dry; remove and serve.

■ Garnish with cucumber slices.

* A mixture of rice wine and the juice of smashed ginger root.

鴨肫⋯⋯⋯6個
薑酒⋯⋯⋯1大匙
青椒（切塊）1個
菠蘿（切片）1杯
「炸油」⋯⋯6杯

① ⎧ 葱（3公分長）6枝
⎨ 紅辣椒（切片）1條
⎩ 酸薑片⋯1½大匙

② ⎧ 糖⋯⋯⋯⋯2大匙
⎪ 醋⋯⋯⋯⋯2大匙
⎪ 番茄醬⋯⋯2大匙
⎨ 水⋯⋯⋯⋯2大匙
⎪ 鹽⋯⋯⋯⋯1小匙
⎪ 麻油⋯⋯⋯1小匙
⎩ 太白粉⋯⋯半大匙

❶ 鴨肫每個切4塊，去皮劃花，以薑酒拌醃，菠蘿加鹽半大匙醃２０分鐘，略擠去水份。

❷ 「炸油」燒熱投入醃過的鴨肫及青椒塊泡約三十秒即撈出。

❸ 油３大匙燒熱將①料及菠蘿片炒香，再將炸好的鴨肫、青椒倒入，並加酒一大匙及②料炒拌，
最後淋上少許熱油炒勻即可盛於菜盤內。

■ 圍邊用材料：炸雲吞皮。薑片拍碎加酒擠出的汁叫薑酒。

菠蘿炒肫球 Stir-Fried Sweet and Sour Duck Gizzards

廣東菜 Cantonese
12人份 12 servings

6 duckling gizzards
1 T. ginger wine
1 medium-sized green pepper
1 C. thinly sliced pineapple
6 C. oil for frying

① ⎧ 6 1-inch sections green onion
⎨ 1 hot red pepper, thinly sliced
⎩ 1½ T. pickled ginger root, thinly sliced

② ⎧ 2 T. sugar
⎪ 2 T. vinegar
⎪ 2 T. tomato ketchup
⎨ 2 T. water
⎪ 1 t. salt
⎪ 1 t. sesame oil
⎩ ½ T. cornstarch

❶ Cut each gizzard into 4 pieces; remove any white membrane covering exterior; score each piece lengthwise and crosswise and rinse in cold water. Mix gizzard pieces with ginger wine and let sit 20 minutes; remove seeds from green pepper and cut into bite-size pieces; mix pineapple slices with ½T. salt; let sit 20 minutes and squeeze lightly to remove some juice; drain slice.

❷ Heat oil for deep-frying; deep-fry gizzard and green pepper for 30 seconds; remove and drain.

❸ Heat pan and 3T. oil; stir-fry ① and pineapple slices until fragrant; add gizzard, green pepper. 1T. rice wine and ② ; mix together and add 1T. oil. Toss lightly to mix ingredients and remove to serving plate; serve.

■ Garnish with fried "won ton" skins.

炸熟腰果⋯2兩	青椒⋯⋯1個	① 鹽⋯⋯半小匙 酒⋯⋯1小匙 蛋白⋯⋯半個 太白粉半大匙	③ 鹽⋯⋯1小匙、麻油⋯⋯半小匙 味精⋯半小匙、水⋯⋯3大匙 糖⋯⋯半小匙、太白粉1½小匙 胡椒⋯¼小匙
「炸油」⋯⋯3杯	筍⋯⋯⋯1枝		
雞肉⋯⋯⋯半斤	紅蘿蔔⋯半條		
沙拉醬⋯⋯4兩	葱絲⋯1大匙		
豬腰⋯⋯⋯2只	薑絲⋯半大匙	② 薑末⋯⋯1小匙 酒⋯⋯半大匙 鹽⋯⋯半小匙	

❶ 腰果壓碎。

❷ 雞胸肉，切約5公分×1公分粗條，調入①料醃泡20分鐘。

❸ 豬腰對剖切除白筋，橫切5公分×1公分粗條，下②料醃泡20分鐘，用開水煮半分鐘撈出。

❹ 筍、紅蘿蔔先煮熟，和青椒均切粗條（與上項各料同大小）。

❺ 將雞肉、豬腰、青椒泡油1分鐘撈出，留油1大匙，把葱薑炒香，倒入各料，下酒半大匙，及③料炒勻，澆上熟油1大匙，置於盤中，再把沙拉醬擠上，並洒入腰果碎，即可供食。

■ 腰果可用花生米代替。

杏花炒双條 Stir-Fried Chicken and Kidney Salad

廣東菜　Cantonese
12人份　12 servings

2 oz. roasted cashews 3 C. oil for frying ⅔ lb. chicken meat ① ½ t. salt 1 t. rice wine ½ egg white ½ T. cornstarch 2 pork kidneys	② 1 t. chopped ginger root ½ T. rice wine ½ t. salt 1 medium-sized green pepper 1 precooked bamboo shoot ½ precooked carrot 1 T. shredded green onion ½ T. shredded ginger root	③ 1 t. salt ½ t. MSG ½ t. sugar ¼ t. black pepper ½ t. sesame oil 3 T. water 1½ t. cornstarch ½ C. mayonnaise

❶ Crush roasted cashews.

❷ Cut chicken meat into matchstick-sized pieces ⅓-inch thick; mix with ① and let soak 20 minutes.

❸ Cut pork kidneys horizontally in half and remove any white membrane; cut into pieces the size of chicken and mix with ② ; let sit 20 minutes. Cook kidney in boiling water for 20 seconds; remove and drain.

❹ Remove seeds from green pepper; cut green pepper, bamboo shoot and carrot into matchstick-sized pieces ⅓-inch thick.

❺ Heat oil for deep-frying; deep-fry chicken, kidney and green pepper 1 minute over medium heat; remove and drain. Reheat pan and 1T. oil; stir-fry shredded onion and ginger root and add all meat and vegetables; ½T. rice wine and ③ . Toss ingredients together and add 1T. oil; remove and place on serving plate. Using a pastry bag, squeeze mayonnaise in a crisscross pattern on top; sprinkle crushed cashews and serve.

| 里肌肉… 1 斤 | ① | 酒……… 1 大匙
醬油…… 2 小匙
味精…… 1 小匙
太白粉… 1 大匙
水……… 6 大匙
洋葱……… 1 個 | ② | 黑醋………… 1 大匙
番茄醬……… 2 大匙
糖………… 2 小匙
味精……… 半小匙
醬油……… 2 大匙
清水……… 3 大匙
檸檬汁……… 半大匙
紅辣椒(切段)…… 1 枝 |

❶ 里肌肉去白筋，切約 1 公分厚片，用刀拍鬆，調①料拌勻，醃約 1 小時，洋葱切絲。

❷ 油 4 大匙燒熱，用大火煎里肌肉片，煎至兩面呈金黃色鏟出。

❸ 油 4 大匙燒熱，將洋葱炒香，取 ¾ 盛於盤內，（做墊底用），餘 ¼ 部份加酒 1 大匙並倒入②料及煎好的肉片，用大火將汁燒到快乾時，澆上熟油 1 大匙，即可倒在洋葱上。

■ 為增加肉的嫩度，可於里肌肉調①料醃泡時，加小蘇打半小匙或發粉 1 小匙。

■ 圍邊用材料：番茄、巴西利。

中式豬扒　Chinese-Style Pork Steak

廣東菜　Cantonese
12人份　12 servings

| 1⅓ lbs. pork loin | ① | 1　T.　rice wine
2　t.　soy sauce
1　t.　MSG
1　T.　cornstarch
6　T.　water
1　medium-sized onion | ② | 1　T.　worcestershire sauce
2　T.　tomato ketchup
2　t.　sugar
½　t.　MSG
2　T.　soy sauce
3　T.　water
½　T.　lemon juice
1　hot red pepper, shredded |

❶ Remove any fat or tough membrane from pork loin; cut into slices ½-inch thick. Using blunt edge of cleaver, pound meat lightly to tenderize; mix with ① and let sit 1 hour. Shred onion.

❷ Heat pan and 4T. oil; fry pork slices on both sides until golden brown; remove.

❸ Reheat pan and 4T. oil; stir-fry onion until soft; remove ¾ and place on serving plate. Add 1T. rice wine, ② and pork slices to remaining onion shreds; cook over high heat until sauce is near-dry. Add 1T. oil and toss ingredients lightly to mix; remove and portion over onions on serving plate; serve.

■ Garnish with tomato slices and parsley.

■ To further tenderize pork, add ½T. baking soda or 1t. baking powder to ①

里肌肉…半斤　　　醬油…２大匙　　　葱（５公分長）……半杯

①{
蒜末…１小匙
醬油…１大匙
糖……半大匙
酒……１大匙
太白粉１大匙
}

②{
糖……１小匙
味精…半小匙
}

❶ 里肌肉切約１公分厚大薄片，用刀拍鬆，調入①料，泡醃約半小時。

❷ 油３大匙燒熱，將里肌肉兩面煎黃，如油不足，可再加點油見肉片熟了再下②料及葱段拌炒即可起鍋供食。

葱爆里肌 Stir-Fried Pork with Green Onions

北平菜　　　Peking
6人份　6 servings

②{
2 T. soy sauce
1 t. sugar
½ t. MSG
}

½ C. 2-inch sections green onion

①{
⅔ lb. pork loin
1 t. chopped garlic
1 T. soy sauce
½ T. sugar
1 T. rice wine
1 T. cornstarch
}

❶ Remove any fat or tough membrane from pork loin; cut into slices ⅓ inch thick. Using the blunt edge of cleaver, pound meat lightly to tenderize; mix with ① and let sit 30 minutes.

❷ Heat pan and 3T. oil; fry pork slices on both sides until golden brown (add more oil if necessary); add ② and green onion sections; mix together and remove to serving plate; serve.

里肌肉……半斤 　泡菜………1杯 　　　醋………3大匙 　　③{太白粉…1½小匙
醬油……1大匙 　青椒(小)…1個 　　　糖………3大匙 　　　水………1½小匙
①{蛋黃………1個 　蒜末……半小匙 　②{水………3大匙
太白粉…1大匙 　「炸油」……6杯 　　　番茄醬……3大匙
太白粉…6大匙 　　　　　　　　　　　鹽………⅓小匙

❶ 里肌肉切成約2公分厚片用刀背捶鬆後，切塊拌上①料醃約20分鐘，炸時再沾上太白粉6大匙。

❷ 青椒去籽，切塊備用。

❸ 「炸油」燒熱，投入已粘裹太白粉之肉塊，以中火炸約3分鐘，全部撈出，油燒滾，重炸一次，約半分鐘，全部撈起，將油倒出。

❹ 油3大匙燒熱，蒜末炒香加青椒、泡菜及②料燒煮沸滾後以③料勾芡，放入已炸過之肉塊拌炒均勻，即可起鍋。

■ 請參考第26頁廣東泡菜做法。

咕咾肉 Sweet and Sour Pork

廣東菜 Cantonese
6人份 6 servings

⅔ lb. pork loin	1 C. pickled vegetable salad*	3 T. vinegar	③{1½ t. cornstarch
①{1 T. soy sauce	1 small green pepper	3 T. sugar	1½ t. water
1 egg yolk	½ t. chopped garlic	②{3 T. water	
1 T. cornstarch	6 C. oil for frying	3 T. tomato ketchup	
6 T. cornstarch		⅓ t. salt	

❶ Remove any fat or tough membrane from pork loin; cut pork into slices ⅔-inch thick. Using blunt edge of cleaver, lightly pound slices to tenderize; cut meat into bite-size pieces; mix with ① and let soak 20 minutes. Before deep-frying meat, mix with 6T. cornstarch.

❷ Remove seeds from green pepper and cut into bite-size pieces.

❸ Heat oil for deep-frying; deep-fry pork pieces over medium heat for 3 minutes; remove and reheat oil until very hot; re-fry pork pieces another 30 seconds; remove and drain.

❹ Reheat pan and 3T. oil; stir-fry chopped garlic until fragrant, add green pepper and pickled salad and stir-fry briefly; add ② and when mixture begins to boil, add ③ to thicken. Add fried meat pieces and toss lightly to mix together; remove to serving plate and serve.

* To prepare pickled vegetable salad, follow directions on P. 26

①{	里肌肉‥‥‥１２兩	②{	雞蛋‥‥‥‥２個	④{	白醋‥‥‥‥１大匙
	薑酒‥‥‥‥１大匙		麵粉‥‥‥‥半杯		糖‥‥‥‥‥１大匙
	鹽‥‥‥‥‥１小匙		香菜菜‥‥５大匙		番茄醬‥‥‥１大匙
	胡椒‥‥‥‥$\frac{1}{4}$小匙	③{	葱末‥‥‥‥１小匙		水‥‥‥‥‥１大匙
	麻油‥‥‥‥１小匙		薑末‥‥‥‥１小匙		鹽‥‥‥‥‥$\frac{1}{3}$小匙
	「炸油」‥‥‥‥６杯		蒜末‥‥‥‥１小匙		太白粉‥‥‥半小匙

❶ 里肌肉切１公分厚片，輕輕拍鬆，再切條狀，調①料醃２０分鐘。

❷ ②料拌勻備用。

❸ 「炸油」燒熱，肉條與②料拌勻，１條１條放入油鍋內炸呈金黃色，肉熟（２分鐘）撈起。

❹ 油３大匙燒熱，將③料炒香，並倒入④料燒開，加１大匙熟油裝小碗以備沾用。

■ 高麗魚條：肉改用魚肉，其他用料，做法相同。

■ 高麗明蝦：肉改用明蝦或小蝦，其他用料，做法相同

高麗肉條 Deep-fried Pork Strips

廣東菜 Cantonese
12人份 12 servings

①{	1 lb. pork loin	②{	2 eggs	④{	1 T. vinegar
	1 T. ginger wine		½ C. flour		1 T. sugar
	1 t. salt		5 T. coriander		1 T. tomato ketchup
	¼ t. black pepper		6 C. oil for frying		1 T. water
	1 t. sesame oil	③{	1 t. chopped green onion		⅓ t. salt
			1 t. chopped ginger root		½ t. cornstarch
			1 t. chopped garlic		

❶ Slice pork into pieces ⅓ inch thick; pound and cut into strips, mix with ① and let soak 20 minutes.

❷ Mix ② evenly for use.

❸ Heat oil, mix ② thoroughly with meat strips, fry them in the oil one by one, until the color becomes golden brown, and meat well-cooked (about 2 minutes), remove.

❹ Heat pan and 3T. oil; stir-fry ③ fragrant, add ④ and let liquid come to boil; add 1T. oil and pour into a small bowl for dipping.

■ Deep-fried Fish Strips, Deep-fried Shrimp Strips: Change pork to fish or shrimps, the cooking method is same as the above.

小排骨……1斤	①	豆豉………3大匙	②	酒…………半大匙
		蒜末………1大匙		醬油………5大匙
		葱末………1大匙		糖………1½小匙
		薑末………1大匙		紅辣椒………1條
				葱花………1大匙

❶ 小排骨切成約３０塊（１寸大小）。

❷ 豆豉輕洗剁碎備用。

❸ 油３大匙燒熱，放進小排骨爆出油，用鍋鏟，鏟到一邊，以中火將①料炒香，再下②料並把全部材料炒拌均勻，燒煮１分鐘盛起，置中碗蒸約４０分鐘取出，放菜盤，上洒紅辣椒末及葱花增加美觀。

豆豉蒸排骨 Steamed Spareribs with Fermented Black Beans

廣東菜　Cantonese
12人份　12 servings

1⅓ lbs. small spareribs	①	3 T. fermented black beans	②	½ T. rice wine
		1 T. chopped garlic		5 T. soy sauce
		1 T. chopped green onion		1½ t. sugar
		1 T. chopped ginger root		1 hot red pepper, chopped
				1 T. chopped green onion

❶ Using a cleaver or heavy knife, cut spareribs into 30 pieces.

❷ Lightly rinse fermented black beans; drain and chop finely.

❸ Heat pan and 3T. oil; stir-fry spareribs for 1 minute over high heat; push to side of pan and add ① ; stir-fry over medium heat until fragrant and add ② ; mix together and cook 1 minute; remove and place in a heatproof bowl. Place bowl in steamer and steam 40 minutes over high heat. Remove and place on serving plate; sprinkle with chopped red pepper and green onion; serve.

小排骨……1 斤　　　┌醬油………半大匙　　┌辣醬油……1 大匙
「炸油」……6 杯　　　│鹽…………半小匙　　│番茄醬……1 大匙
　　　　　　　　　①│糖…………1 小匙　　②│糖…………半大匙
　　　　　　　　　　│酒…………半大匙　　│麻油…………¼ 小匙
　　　　　　　　　　│蒜末………半大匙　　└水…………2 大匙
　　　　　　　　　　└太白粉……3 大匙

❶ 排骨切２０塊，調上①料拌醃約２０分鐘，炸時再加太白粉３大匙攪勻。
❷「炸油」燒開，將排骨下鍋中火炸約４分鐘撈起，再將油燒開，炸好排骨再入鍋炸約１分鐘撈起。
❸ 將②料燒開，即倒入炸熟排骨，並大火炒至汁收乾加熱油１大匙拌勻即起，盛於盤內即成。
■ 圍邊用材料：番茄。

京都排骨 "Jing-Du" Spareribs

廣東菜　Cantonese
12人份　12 servings

1⅓ lbs. small spareribs
6 C. oil for frying

① ½ T. soy sauce
½ t. salt
1 t. sugar
½ T. rice wine
½ T. chopped garlic
3 T. cornstarch

② 1 T. worcestershire sauce
1 T. tomato ketchup
½ T. sugar
¼ t. sesame oil
2 T. water

❶ Cut spareribs into 20 sections; mix with ① and let sit 20 minutes. Before deep-frying, mix with 3T. cornstarch.
❷ Heat oil for deep-frying; deep-fry spareribs for 4 minutes over medium heat; remove and heat oil until very hot. Re-fry spareribs for 1 minute over high heat; remove and drain.
❸ Heat ingredients of ② until boiling; add spareribs and 1T. oil; toss lightly to coat spareribs with sauce; remove and drain.
■ Garnish with tomato slices.

小排骨…10兩

① {
咖哩粉……半大匙
蒜末………半大匙
五香粉……半小匙
醬油………1 大匙
鹽…………1 小匙
味精………半小匙
胡椒………¼ 小匙
糖…………半大匙
酒…………半大匙
}

② {
蛋黃…………半個
太白粉…1 ½ 大匙
}

❶ 小排骨切成長方形塊狀，切約12塊。

❷ 把小排骨泡在①料內，醃約30分鐘（需時時翻拌），再與②料（先入蛋黃再拌入太白粉）拌合。

❸ 油4大匙燒熱，鍋移開，把排骨逐塊置入鍋內，再把鍋移火上慢煎，兩面煎熟，如果太乾，可從鍋邊加些油，兩面煎金黃（約需6分鐘）即可。

■ 圍邊用材料：紅蘿蔔、巴西利。

印度煎排骨 India Fried Spareribs

廣東菜　Cantonese
6人份　6 servings

10 oz. spareribs

① {
½　T.　curry powder
½　T.　chopped garlic
½　t.　five-spice powder
1　T.　soy sauce
1　t.　salt
½　t.　MSG
¼　t.　black pepper
½　T.　sugar
½　T.　rice wine
}

② {
½　egg yolk
1½ T. cornstarch
}

❶ Divide spareribs into 12 sections.

❷ Mix spareribs with ① and let sit 30 minutes, turning occasionally; dip each sparerib into yolk and coat with cornstarch.

❸ Heat pan and 4T. oil; place spareribs in pan and fry 6 minutes over medium heat until both sides are golden brown (add more oil if necessary); remove, drain and serve.

■ Garnish with carrot and parsley.

<table>
<tr><td rowspan="5">①</td><td>肥肉（整塊）</td><td>……………半斤</td></tr>
<tr><td>里肌肉</td><td>……………半斤</td></tr>
<tr><td>雞肝</td><td>……………３只</td></tr>
<tr><td>紅蘿蔔</td><td>……………１大條</td></tr>
<tr><td>土司（麵包）</td><td>………４片</td></tr>
</table>

②
酒……………１大匙
糖……………１大匙
鹽……………半小匙
味精…………１小匙
醬油…………１大匙
蒜末…………１小匙

❶ 將①項各料切成直徑５公分圓形薄片（各１２片）。

❷ 把切好之肥肉、里肌肉、雞肝放在②料內泡約半小時（紅蘿蔔不需要泡）。

❸ 用串針先插上紅蘿蔔，然後插里肌肉、雞肝、肥肉，如此每四種為一組，每數組一串，用烤箱（４００°～４５０°）烤約２５分鐘，與土司一併食用。

■ 圍邊用材料：小黃瓜。

燒金錢雞 Baked Pork Rolls

廣東菜　Cantonese
6人份　6 servings

①
⅔ lb. pork fat
⅔ lb. pork loin
3 chicken livers
1 big carrot
4 slices white bread

②
1 T. rice wine
1 T. sugar
½ t. salt
1 t. MSG
1 T. soy sauce
1 t. chopped garlic

❶ Slice each ingredient in ① into 12 pieces; trim slices into circles 2-inches wide.

❷ Mix pork fat, loin and liver slices with ② ; let sit 30 minutes (don't marinate carrot slices).

❸ Place one slice each of carrot, pork loin, liver and pork fat on a skewer; place other slices in same order on skewers. Preheat oven to 450°; place skewers on broiler pan and bake 25 minutes until lightly brown; remove slices from skewers, discarding carrot slices (used only to impart flavor and separate meat) and place on serving plate; serve with bread (each slice cut to 4 pieces) to make miniature sandwiches.

■ Garnish with cucumber slices

里肌肉……半斤

① 酒………1小匙、糖………1½小匙
醬油……1½大匙、胡椒………¼小匙
鹽………1小匙、麻油………1小匙
味精………半小匙

雞肝………6只
沙茶醬………3大匙
葱(4公分長)24枝
牙籤………24枝

❶ 里肌肉切24片（6公分×4公分），調入①料，醃約20分鐘待用。
❷ 雞肝每只切4塊，共計24塊，用開水燙煮1分鐘取出。
❸ 里肌肉一片，上面塗少許沙茶醬，然後擺上雞肝1片，葱段1枝，用手捲成筒形，用牙籤從中間串上，按此法，全部做好待用。
❹ 燒熱平底鍋（不放油），擺進肉串捲，密蓋鍋，兩面烤至金黃色，約需6～7分鐘，置於菜盤即成。
■ 此道亦可用烤箱，以500度烤至兩面呈金黃色。
■ 圍邊用材料：香菜。

沙茶肉串捲 Broiled Pork Slices with "Sha Cha Jiang"

廣東菜 Cantonese
12人份 12 servings

⅔ lb. pork loin

① 1 t. rice wine • 1½ t. sugar
1½ T. soy sauce • ¼ t. black pepper
1 t. salt • 1 t. sesame oil
½ t. MSG

6 chicken livers
3 T. "sha cha jiang"*
24 1½-inch sections green onion
24 skewers

❶ Remove any fat or tough membrane from outside of pork loin; cut into 24 thin slices 2-inches long and 1½-inches wide; mix slices with ① and let sit 20 minutes.
❷ Cut each chicken liver into 4 pieces; precook in boiling water for 1 minute; remove and drain.
❸ Rub "sha cha jiang" on each slice of pork; place a piece of chicken liver and one section of green onion, in center of pork slice; roll up pork slice jelly-roll style to enclose liver and onion; repeat procedure to make 24 rolls and place finished rolls on skewers.
❹ Place skewered rolls under broiler and broil 5 minutes on each side until golden brown; remove and serve.
■ Garnish with coriander
* "Sha cha jiang" is a sauce made of peanut oil, peanuts, green onion oil, coriander seed, garlic powder, hot pepper powder, star of anise, Szechuan peppercorns, and dried shrimp. It may be purchased in a Chinese grocery store. If unavailable, substitute hoisin sauce.

① 絞肉‥‥‥‥‥‥‥‥‥‥‥６兩
  酒‥‥‥‥‥‥‥‥‥‥‥半大匙
  醬油‥‥‥‥‥‥‥‥‥‥１大匙
  味精‥‥‥‥‥‥‥‥‥‥半小匙
  胡椒‥‥‥‥‥‥‥‥‥‥¼小匙
  蛋‥‥‥‥半個（或水２大匙）
  太白粉‥‥‥‥‥‥‥‥‥半大匙

② 荸薺末‥‥‥‥２大匙
  蝦米末‥‥‥‥１大匙
  葱薑末（各）１小匙
  太白粉‥‥‥‥１大匙

  糯米‥‥‥‥‥‥¾杯
  紅蘿蔔‥‥‥‥半條
  香菜葉‥‥２０片

❶ 絞肉調①料攪勻，用手甩打（前後約５分鐘）後，加②料拌勻成肉餡備用。

❷ 預先泡淨糯米（約１小時）瀝乾水份，置於盤內。

❸ 將肉餡做成直徑約３公分的小丸子（可做約２０個）分別放進糯米內粘裹，粘勻後置於蒸盤（不必擦油），放進蒸鍋內用大火蒸約３０分鐘，即可取出盛盤。

❹ 紅蘿蔔削皮，刨成細末，洒在珍珠丸子上並配香菜葉即成。

■ 珍珠丸子係湖北菜之糯米丸子改良。

珍珠丸子 Pearl Balls

湖南菜　　Hunan
6人份　　6 servings

① 6 oz. Chopped pork
  ½ T. rice wine
  1 T. soy sauce
  ½ t. MSG
  ¼ t. black pepper
  ½ T. cornstarch

② 2 T. chopped water chesnuts
  1 T. chopped dried shrimp
  1 t. chopped green onion
  1 t. chopped ginger root
  1 T. cornstarch

  ¾ C. glutinous rice
  ½ carrot
  20 sprigs of coriander

❶ Mix chopped pork with ① ; stir vigorously for 5 minutes to combine ingredients thoroughly; add ② and mix well to combine ingredients. (filling)

❷ Rinse rice until water runs clear; place in water to cover and soak 1 hour; remove and drain; pour onto spread rice on a flat plate.

❸ Divide filling into 20 portions and roll into 1-inch balls; roll balls in soaked rice to completely coat outside; place on a heatproof plate ½ inch apart and steam over high heat for 30 minutes; remove.

❹ Shreds carrot and sprinkle over rice balls; add 1 sprig coriander and serve.

里肌肉…半斤
①{
鹽……半小匙
酒……1小匙
蛋黃……1個
太白粉半大匙
「炸油」…6杯

冬菇…………3朵
②{
醬油………半大匙
麻油…………$\frac{1}{4}$小匙
葱(4公分長)12枝
芥蘭菜…………半斤
③{
薑…………6片
葱(3公分長)…6枝

酒……………半大匙
④{
醬油…1小匙、胡椒…$\frac{1}{4}$小匙
鹽…$\frac{1}{4}$小匙、麻油…$\frac{1}{4}$小匙
味精…半小匙、水…1$\frac{1}{2}$大匙
糖…$\frac{1}{4}$小匙、太白粉1小匙

❶ 里肌肉切12薄片（6公分×4公分）、調①料拌醃，冬菇泡軟切12條、入②料拌勻。

❷ 芥蘭菜去老葉，燙熟撈起，漂涼。

❸ 將醃好肉片攤開放上冬菇條及葱段捲好，沾上太白粉，入油鍋炸3分鐘呈金黃色撈出。

❹ 油4大匙燒熱，③料炒香，將芥蘭菜加鹽$\frac{1}{4}$小匙拌炒後，將炸好肉捲及酒半大匙加入，再以④料拌炒均勻，即可盛入菜盤上。

碧綠野雞捲 Stir-Fried Pork Rolls with Broccoli

廣東菜　Cantonese
6人份　6 servings

①{
⅔ lb. pork loin
½ t. salt
1 t. rice wine
1 egg yolk
½ T. cornstarch
6 C. oil for frying

②{
3 Chinese black mushrooms
½ T. soy sauce
¼ t. sesame oil
12 1½-inch sections green onion
⅔ lb. Chinese broccoli*

③{
6 slices ginger root
6 1-inch sections green onion

④{
½ T. rice wine
1 t. soy sauce
¼ t. salt
½ t. MSG
¼ t. sugar
¼ t. black pepper
¼ t. sesame oil
1½ T. water
1 t. cornstarch

❶ Remove any fat or tough membrane from pork loin; cut loin into 12 slices, 2-inches long and 1½ inch wide; mix with ① and let sit 20 minutes. Soften black mushrooms in warm water; remove stems and cut caps into 12 pieces about 1½ inch long; mix with ② and let sit 20 minutes.

❷ Trim any wilted leaves from broccoli; cut into 4-inch sections; precook in boiling water 1 minute; remove and plunge into cold water; remove and drain.

❸ Place one piece black mushroom and 1 section green onion in center of pork loin slice; roll up pork loin jelly roll-style to enclose mushroom and onion; coat roll with cornstarch. Repeat for 11 other rolls. Heat oil for deep-frying; deep-fry rolls over medium heat for 3 minutes until golden brown; remove and drain.

❹ Heat pan and 4T. oil; stir-fry ③ until fragrant; add broccoli sections and ¼t. salt; mix and add fried pork rolls, 1½T. wine, and ④ ; toss lightly to mix ingredients and remove to serving plate; serve.

* If Chinese broccoli is unavailable, substitute American broccoli and cut stalks into ⅓-inch thick pieces.

里肌肉………半斤

① 醬油……1大匙
酒………1小匙
水………3大匙
太白粉…2小匙
「炸油」…3杯

② 甜麵醬…1⅓大匙
酒………半大匙
醬油……1大匙
糖………2小匙
味精……半小匙
葱絲………半杯

❶ 里肌肉切成細絲，拌上①料。

❷ 甜麵醬調上②料拌勻。

❸ 先將葱絲鋪在盤底。

❹ 「炸油」3杯燒熱，中火將肉絲泡熟撈出，留3大匙油，將拌好之甜麵醬炒香，隨即放入肉絲拌炒，加1大匙油，即可盛出，置在葱絲上。

京醬肉絲 Shredded Pork with Sweet Bean Paste

北平菜　Peking
6人份　6 servings

⅔ lb. pork loin

① 1 T. soy sauce
1 t. rice wine
3 T. water
2 t. cornstarch
3 C. oil for frying

② 1⅓ T. sweet bean paste ("tien mien jiang")
½ T. rice wine
1 T. soy sauce
2 t. sugar
½ t. MSG
½ C. shredded green onion

❶ Remove any fat or fibrous membrane from pork loin; shred loin and mix with ① ; let sit 20 minutes.

❷ Mix sweet bean paste with ② .

❸ Place shredded green onion on serving plate.

❹ Heat 3C. oil for deep-frying; deep-fry pork shreds over medium heat until color changes; remove and drain. Remove all but 3T. oil from pan; reheat and add sweet bean paste mixture; stir-fry until fragrant and add shredded pork; add 1T. oil and toss lightly to mix; portion onto shredded onion on serving plate; serve.

①
里肌肉……半斤
醬油……1大匙
酒………1小匙
水………3大匙
太白粉…2小匙
木耳……10朵
荸薺………2兩
「炸油」……3杯

② {
辣豆瓣醬………1大匙
葱、薑、蒜末各1大匙
}

③ {
酒……1大匙
醬油…1大匙
味精…¼小匙
糖……2小匙
麻油…半小匙
黑醋…1小匙
水…1½大匙
太白粉1小匙
}

❶ 里肌肉去筋切成細絲拌上①料，木耳用温水泡軟切絲。

❷ 荸薺用沸水略煮撈起，漂涼再切碎。

❸ 「炸油」燒熱用中火把肉絲泡熟撈起，留油3大匙，將②料炒香，續入木耳、荸薺略炒隨即入肉絲、及③料迅速炒拌均勻即成。

魚香肉絲 Stir-Fried Shredded Pork with Fish Flavor　四川菜　Szechuan
6人份　6 servings

① ⅔ lb. pork loin
1 T. soy sauce
1 t. rice wine
3 T. water
2 t. cornstarch
10 dried wood ears
2 oz. water chestnuts
3 C. oil for frying

② 1 T. hot bean paste ("la do ban jiang")
1 T. chopped green onion
1 T. chopped ginger root
1 T. chopped garlic

③ 1 T. rice wine
1 T. soy sauce
¼ t. MSG
2 t. sugar
½ t. sesame oil
1 t. worcestershire sauce
1½ T. water
1 t. cornstarch

❶ Remove any fat or tough membrane from pork loin; cut pork into shreds the size of matchsticks; mix with ① and let sit 20 minutes. Soften wood ears in warm water until soft and expanded; remove, drain and shred.

❷ Precook water chestnuts in boiling water for 1 minute; remove, drain and chop.

❸ Heat oil for deep-frying; deep-fry meat shreds over medium heat until changed in color; remove and drain. Remove all but 3T. oil from pan; reheat and stir-fry ② until fragrant; add wood ears, water chestnuts and mix together; add pork shreds, ③ and toss lightly; remove to serving plate and serve.

里肌肉……半斤
「炸油」……3杯

① 醬油………1大匙
酒…………1小匙
水…………3大匙
太白粉……2小匙

葱（3公分長）6枝
花瓜…………¾杯

② 花瓜汁……2大匙
醬油………2大匙

❶ 里肌肉切細絲拌上①料。

❷ 花瓜亦切細絲。

❸ 「炸油」燒熱，以中火把肉絲泡熟盛出，留油三大匙投葱段炒香，隨即放入肉絲、花瓜絲及②料，拌勻即成。

味全花瓜炒肉絲 Stir-Fried Pork with Pickled Cucumber 台灣菜 Taiwanese 6人份 6 servings

⅔ lb. pork loin
3 C. oil for frying

① 1 T. soy sauce
1 t. rice wine
3 T. water
2 t. cornstarch

6 1-inch sections green onion
¾ C. Wei-Chuan pickled cucumber

② 2 T. pickled cucumber liquid
2 T. soy sauce

❶ Remove any fat or tough membrane from pork loin; cut pork loin into shreds the size of matchsticks; mix with ① and let sit 20 minutes.

❷ Cut pickled cucumbers into shreds the same size as pork.

❸ Heat oil for deep-frying; deep-fry pork shreds until color changes; remove and drain. Remove all but 3T. oil from pan; reheat and stir-fry green onion until fragrant. Add pork shreds, pickled cucumber and ② ; toss lightly to mix together and remove to serving plate; serve.

<table>
<tbody>
<tr><td>①</td><td>里肌肉……6兩
鹽………半小匙
酒………1小匙
水………2大匙
太白粉…半大匙
「炸油」……3杯</td><td>②</td><td>葱絲………1大匙
薑絲………1大匙
紅椒絲……1大匙
青椒絲……¼杯</td><td>④</td><td>鹽………半小匙
味精……¼小匙
胡椒……¼小匙
麻油……¼小匙
水……1½大匙
太白粉…1小匙</td></tr>
<tr><td></td><td></td><td>③</td><td>榨菜絲………半杯
熟筍絲………半杯
熟紅蘿蔔絲…¼杯</td><td></td><td></td></tr>
</tbody>
</table>

❶ 里肌肉去白筋切細絲，以①料拌勻。

❷ 「炸油」燒熱，用中火把肉絲泡熟撈起，留油1大匙，先炒香②料，再倒入③料及肉絲略炒。以④料拌炒，加熟油1大匙，即可盛於盤上。

榨菜炒肉絲 Stir-Fried Pork and Szechuan Mustard Green

廣東菜 Cantonese
6人份 6 servings

①	6 oz. pork loin ½ t. salt 1 t. rice wine 2 T. water ½ T. cornstarch 3 C. oil for frying
②	1 T. shredded green onion 1 T. shredded ginger root 1 T. shredded hot red pepper ¼ C. shredded green pepper
③	½ C. shredded Szechuan pickled mustard green ½ C. shredded precooked bamboo shoot ¼ C. shredded precooked carrot
④	½ t. salt ¼ t. MSG ¼ t. black pepper ¼ t. sesame oil 1½ T. water 1 t. cornstarch

❶ Remove any fat or tough membrane from pork loin; cut into shreds; mix with ① and let sit 20 minutes.

❷ Heat oil for deep-frying; deep-fry meat shreds until color changes; remove and drain. Remove all but 1T. oil and stir-fry ② until fragrant; add ③ and pork shreds; mix together and add ④ ; add 1T. oil toss lightly. Remove to serving plate and serve.

①	里肌肉……6兩 鹽………半小匙 酒………1小匙 水………2大匙 太白粉……2小匙 「炸油」……3杯	②	鹹菜(切丁)………1杯 糖……………半小匙 油炸花生米(脫皮)半杯 蒜末……………1大匙 紅辣椒(切丁)…1大匙	③	酒………1大匙 醬油……1大匙 豆瓣醬…1大匙 味精……半小匙 糖………半小匙 麻油……半小匙

❶ 里肌肉切約1公分大小之四方小丁粒，拌上①料，醃約20分鐘。③料調好在碗內。

❷ 鍋燒熱（不放油）乾炒鹹菜，加糖半小匙，炒勻後盛起。

❸ 「炸油」3杯燒熱，倒入醃過之肉丁（中火）用鍋鏟翻動肉丁，呈白色時撈出留油2大匙，將②料炒香隨入③料，略炒並倒入泡過油之肉丁及炒乾之鹹菜，最後加油炸花生米拌勻即可。

鹹菜花生炒肉丁 Stir-Fried Pork with Peanuts and Mustard Cabbage

廣東菜 Cantonese 12人份 12 servings

①	6 oz. pork loin ½ t. salt 1 t. rice wine 2 T. water 2 t. cornstarch 3 C. oil for frying	②	1 C. diced pickled cabbage ½ t. sugar ½ C. roasted peanuts (salted and deshelled) 1 T. chopped garlic 1 T. diced hot red pepper	③	1 T. rice wine 1 T. soy sauce 1 T. soy bean paste ("do ban jiang") ½ t. MSG ½ t. sugar ½ t. sesame oil

❶ Remove any fat or white membrane from pork loin; dice pork loin and mix with ① and let sit 20 minutes.

❷ Heat pan (no oil) and stir-fry pickled cabbage and ½t. sugar until sugar dissolves; remove.

❸ Reheat pan and 3C. oil; stir-fry diced pork over medium heat until it changes color; remove and drain. Remove all but 2T. oil from pan; reheat and stir-fry ② until fragrant; add ③ and stir-fry briefly. Add pork, pickled cabbage and peanuts; toss lightly to mix ingredients; remove and serve.

猪後腿肉 ‥‥‥‥半斤		酒‥‥‥‥‥‥‥‥半大匙	
豆腐干‥1塊(1杯)		辣豆瓣醬‥‥‥‥‥1大匙	
青椒‥‥‥‥‥‥1個	①	甜麵醬‥‥‥‥‥‥1大匙	
蒜苗‥‥‥‥‥‥1枝		醬油‥‥‥‥‥‥‥2大匙	
		糖‥‥‥‥‥‥‥‥1小匙	

❶ 猪肉洗淨，整塊放入冷水中，用小火煮約３０分鐘，待冷後，切薄片。

❷ 豆腐干切薄片，青椒切滾刀塊，蒜苗切斜段分蒜白及蒜葉。

❸ 油３大匙燒開，先爆炒肉片，再下蒜白、豆腐干、青椒同炒盛起。

❹ 油４大匙燒熱，將①料（調匀）炒香，隨即倒入各料拌炒，最後洒上蒜苗葉即成。

回鍋肉 Double-Cooked Pork Slices

四川菜　Szechuan
6人份　6 servings

⅔　lb. fresh ham
1　square pressed bean curd
1　medium-sized green pepper
1　stalk long garlic*

① ½　T. rice wine
1　T. hot bean paste ("la do ban jiang")
1　T. sweet bean paste ("tien mien jiang")
2　T. soy sauce
1　t. sugar

❶ Place pork in water to cover and simmer covered for 30 minutes; remove and drain; cut into paper-thin slices.

❷ Cut pressed bean curd into slices ⅛ inch thick; remove seeds from green pepper and cut into bite-size pieces; cut garlic stalk into diagonal slices ¼-inch thick; separate white and green sections.

❸ Heat pan and 3T. oil; stir-fry pork slices over high heat and add white part of garlic stalk, bean curd and green pepper; stir-fry together and remove.

❹ Reheat pan and 4T. oil; stir-fry ① (already mixed to a fine paste) until fragrant. Add precooked ingredients and green sections garlic stalk; toss lightly to mix ingredients and remove to serving plate; serve.

* If garlic stalk is unavailable, substitute leeks or green onions.

火腿（７公分寬）……１斤
冰糖壓碎（或糖）…４大匙
紅棗………………４兩
土司麵包……………半條

① 桂花醬（如無可免）…１小匙
　冰糖（或糖）…………６大匙
　酒釀（或酒）…………２大匙

② 太白粉…１小匙
　水………１大匙

❶ 火腿削淨黑皮，刷洗乾淨，在水裏煮３０分鐘至熟撈起，紅棗加水４杯煮１５分鐘撈起備用。

❷ 將煮熟火腿切成７公分×４公分×０.２公分四方薄片，整齊排在中型湯碗内，加入冰糖，再鋪上紅棗，加入調勻①料蒸２小時後，將湯汁濾出留用，蜜汁火腿倒扣在大盤上。

❸ 蒸火腿餘汁（約１杯，不夠加水）煮開，以②料勾成薄汁，淋在火腿上即可。

❹ 土司麵包切去硬邊，並切成厚１.５公分與火腿同大小之麵包夾（第一、三刀切斷，第二刀不切斷）略蒸，與火腿夾食。

■ 此爲湖南名菜。

蜜汁火腿 Glazed Ham Slices

湖南菜　Hunan
12人份 12 servings

1⅓ lbs. ham (3 inch wide slices)
4　T.　sugar or rock sugar (ground)
4　oz. Chinese red dates
½　loaf white bread

① 1　t.　"guei hwa" sauce (if unavailable, omit)
6　T.　rock sugar
2　T.　fermented rice wine (if unavailable, substitute rice wine)

② 1　t.　cornstarch
1　T.　water

❶ Peel off skin off ham with a knife; scrub clean; boil in water for 30 minutes until cooked; remove from water. Boil Chinese red dates in 4 cups water for 15 minutes; remove from water.

❷ Cut the cooked ham into very thin slcies, 2¾" x 1½" x 1/16"; arrange slices in a medium-sized soup bowl; add rock sugar, Chinese red dates on top; add ① and steam for 2 hours; save the juice that remains after steaming. Remove glazed ham slices to a large dish.

❸ Bring the remaining juice to a boil (about 1C., add water if not enough); mix ② together; pour slowly over ham; serve.

❹ Cut off crust of bread; cut into ⅜" slices; the first slice do not cut through to bottom, the second cut all the way through; slice entire loaf in this manner. Steam slightly; place ham slices between bread and serve as sandwiches.

五花肉…１２兩　①{蒜末………半大匙　　②{酒…………１大匙　③{太白粉……１小匙
醬油……５大匙　　{紅豆乳……２塊　　　{味精………半小匙　　{水…………１小匙
「炸油」……３杯　　葱…………２枝　　　{糖…………２小匙
芋頭………１斤　　燙熟油菜…１４棵　　　{水…………半杯

❶ 五花肉盛鍋，加水（要淹滿）小火煮，約３０分鐘取出，用大針將肉皮插勻（以免炸時肉皮起大泡），拭乾水份趁熱以５大匙醬油醃泡肉皮備用。

❷ 芋頭去皮洗淨，切約２寸長、１寸寬之長方形薄片。

❸ 「炸油」燒開，將五花肉下鍋炸（肉皮面向鍋底蓋鍋，以免油爆），用中火炸至金黃色撈出（約３分鐘），浸冷水待涼，取出切片（與芋頭片同大小）。芋頭片亦入油鍋炸至呈金黃色取出。

❹ 將油４大匙燒熱，把①料炒香，隨入肉片同炒數下，再加醃肉醬油及②料煮開（２分鐘）取出。

❺ 備中碗一只，按照肉一片（肉皮貼碗），芋頭一片，順序排滿，剩餘材料把碗填滿，肉汁倒入碗內，上面擺２枝葱，蒸約１小時半，蒸爛倒出汁，反扣菜盤中，另鍋將餘汁加③料太白粉水勾汁澆上，用油菜圍邊。

南乳扣肉　Steamed Pork in Preserved Bean Sauce

廣東菜　Cantonese
12人份　12 servings

1 lb. fresh bacon (unsliced)	①{ ½ T. chopped garlic	②{ 1 T. rice wine · 2 t. sugar
5 T. soy sauce	2 squares fermented	½ t. MSG · ½ C. water
3 C. oil for frying	bean curd ("do fu ru")	③{ 1 t. cornstarch
1⅓ lbs. taro root or sweet potato	2 stalks green onion	1 t. water
	8 oz. spinach	

❶ Place fresh bacon in a pot with water to cover; cook 30 minutes over medium heat; remove and drain. Lightly pierce skin of bacon (to prevent big bubbles during deep-frying); dry outside of bacon and rub 5T. soy sauce over skin; drain and retain soy sauce.

❷ Peel taro and rinse; drain and cut into 1-inch by 2-inch thin slices.

❸ Heat oil for deep-frying; deep-fry bacon (skin-side towards bottom of pan) over medium heat for 3 minutes until golden brown (cover to prevent oil from splashing); remove and rinse in cold water. Cut meat into slices the same size as taro; reheat oil for deep-frying and deep-fry taro slices until golden brown; remove and drain.

❹ Heat pan and 4T. oil; stir-fry ① until fragrant and add meat slices, retained soy sauce and ② ; let liquid come to a boil and cook 2 minutes; remove.

❺ In a medium-sized heatproof soup bowl, arrange taro and pork slices alternately (skin side down); pack pieces securely into bowl; add soup and place 2 stalks green onion on top. Place bowl in steamer and steam over high heat for 1½ hours (pork should be very tender); drain soup into a bowl (retain) and invert pork and taro slices onto serving plate. Heat retained liquid until boiling and add ③ to thicken; pour over pork and taro. Heat pan and 3T. oil; add spinach and ½t. salt; stir-fry until limp (add a little water if necessary) and remove; arrange around pork and taro as illustrated; serve.

五花猪肉(寬七、八公分)…12兩	梅乾菜…………4兩	① 酒……1大匙、糖……2小匙
醬油…………………5大匙	葱(3公分長)…6枝	味精…半小匙、清水……半杯
「炸油」…………………3杯	薑…………6片	

❶ 五花肉盛鍋，加水(要淹滿)，小火煮約30分鐘取出，用大針將肉皮插勻 (以免炸時，肉皮起大泡) ，拭乾水份，趁熱以5大匙醬油，醃泡肉皮備用。

❷ 「炸油」燒開，將五花肉下鍋炸(肉皮面向鍋底蓋鍋以免油爆)，用中火炸至金黃色撈出 (約3分鐘) ，浸冷水待涼，取出，切約1公分厚的長方片，並整齊的排列在中碗內(肉皮朝下)。

❸ 梅乾菜用温水洗淨切碎。

❹ 油4大匙燒熱，將葱段、薑片炒香，隨加梅乾菜、醃肉醬油及①料燜煮5分鐘後，放在已排好之肉片上面，用大火蒸約1小時，倒出餘汁，反扣入菜盤內再把餘汁澆上，即可上桌供食。

■ 應用材料：梅乾菜可用鹹菜、冬菜取代。

梅菜扣肉 Steamed Pork with "Mei Gan Tsai"

四川菜　Szechuan
12人份　12 servings

1　lb. fresh bacon (cut to a piece 3-inches thick)
5　T. soy sauce
3　C. oil for frying

4　oz. "mei gan tsai"*
6　1-inch sections green onion
6　slices ginger root

① 　1　T. rice wine
½　t. MSG
2　t. sugar
½　C. water

❶ Place fresh bacon in a pot with water to cover; cook 30 minutes over medium heat; remove and drain. Lightly pierce skin of bacon (to prevent big bubbles during deep-frying); dry outside of bacon and rub 5T. soy sauce over skin; drain bacon and retain soy sauce.

❷ Heat oil for deep-frying; deep-fry bacon (skin-side towards bottom of pan) over medium heat for 3 minutes until golden brown (cover to prevent oil from splashing); remove and rinse in cold water; drain. Cut bacon into slices ⅓-inch thick and arrange slices in a medium-sized soup bowl, skin side down; pack pieces securely.

❸ Lightly rinse "mei gan tsai" in warm water; chop finely.

❹ Heat pan and 4T. oil; stir-fry green onion and ginger until fragrant; add "mei gan tsai", retained soy sauce and ① ; simmer 5 minutes covered; remove and spoon mixture over bacon slices in bowl. Place bowl in a steamer and steam 1 hour over high heat; remove and drain soup into a bowl. Invert pork onto serving plate and pour soup over top; serve.

* "Mei gan tsai" is a Chinese herb which may be purchased at a Chinese herbal drugstore. If unavailable, substitute pressed mustard green.

	牛肉⋯⋯⋯⋯8兩	葱（3公分長）⋯6枝	酒⋯⋯⋯⋯半大匙	
	醬油⋯⋯⋯1大匙	薑⋯⋯⋯⋯6片	蠔油⋯⋯1½大匙	
	酒⋯⋯⋯⋯1小匙		味精⋯⋯¼小匙	
①	小蘇打⋯⋯¼小匙		糖⋯⋯⋯¼小匙	②
	清水⋯⋯⋯5大匙		胡椒⋯⋯¼小匙	
	太白粉⋯⋯2小匙		麻油⋯⋯¼小匙	
	熟油⋯⋯⋯1大匙		清水⋯⋯1½大匙	
	「炸油」⋯⋯3杯		太白粉⋯⋯1小匙	

❶ 牛肉洗淨除筋，橫紋切成薄片，調①料醃約1小時，下鍋前加熟油（泡油時容易鏟開）。

❷ 「炸油」燒熱，把牛肉倒入，中火泡約２０秒鐘，至牛肉九分熟時，即刻撈出；留油2大匙，爆炒葱薑，隨入牛肉及酒半大匙和②料，迅速拌炒，即可起鍋。

■ 圍邊用材料：香菜。

蠔油牛肉 Stir-Fried Beef with Oyster Sauce

廣東菜 Cantonese
6人份　6 servings

	8 oz. flank steak or beef tenderloin	6 1-inch sections green onion	½ T. rice wine
①	1 T. soy sauce	6 slices ginger root	1½ T. oyster or soy sauce
	1 t. rice wine		¼ t. MSG
	5 T. water		¼ t. sugar
	2 t. cornstarch		② ¼ t. black pepper
	1 T. oil		¼ t. sesame oil
	3 C. oil for frying		1½ T. water
			1 t. cornstarch

❶ Remove any fat or tough membrane from beef; cut across grain into thin bite-size pieces; mix with ① and let soak 1 hour; and ½T. oil* and mix.

❷ Heat oil; deep-fry meat slices over medium heat for 20 seconds until changed in color; remove and drain. Remove all but 2T. oil from pan and reheat; stir-fry green onion and ginger until fragrant; add beef slices, ½T. rice wine and ② ; toss lightly to mix ingredients and remove to serving plate; serve.

■ Garnish with coriander.

* The 1T. oil added to beef slices prevents slices from sticking together during deep-frying.

牛肉……8兩　　　｜醬油……1大匙　　　｜青椒…………6個　　　｜鹽……半小匙、麻油…半小匙
熟油…1大匙　　　｜酒………1小匙　　　｜葱(切碎)…半大匙　　　｜味精…半小匙、清水…3大匙
「炸油」…3杯　①｜小蘇打…¼小匙　②｜薑(切碎)…半大匙　③｜糖……半小匙、太白粉2小匙
　　　　　　　　　｜清水……5大匙　　　｜蒜(切碎)…1大匙　　　｜胡椒…¼小匙
　　　　　　　　　｜太白粉…2小匙　　　｜豆豉(切碎)1大匙

❶ 牛肉除筋，橫紋切絲調①料醃約1小時，泡油前加熱油，可使牛肉容易鏟開。青椒切絲，②料
　、③料各備在小碗。

❷ 「炸油」燒熱，把牛肉倒入，中火泡熟（需用鍋鏟攪開）20秒鐘至牛肉九分熟時，即刻撈出，
　，留油4大匙炒青椒，並下水2大匙以保持青椒之青綠盛出。

❸ 油4大匙燒熱，中火炒香②料，隨入牛肉，青椒、酒、③料，大火迅速炒拌，即可起鍋。

■ 牛肉切絲、切片，配料用荸薺、木耳、豌豆角、芹菜、包心菜、芥蘭菜、白菜、青江菜、嫩薑
　、葱、紅蘿蔔、毛菇、草菇、番茄等等可依個人喜愛調配。

青椒牛肉絲 Stir-Fried Beef with Green Peppers

廣東菜 Cantonese
12人份 12 servings

8　oz. flank steak or beef
　　　tenderloin
1　T. soy sauce
1　t. rice wine
① ¼　t. baking soda
5　T. water
2　t. cornstarch
1　T. oil
3　C. oil for frying

6　green peppers
½　T. chopped green onion
½　T. chopped ginger root
② 1　T. chopped garlic
1　T. chopped fermented
　　　black beans

½　t. salt　・½ t. sesame oil
½　t. MSG　・3 T. water
③ ½　t. sugar　・2 t. cornstarch
¼　t. black pepper

❶ Remove any fat or tough membrane from beef; cut into shreds; mix with ① and let soak for 1 hour; before frying, add 1T. oil (this prevents meat from sticking together during deep-frying). Cut green peppers into shreds; mix ② and ③ in separate bowls.

❷ Heat oil for deep-frying; deep-fry meat slices over medium heat for 20 seconds and until color changes; remove and drain; remove all but 4T. oil from pan; stir-fry green peppers, adding 2T. water as it fries.

❸ Heat 4T. oil for frying; stir-fry ② until fragrant; add beef, green peppers, rice wine, and ③ ; mix together quickly over high heat. Remove to serving plate; serve.

■ According to preference, beef may be cut into shreds or slices. Water chestnuts, dried wood ears, peas, celery, Chinese cabbage, green cabbage, ginger root, green onion, carrots, button mushrooms, straw mushrooms, tomatoes, etc. may be substituted for green pepper.

牛肉⋯⋯⋯⋯⋯1斤		辣豆瓣醬⋯⋯2小匙		麻油⋯1小匙
紅蘿蔔絲⋯⋯⋯1杯	①	葱薑末⋯(各)1小匙	③	猪油⋯1小匙
芹菜(3公分長)⋯1杯		酒⋯⋯⋯⋯⋯1小匙		醋⋯⋯半小匙
蒜苗切斜薄片⋯⋯½杯	②	醬油⋯⋯⋯⋯1大匙		花椒粉⅓小匙
		味精⋯⋯⋯⋯半小匙		
		糖⋯⋯⋯⋯⋯1小匙		

❶ 牛肉切細絲。

❷ 油1杯燒熱,將牛肉絲大火炸約8分鐘撈出;鍋洗淨(以免粘鍋),另放油1杯,再把牛肉絲放入,中火炸6分鐘到乾撈起。

❸ 油4大匙先炒香①料再將紅蘿蔔絲及蒜苗略炒,隨下芹菜,炸乾牛肉及②料炒勻,最後加③料炒拌,置於菜盤,上面洒⅓小匙花椒粉即可。

干扁牛肉絲 Stir-Fried Beef with Vegetables

四川菜　Szechuan
12人份　12 servings

1⅓ lbs. flank steak		2 t. hot bean paste ("la do ban jiang")		1 t. sesame oil
1 C. shredded carrot	①	1 t. chopped green onion	③	1 t. lard or vegetable shortening
1 C. 1-inch sections celery		1 t. chopped ginger root		½ t. worcestershire sauce
¼ C. Chopped garlic		1 t. rice wine		⅓ t. Szechuan peppercorn powder
	②	1 T. soy sauce		
		½ t. MSG		
		1 t. sugar		

❶ Cut flank steak into shreds.

❷ Heat 1C. oil for deep-frying; deep-fry flank steak over high heat for 8 minute; remove and drain. Remove oil and reheat 1C. clean oil for deep-frying; re-fry flank steak over medium heat for 6 minutes until shreds are very crisp; remove and drain.

❸ Heat pan and 4T. oil; stir-fry ① until fragrant; add carrot shreds and minced garlic; stir-fry until carrot is tender; add celery sections, beef shreds and ② . Continue to stir-fry and add ③ ; toss ingredients lightly to mix and remove to serving plate; sprinkle Szechuan peppercorn powder on top. Serve.

牛腩…………1斤半	葱…………2枝	②{ 牛肉湯汁………半杯
粉皮…………１〇張	薑…………2片	味精…………半小匙
	醬油…………半杯	
	①{ 糖…………１大匙	
	花椒粒………半小匙	
	八角…………1朶	
	水…………5杯	
	酒…………2大匙	

❶ 牛肉整塊切3公分厚與①料盛快鍋以中火燒煮５〇分鐘（至湯汁剩約1杯），待冷將牛肉撈起切片，粉皮切條，以熱水略洗備用。

❷ 備中碗1個先擺牛肉，再置粉皮淋上②料蒸２〇分鐘，即可倒扣在盤上供食。

■ 可用大白菜或白蘿蔔與煮熟牛肉（各切塊）連同牛肉汁一起紅燒食之，也可以炒熟青菜圍邊取代粉皮。

■ 圍邊用材料：香菜。

紅燒牛腩 Red-Cooked Beef Slices

2　lbs. brisket of beef
10 bean thread sheets*[1] ("fen pi")

①{
2　stalks green onion
2　slices ginger root
½　C. soy sauce
1　T. sugar
½　t. Szechuan peppercorns
1　star anise
5　C. water
2　T. rice wine

②{
½　C. beef stock from steaming
½　t. MSG

❶ Place beef and ① in a pressure cooker*[2]; cook 50 minutes over medium heat until liquid is reduced to 1C.; remove beef and let cool (retain soup for ②); cut beef into paper-thin slices. Cut bean thread sheets into ½-inch strips; lightly rinse in hot water; drain.

❷ In a medium-sized soup bowl, arrange beef slices in a circular pattern, pack tightly and put bean thread slices on top; pour ② on top and place bowl in steamer; steam 20 minutes over medium heat. Remove and drain soup into a bowl; invert meat onto serving plate; pour soup on top and serve.

*[1] If bean thread sheets are unavailable, substitute stir-fried spinach or broccoli and arrange around steamed beef slices on serving plate.

*[2] If no pressure cooker is available, place ingredients in a covered pot or casserole and cook covered 2 hours over medium heat until tender. Garnish with coriander.

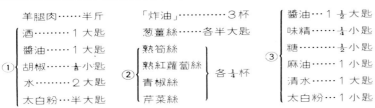

① 羊腿肉……半斤　酒………1大匙　醬油……1大匙　胡椒……⅛小匙　水………2大匙　太白粉…半大匙

② 「炸油」………3杯　葱薑絲……各半大匙　熟筍絲　熟紅蘿蔔絲　青椒絲　芹菜絲　各¼杯

③ 醬油…1½大匙　味精……¼小匙　糖………½小匙　麻油……1小匙　清水……1大匙　太白粉…1小匙

❶ 羊肉切絲調①料醃約２０分鐘。

❷ 「炸油」燒熱，中火將羊肉絲泡熟撈出，留油４大匙炒葱薑及②料各絲並入泡熟羊肉絲及③料拌炒均勻即成。

炒羊肉丝　Stir-Fried Lamb with Assorted Vegetables
廣東菜　Cantonese
12人份　**12 servings**

① ⅔ lb. leg of lamb meat
1 T. rice wine
1 T. soy sauce
⅛ t. black pepper
2 T. water
½ T. cornstarch

② 3 C. oil for frying
½ T. shredded green onion
½ T. shredded ginger root
¼ C. shredded precooked bamboo shoot
¼ C. shredded precooked carrot
¼ C. shredded green pepper
¼ C. shredded celery

③ 1½ T. soy sauce
¼ t. MSG
½ t. sugar
1 t. sesame oil
1 T. water
1 t. cornstarch

❶ Shred lamb meat; mix with ① and let sit 20 minutes.

❷ Heat oil for deep-frying; deep-fry lamb shreds over medium heat until changed in color; remove and drain.   Remove all but 4T. oil from pan; reheat and stir-fry shredded onion and ginger until fragrant; add ② and stir-fry briefly; add lamb shreds and ③ ; lightly toss ingredients to mix together and remove to serving plate; serve.

熟豬肚絲⋯2杯　紅辣椒絲2大匙　　　酒⋯⋯⋯⋯⋯半大匙
鮮筍絲⋯⋯1杯 ① 嫩薑絲⋯2大匙　　　醬油⋯⋯⋯⋯半大匙
鹹菜絲⋯⋯1杯　　葱絲⋯⋯2大匙　　　鹽⋯⋯⋯⋯⋯1小匙
　　　　　　　　　　　　　　　　② 味精⋯⋯⋯⋯半小匙
　　　　　　　　　　　　　　　　　胡椒、麻油各¼小匙
　　　　　　　　　　　　　　　　　水⋯⋯⋯⋯⋯4大匙
　　　　　　　　　　　　　　　　　太白粉⋯⋯⋯1小匙

❶ 油4大匙燒熱，先炒香①料，隨下筍絲、鹹菜絲炒熟再入肚絲略炒，加酒半大匙及②料迅速炒
　拌均勻即可。
■ 熟豬肚參照本書第２１６頁鮑魚豬肚湯內豬肚處理法。
■ 應用材料：鹹菜絲可用西芹菜絲取代。

鹹菜炒肚絲　Stir-Fried Stomach and Szechuan Mustard Green

台灣菜　Taiwanese
12人份 **12 servings**

2 C. precooked shredded pork stomach
1 C. precooked shredded bamboo shoot
1 C. shredded pickled cabbage*

①
2 T. shredded hot red pepper
2 T. shredded ginger root
2 T. shredded green onion

②
½ T. rice wine
½ T. soy sauce
1 t. salt
½ t. MSG
¼ t. black pepper
¼ t. sesame oil
4 T. water
1 t. cornstarch

❶ Heat pan and 4T. oil; stir-fry ① until fragrant; add bamboo shoot and pickled cabbage; stir-fry to mix together and add shredded stomach; briefly stir-fry and add ½T. rice wine and ② ; toss ingredients lightly to mix together and remove to serving plate; serve.
■ For directions for precooked pork stomach, see "Abalone with pork stomach in broth" on P. 216.
* If pickled cabbage is unavailable, you may substitute celery.

①	②	③	④
猪肝……半斤 酒……1小匙 醬油…1大匙	葱（3公分長）…6枝 薑…………6片 大蒜（拍碎）…3粒	熟豌豆角……12片 熟紅蘿蔔片…12片 熟筍片………12片 「炸油」…………3杯	鹽………半小匙 味精……¼小匙 糖………半小匙 醋………半小匙 胡椒……¼小匙 麻油……¼小匙 水……1½大匙 太白粉…1小匙

❶ 猪肝洗淨，切片，調上①料，拌勻醃20分鐘。

❷ 「炸油」燒熱，中火把猪肝泡熟，見顏色轉白撈出，留油3大匙，把②料炒香，並入③料略炒後，放入猪肝及④料炒拌均勻即成。

生炒猪肝 Stir-Fried Liver with Assorted Vegetables

北平菜　　Peking
6人份　6 servings

①	②	③	④
⅔ lb. beef, pork 1 t. rice wine 1 T. soy sauce	6 1-inch sections green onion 6 slices ginger root 3 cloves garlic, smashed	12 pods precooked snow peas 12 slices precooked carrot 12 slices precooked bamboo shoot 3 C. oil for frying	½ t. salt ¼ t. MSG ½ t. sugar ½ t. vinegar ¼ t. black pepper ¼ t. sesame oil 1½ T. water 1 t. cornstarch

❶ Rinse liver and cut into slices ¼-inch thick; mix with ① and let sit 20 minutes.

❷ Heat oil for deep-frying; deep-fry liver slices over medium heat until color changes (about 20 seconds); remove and drain. Remove all but 3T. oil and reheat; stir-fry ② until fragrant; add ③ and briefly stir-fry; add liver slcies and ④; toss lightly to mix ingredients and remove to serving plate; serve.

①	猪腰 1 付⋯⋯⋯⋯ 2 個 葱（3公分長）⋯⋯ 6 枝 薑⋯⋯⋯⋯⋯ 6 片 大蒜（拍碎）⋯⋯⋯ 3 粒	②	熟豌豆角⋯ 1 2 片 熟紅蘿蔔⋯ 1 2 片 熟筍片⋯⋯ 1 2 片	③	酒⋯⋯ 1 小匙、醋⋯⋯ 半小匙 醬油⋯ 2 小匙、胡椒⋯ ¼ 小匙 鹽⋯⋯ 1 小匙、麻油⋯ ¼ 小匙 味精⋯ 半小匙、水⋯⋯ 1 大匙 糖⋯⋯ 半小匙、太白粉 1 小匙

❶ 猪腰橫切開成二半，挖去白筋，每片之內部（外面亦可）先用刀直劃5或6刀，再橫切斜薄片
（ 第一、二刀不斷，第三刀切斷 ），泡在水內備用。

❷ 豌豆角折去兩端之硬筋，與猪腰分別放入滾水中川燙２０秒撈出，泡入冷水內備用。

❸ 油４大匙燒熱，把①料炒香，並將②料略炒，放入腰花及③料拌炒數下，即刻起鍋。

■ 燙猪腰需注意，水剛燒滾，燙約２０秒即可撈出。

炒腰花 Stir-Fried Kidney with Assorted Vegetables

北平菜　Peking
12人份 **12 servings**

①	2　pork kidneys (about 1lb.) 6　1-inch sections green onion 6　slices ginger root 3　cloves garlic, smashed	②	12 pods snow peas 12 slices precooked carrot 12 slices precooked bamboo shoot	③	1　t.　rice wine 2　t.　soy sauce 1　t.　salt ½　t.　MSG ½　t.　sugar ½　t.　vinegar ¼　t.　black pepper ¼　t.　sesame oil 1　T.　water 1　t.　cornstarch

❶ Slice each kidney in half horizontally and remove any white membrance from center; score surface vertically; cut diagonally into thin slices and place slices in water.

❷ Remove stems from snow peas and pull away any veiny strings; blanch in boiling water for 1 minute; remove and cook kidney slices in simmering water for 20 seconds; remove and place snow peas and kidneys separately in cold water to cool; drain.

❸ Heat pan and 4T. oil; stir-fry ① until fragrant and add ② ; briefly stir-fry and add kidney slices and ③ ; toss ingredients lightly to mix and remove to serving plate; serve.

<table>
<tr><td rowspan="1">①{</td><td>豬肚尖（6兩）2杯
薑酒⋯⋯⋯1大匙
鹽⋯⋯⋯⋯半小匙
豬腰（大2只）2杯</td><td>香菜（5兩）⋯⋯3杯
葱段（3公分長）6枝
薑⋯⋯⋯⋯⋯6片</td><td>②{</td><td>酒⋯⋯⋯⋯1大匙
鹽⋯⋯1½小匙
味精⋯⋯⋯1小匙
胡椒⋯⋯¼小匙
麻油⋯⋯⋯1小匙
太白粉⋯1小匙
水⋯⋯⋯⋯1大匙</td></tr>
</table>

❶ 肚尖對切成二片，除去內層豬肚切約5公分×1公分×1公分粗條，以①料醃約20分鐘。

❷ 豬腰剖開，除去白筋切同肚尖大小粗條，香菜略切備用。

❸ 4杯水燒開，將肚尖豬腰各入開水內泡20秒見顏色轉白撈起，另將豬腰泡在冷水備用。

❹ 油4大匙燒熱，先炒葱、薑，隨入肚尖豬腰爆炒再加香菜略炒，最後下酒1大匙及②料炒拌均勻即可。

■ 肚尖係豬肚厚的部份約10公分，參照本書第216頁鮑魚豬肚湯內豬肚處理法❶。

生炒双脆 Stir-Fried Stomach and Kidney

6　oz. base of pork stomach	5　oz. (3C.) coriander	1　T. rice wine
①{ 1　T. ginger wine ½　t. salt 2　pork kidneys (about 1lb.)	6　1-inch sections green onion 6　slices ginger root	②{ 1½ t. salt • 1　t. sesame oil 1　t. MSG • 1　t. cornstarch ¼　t. black pepper • 1 T. water

❶ Slice base of stomach horizontally into half; cut into matchstick-sized pieces 2 inches long; mix with ① and let sit 20 minutes.

❷ Slice kidneys in half horizontally; remove any white membrane from middle, cut into pieces the same size as pork stomach, lightly chop coriander.

❸ Boil 4C. water; cook pig's stomach and kidney separately, 20 seconds until changed in color; remove and place kidney slices in cold water to cool; drain.

❹ Heat pan and 4T. oil; stir-fry green onion and ginger until fragrant; add stomach, kidney and stir-fry over high heat; add coriander and lightly stir-fry; add 1T. rice wine and ② ; toss lightly to mix ingredients and remove to serving plate; serve.

蝦仁⋯⋯⋯¼杯
①{ 鹽⋯⋯⋯⅛小匙
太白粉⋯半小匙

②{ 里肌肉絲⋯¼杯
太白粉⋯半小匙

③{ 猪腰⋯⋯⋯¼杯
生魷魚⋯⋯¼杯
猪肝⋯⋯⋯¼杯

④{ 綠豆芽⋯⋯1杯
青椒⋯⋯⋯¼杯

⑤{ 葱薑⋯1大匙
叉燒肉⋯¼杯
冬菇⋯1大匙
「炸油」⋯3杯
炸米粉⋯1兩

⑥{ 鹽⋯⋯半小匙、麻油⋯⋯¼小匙
味精⋯¼小匙、水⋯1½大匙
糖⋯¼小匙、太白粉⋯1小匙
胡椒⋯¼小匙

❶ 蝦調①料，里肌肉絲調上太白粉，其他各料全部切絲備用。

❷ 油三杯燒熱，分別將①②③各料泡油撈出，留油3大匙，入④料加鹽¼小匙大火炒勻盛起，再下2大匙油將⑤料炒香，最後再把以上各料（米粉除外）放入，下酒1小匙，再倒入⑥料加1大匙熟油拌勻即可。

❸ 米粉做底，炒好各料盛在其上。

■ 炸米粉時「炸油」先燒沸，再用中火炸。

李公什碎 Li's Chop Suey

廣東菜　Cantonese
6人份　6 servings

①{ ¼ C. raw, shelled shrimp
⅛ t. salt
½ t. cornstarch

②{ ¼ C. shredded pork loin
½ t. cornstarch

③{ ¼ C. shredded pork kidney
¼ C. shredded squid meat
¼ C. shredded beef, chicken or pork liver

④{ 1 C. bean sprouts
¼ C. shredded green pepper

⑤{ 1 T. chopped green onion
1 T. chopped ginger root
¼ C. shredded roasted pork
1 T. shredded Chinese black mushroom
3 C. oil for frying
1 oz. fried rice noodles*

⑥{ ½ t. salt
¼ t. MSG
¼ t. sugar
¼ t. black pepper
¼ t. sesame oil
1½ T. water
1 t. cornstarch

❶ Clean and devein shrimp and mix with ① ; mix cornstarch with shredded pork; let sit 20 minutes.

❷ Heat oil for deep-frying; separately deep-fry ingredients of ① , ② and ③ until changed in color; remove and drain. Remove all but 3T. oil from pan and briefly stir-fry ④ and ¼t. salt over high heat; remove. Reheat pan and 2T. oil; stir-fry ⑤ until fragrant; add all vegetables and meats except fried rice noodles; continue to stir-fry and add 1t. rice wine, ⑥ and 1T. oil; mix together and remove.

❸ Arrange fried rice noodles on serving plate; portion stir-fried mixture on top and serve.

* To deep-fry rice noodles: heat oil until very hot; add rice noodles and deep-fry briefly until expanded; remove and drain.

<table>
<tr><td rowspan="3">①</td><td>猪大腸頭…6條</td></tr>
<tr><td>薑酒……1大匙</td></tr>
<tr><td>醋………1大匙</td></tr>
</table>

②	
水……3杯	
醬油…半杯	
糖…2大匙	
酒…2大匙	
葱……2枝	
薑……2片	
八角…1朵	

「炸油」……3杯
葱薑末…各1小匙
酒…………半大匙

③	
水…………1杯	
醬油…2½大匙	
味精……半小匙	
糖………1大匙	
太白粉…1小匙	

④	
蒜末……1大匙	
香菜末…1大匙	

❶ 大腸加入①料醃２０分鐘後，將１條大腸套入另一條裏面，依次做好３條備用。

❷ 快鍋內放入②料及大腸煮３０分鐘，以筷子能插入大腸的程度即可撈起起待涼。

❸ 「炸油」燒開，入大腸炸３分鐘至皮脆，表面呈金黃色，撈起切成２公分長。

❹ 油２大匙燒熱，葱薑末炒香，下酒及③料燒開，再入大腸以中火煮２分鐘，盛盤上灑④料即成。

■ 猪大腸頭處理法：將大腸頭前端切掉並除污油，再將大腸頭內外各以鹽、醋搓揉至無黏液時，用水冲洗乾淨至無臭味後即可使用。

紅燒肥腸 Red-Cooked Tripe Sections

北平菜　Peking
6人份　6 servings

6　4-inch sections pork tripe*[1]
① 1　T.　ginger wine
1　T.　vinegar

② 3　C.　water
½　C.　soy sauce
2　T.　sugar
2　T.　rice wine
2　stalks green onion
2　slices ginger root
1　star anise

3　C.　oil for frying
1　t.　chopped green onion
1　t.　chopped ginger root
½　T.　rice wine
③ 1　C.　water
2½ T.　soy sauce
½　t.　MSG
1　T.　sugar
1　t.　cornstarch

④ 1　T.　chopped garlic
1　T.　chopped coriander

❶ Mix tripe sections with ① ; let soak 20 minutes; place 1 section tripe in the hole of another section so that there are now three "double" sections.

❷ Place ② and tripe sections in pressure cooker*[2]; cook 30 minutes over medium heat; test sections with chopstick for tenderness; remove, drain sections and let cool.

❸ Heat oil for deep-frying; deep-fry tripe sections 3 minutes until golden brown and crunchy; remove, drain and cut sections into ⅔-inch slices.

❹ Heat pan and 2T. oil; stir-fry onion and ginger until fragrant; add rice wine, ③ and let liquid come to boil; add tripe slices and cook covered over medium heat for 2 minutes; remove to serving plate and sprinkle ④ on top; serve.

*[1] Tripe must be pre-conditioned before using in recipe; remove any fat from exterior; rub tripe interior and exterior with salt and vinegar; rinse and repeat this procedure until tripe is rid of any slimy covering; drain and use as directed.

*[2] If no pressure cooker is available, place ingredients in covered pan or casserole and cook 1 hour over medium heat; until tripe is tender.

鯧魚 1 條…10 兩
鹽…………1 小匙
① 里肌肉絲…2 大匙
多菇絲……1 大匙
榨菜絲……2 大匙
薑絲………1 大匙

② 醬油…半小匙
味精…¼小匙
糖…¼小匙
酒……1 小匙

③ 胡椒…¼小匙
麻油…半小匙
葱絲…2 大匙

❶ 魚加鹽 1 小匙抹勻，置於蒸盤上，盤底擺一雙筷子。

❷ 將①料調上②料後，擺於魚上，水開用大火蒸熟（約 15 分鐘）。

❸ 取出魚置於菜盤（蒸汁留用），加入③料，上面擺葱絲，燒滾 2 大匙油，澆熟葱絲並淋上蒸汁即可。

清蒸海鮮 Steamed Pomfret

廣東菜　Cantonese
6人份　6 servings

1　whole pomfret* (about 10 oz.)
1　t.　salt
① 2　T. shredded pork loin
1　T. shredded Chinese black mushroom
2　T. shredded Szechuan pickled mustard green
1　T. shredded ginger root

② ½　t.　soy sauce
¼　t.　MSG
¼　t.　sugar
1　t.　rice wine

③ ¼　t.　black pepper
½　t.　sesame oil
2　T. shredded green onion

❶ Rub fish exterior with salt; place 2 chopsticks on a heatproof plate to form a rack for fish; place fish on chopsticks.

❷ Mix ① and ② ; sprinkle mixture on top of fish and place plate in a steamer. Steam 10 minutes over high heat until meat is flaky and tender.

❸ Remove fish to serving plate (retain liquid); pour ③ on top of fish and sprinkle 2T. shredded green onion on top. Heat 2T. oil until very hot; pour on top of green onion. Heat retained liquid and pour over fish; serve.

* If pomfret is unavailable, substitute mackerel, haddock or striped bass.

鯉魚………1 斤	里肌肉…………2 兩	網油………………3 兩
① 鹽………1 小匙	② 豆豉………2 大匙	（３０公分×２０公分）
酒………1 大匙	葱薑末(各)…1 大匙	
胡椒……¼ 小匙	紅辣椒末……1 大匙	
	醬油…………1 大匙	

❶ 魚從腹部剖開，但背部需連着，然後在背部正面直劃刀，調上①料擺在蒸盤備用。

❷ 里肌肉切細丁粒。

❸ 油３大匙燒熱，將里肌肉及②料炒香，加醬油１大匙取出，倒勻在魚上，網上網油，蒸約１５分鐘（需大火），蒸熟擺在菜盤即可。

■ 蒸魚除鯉魚外，可用鯰魚、虱目魚或其他新鮮魚代替，家庭做可免用網油。

■ 圍邊用材料：香菜。

豆豉蒸魚 Steamed Carp with Fermented Black Beans　湖南菜 12人份　Hunan 12 servings

1 carp (about 1⅓ lbs.) *¹	2 oz. pork loin	1 10-by-7-inch piece pork net oil
① 1 t. salt	② 2 T. fermented black beans	or caul fat (3oz.) *²
1 T. rice wine	1 T. chopped green onion	
¼ t. black pepper	1 T. chopped ginger root	
	1 T. chopped hot red pepper	
	1 T. soy sauce	

❶ Make a long vertical cut along the underside of the fish, slicing the fish in half, but leaving the halves connected along the back. Mix fish with ① and place opened fish flat on serving plate; lightly score each half two or three times.

❷ Dice pork loin.

❸ Heat pan and 3T. oil; stir-fry diced pork until it changes color; push to side of pan and add ② ; stir-fry until fragrant and add 1T. soy sauce. Remove mixture and portion over fish. Place pork net oil on top, and carefully tuck in edges under fish. Place in steamer and steam 15 minutes over high heat; remove to serving plate and serve immediately.

*¹ Trout or sea bass may be substituted.

*² In family cooking or if unavailable, omit pork net oil.

■ Garnish with coriander.

鯧魚…………1斤	瘦火腿………2兩	葱（３公分長）１０枝
① 鹽…………２小匙	冬菇…………5朵	
味精……半小匙	醬油………半大匙	
酒…………１大匙	雞油………１大匙	
薑…………6片		

❶ 火腿蒸熟，冬菇泡軟均切薄片。

❷ 魚一面每隔２公分處切數條深刀痕（觸骨），將①料抹勻，按照火腿一片，冬菇一片順序夾在每一個刀痕內（盤底橫放二根筷子），淋上醬油半大匙，雞油１大匙備用。

❸ 將水燒開，擺進鯧魚用大火蒸約１５分鐘。蒸熟魚汁倒出，將魚放在菜盤中，上擺葱段，澆上燒開的熟油２大匙，再將蒸熟魚汁淋上即可。

■ 如無雞油，可用麻油或其他油代替。

雞油海鮮 Steamed Pomfret with Ham and Mushroom Slices

廣東菜　Cantonese
12人份　**12 servings**

1 whole pomfret*[1] (about 1⅓ bs.)	2 oz. precooked Chinese ham	10 1-inch sections green onion
① 2 t. salt	5 pre-softened Chinese black mushrooms	
½ t. MSG	½ T. soy sauce	
1 T. rice wine	1 T. melted chicken fat*[2]	
6 slices ginger root		

❶ Cut Chinese ham and Chinese mushrooms into thin, bite-size slices.

❷ Rinse and drain fish; on one side make diagonal cuts every ⅔ of an inch, slicing through meat to central bone; rub ① mixutre over fish and into cuts; let sit 20 minutes. Taking a piece of ham and black mushroom, place in a diagonal cut as illustrated; repeat for other slices until all of the cuts are filled. Place 2 chopsticks on a heatproof platter and place fish on platter; pour soy sauce and chicken fat over fish.

❸ Place fish in steamer and steam over high heat for 15 minutes; remove and drain off liquid to a bowl (retain); place fish on serving plate and place onion sections on top of fish. Heat 2T. oil until smoking; pour over fish. Pour retained liquid on top and serve.

*[1] If pomfret is unavailable, substitute sea bass, flounder or blue fish.

*[2] You may substitute sesame oil or vegetable oil.

<table>
<tbody>
<tr><td>①</td><td>石斑魚……1斤半
葱………2枝
薑………2片
酒………1大匙
水………20杯</td></tr>
<tr><td>②</td><td>葱………2枝
薑………2片
酒………1大匙
鹽………1大匙</td></tr>
</tbody>
</table>

③ 胡椒………¼小匙
葱絲………半杯
薑絲………¼杯
油………4大匙

④ 煮魚湯………¾杯
鹽………1小匙
醬油………1大匙
味精………半小匙

❶ 油3大匙燒熱，將①料之葱薑炒香，下酒及水燒沸，放入魚川燙20秒撈出，用刀刮去鱗，仔細洗淨，調入②料醃約半小時。

❷ 利用川燙魚水，把已醃過之魚放入，待沸立即熄火，蓋鍋浸泡15分鐘撈起，置菜盤。

❸ 把③料洒在魚上，油半杯澆沸，澆在③料之葱薑絲上，並燒開④料淋在魚上即成。

■ 殺魚時，魚肚皮勿開太大，以保持魚態之完整。

豉油王海鮮 Poached Fish with Shredded Onion and Ginger
廣東菜　Cantonese
12人份　12 servings

① 1　whole sea bass or flounder (2 lbs.)
2　stalks green onion
2　slices ginger root
1　T. rice wine
20 C. water

② 2　stalks green onion
2　slices ginger root
1　T. rice wine
1　T. salt

③ ¼　t.　black pepper
½　C.　shredded green onion
¼　C.　shredded ginger root
4　T.　oil

④ ¾　C.　fish stock
1　t.　salt
1　T.　soy sauce
½　t.　MSG

❶ Rinse fish and drain. Heat pan and 3T. oil and stir-fry green onion and ginger from ① until fragrant; add wine and water and bring liquid to a boil; add fish and cook 20 seconds; remove, drain and lightly scrape skin to clean. (retain liquid) Rub fish with ② and let sit 30 minutes.

❷ Place retained liquid from ① in a pan and bring liquid to a boil; add fish and turn off heat; let sit covered, for 15 minutes; remove and drain. Place fish on serving plate. (retain ¾C. stock for ④).

❸ Sprinkle ③ over fish; heat 4T. oil until very hot and pour over fish. Heat ④ until boiling and pour over fish; serve.

桂魚（石斑魚）…1條（1斤4兩）

①{
酒……半大匙
醬油…1小匙
鹽……半小匙
味精…¼小匙
胡椒…¼小匙
麻油…半小匙
葱………2枝
薑………2片
}

②{
熟火腿…14片
冬菇……14片
太白粉…半小匙
水………1小匙
}

❶ 用刀將兩面魚肉片出，切成2公分×5公分長方塊計14片調①料，醃20分鐘備用。

❷ 將魚之中間大骨切除，留魚頭及背脊連尾。由魚頭底剖開擺平置大盤一端，魚頭洒少許鹽，按照魚肉一片、火腿一片、冬菇一片，順序分別排列於兩旁（如圖）。水開大火蒸約8分鐘。

❸ 蒸熟魚汁半杯以②料勾汁淋於魚身，再燒滾2大匙熟油澆上即可。

■ 圍邊用材料：菠蘿、櫻桃、香菜。

麒麟蒸桂魚 Steamed Fish with Mushrooms and Ham

廣東菜 Cantonese
12人份 12 servings

1 whole grouper haddock, mackerel or flounder (about 1⅓ lbs.)

①{
½ T. rice wine
1 t. soy sauce
½ t. salt
¼ t. MSG
¼ t. black pepper
½ t. sesame oil
2 stalks green onion
2 slices ginger root
}

14 thin slices Chinese ham
14 slices pre-softened Chinese black mushroom

②{
½ t. cornstarch
1 t. water
}

❶ Slice fillets from sides of fish, cutting to within one inch of dorsal fin; cut fillet sections into 14 pieces 2-inches long and ⅔-inch wide; mix with ① and let sit 20 minutes.

❷ Remove central bone from fish, leaving head and tail connected; make a vertical cut in head underneath mouth of fish to flatten bottom of head; place piece on a heatproof plate and sprinkle lightly with salt. Arrange slices of fish, ham and mushrooms alternately, as illustrated around fish; place in steamer and steam 8 minutes over high heat; remove and place on serving plate.

❸ Drain ½C. soup from steaming and heat; when liquid comes to a boil, add ② to thicken; pour over fish. Heat 2T. oil until very hot; pour over fish and serve.

■ Garnish with pineapple slices, cherries and coriander.

| 魚 1 條 1 斤 8 兩 | ① | 酒‥‥‥‥1 大匙
葱‥‥‥‥2 枝
薑‥‥‥‥2 片
胡椒‥‥½ 小匙
鹽‥‥‥‥1 小匙 | | 蛋黃‥‥‥1 個
太白粉‥‥1 杯
「炸油」‥10 杯 | ③ | 糖‥‥‥‥‥6 大匙
醋‥‥‥‥‥6 大匙
番茄醬‥‥‥6 大匙
水‥‥‥‥‥6 大匙
鹽‥‥‥‥½ 小匙
太白粉‥1½ 小匙 | ④ | 葱絲‥‥‥‥2 大匙
薑絲‥‥‥‥1 大匙
紅辣椒絲‥半 大匙
香菜‥‥‥‥2 大匙 |
| | | | ② | 蒜末‥‥1 大匙
洋葱絲‥半 杯
青椒絲‥¼ 杯 | | | | |

❶ 魚身兩面每隔約 1、5 公分用刀斜切（刀深需觸及大骨），將①料擠汁擦勻魚身（需在每一切開之魚片縫擦均勻）醃約半小時。炸時塗上蛋黃及沾裹太白粉（約 1 杯）於魚身各處需仔細敷緊按魚在水中游水的姿式備好在盤內。

❷ 燒開「炸油」提起魚尾，也將魚頭順着魚在水中游水的姿式投入用鍋鏟淋熱油於魚身多次，使魚身花紋定型並以大火炸約 10 分鐘魚肉熟外皮脆即撈出。

❸ 將油 2 大匙燒熱，把②料炒香放入③料燒滾攪拌，最後加入熱油 1 大匙（使其有光澤）即可淋在魚身，上洒④料以增加美觀。

糖醋魚 Sweet and Sour Fish

| ① | 1 yellow fish* (about 2 lbs.)
1 T. rice wine
2 stalks green onion
2 slices ginger root
¼ t. black pepper
1 t. salt
1 egg yolk
1 C. cornstarch
10 C. oil for frying | ② | 1 T. chopped garlic
½ C. shredded onion
¼ C. shredded green pepper | ④ | 2 T. shredded green onion
1 T. shredded ginger root
½ T. shredded hot red pepper
2 T. chopped coriander |
| | | ③ | 6 T. sugar
6 T. vinegar
6 T. tomato ketchup
6 T. water
½ t. salt
1½ t. cornstarch | | |

❶ Rinse fish lightly; drain. On each side of the fish, make diagonal cuts through meat to the bone at every ½ inch; rub fish with ① mixture, making sure to reach meat inside diagonal cuts, let soak 30 minutes. Before deep-frying, dip fish in egg yolk and coat with cornstarch. (Once again, make sure to thoroughly coat inside of cuts.) Place fish on serving plate and press down lightly to flatten bottom of fish.

❷ Heat oil for deep-frying; taking fish by the tail, place in hot oil so that fish is completely immersed; ladle hot oil over fish. After diagonal cuts have "opened" (see picture) and batter has become lightly crispy, cook 10 minutes until golden brown; remove, drain and place on serving plate.

❸ Heat pan and 2T. oil; stir-fry ② until fragrant and add ③ ; when liquid reaches a boil and has become thick, add 1T. oil and mix together; pour over fish and sprinkle ④ on top; serve.

* If yellow fish is unavailable, substitute haddock, mackerel or sea bass.

①	活草魚…1斤8兩 葱…………2枝 薑…………2片 酒…………1大匙 鹽…………1大匙	③	嫩薑絲……2大匙 洋葱絲……2大匙 紅辣椒絲…1大匙 青椒絲……2大匙	④	醋………6大匙 糖………6大匙 番茄醬…3大匙 水………3大匙 鹽………1小匙	⑤	太白粉…半大匙 水………1大匙 香菜………少許
②	油…………1大匙 酒…………1大匙 水…………15杯						

❶ 將活魚殺好洗淨調①料醃約２０分鐘。

❷ 鍋燒熱，下②料之油、酒，隨即加水１５杯待滾，醃好之魚下鍋煮，蓋好鍋蓋（水要滿過魚身）待滾，速予熄火，燜約２０分鐘。

❸ 魚取出置於菜盤，並洒少許胡椒，澆上燒開的滾油４大匙。

❹ 油４大匙燒熱，將③料炒香，立即加④料燒滾，以⑤料勾汁，加１小匙麻油，澆於魚上，並洒香菜即可。

五柳鮮魚 Poached Fish in Sour Sauce

廣東菜　Cantonese
12人份　**12 servings**

①	1 whole perch* (1⅔ lbs.) 2 stalks green onion 2 slices ginger root 1 T. rice wine 1 T. salt	③	2 T. shredded ginger root 2 T. shredded green onion 1 T. shredded hot red pepper 2 T. shredded green pepper	④	6 T. vinegar 6 T. sugar 3 T. tomato ketchup 3 T. water 1 t. salt	⑤	½ T. cornstarch 1 T. water 1 t. sesame oil 3 sprigs of coriander
②	1 T. oil 1 T. rice wine 15 C. water						

❶ Rinse fish lightly; rub ① mixture over outside of fish; let stand 20 minutes.

❷ Heat pan and 1T. oil from ② ; add rice wine and water. When water comes to a boil, place whole fish in water (water should cover fish); cover and when water reaches a boil, turn off heat. Let sit covered for 20 minutes.

❸ Remove fish to serving plate; sprinkle a little black pepper on top. Heat 4T. oil until smoking; pour over fish.

❹ Heat pan and 4T. oil; stir-fry ③ until fragrant and add ④ . When liquid comes to a boil, add ⑤ to thicken and 1t. sesame oil. When sauce has thickened, pour over fish on serving plate; sprinkle coriander on top and serve.

* If perch is unavailable, substitute flounder, halibut or sea bass.

<table>
<tr><td>①</td><td>活草魚···1斤8兩
葱·············2枝
薑·············2片
酒············1大匙</td></tr>
<tr><td>②</td><td>猪油·······1大匙
酒············1大匙
水··········15杯</td></tr>
</table>

③{ 嫩薑絲······半杯
紅椒絲···1大匙
胡椒······¼小匙

④{ 醬油······3大匙
鹽·········1小匙
糖·········3大匙
黑醋······4大匙
川魚湯···1½杯

⑤{ 太白粉1½大匙
水·········2大匙

❶ 將活魚殺好去鱗及內臟腑洗淨，從腹下剖開，使背部相連，調①料醃約２０分鐘。

❷ 鍋燒熱下②料之猪油、酒，隨即加水１５杯待滾，醃好之魚下鍋川煮，蓋好鍋蓋（水要滿過魚身，且背部朝上）待沸速予熄火，燜約１０分鐘撈起，裝於長盤上。

❸ 將③料均勻的洒在魚身上。

❹ ④料燒開，以⑤料調成薄糊狀，加熱油１大匙澆淋在魚身上。（或洒上少許香菜即成。）

西湖醋魚 Westlake Fish

上海菜　Shanghai
12人份　12 servings

1 whole trout (about 2lbs.)

①{ 2 2-inch sections green onion
2 slices ginger root
1 T. rice wine

②{ 1 T. oil
1 T. rice wine
15 C. water

③{ ½ C. shredded ginger root
1 T. shredded hot red pepper
¼ t. black pepper

④{ 3 T. soy sauce
1 t. salt
3 T. sugar
4 T. worcestershire sauce
1½ C. fish steaming stock

⑤{ 1½ T. cornstarch
2 T. water

❶ Rinse fish lightly; drain and make a long vertical cut along the underside of fish, cutting the fish in half but leaving the halves connected along the back. Mix fish with ① and let sit 20 minutes.

❷ Heat pan and 1T. oil from ② ; add rice wine and water and when water comes to a boil, place fish in water (skin side up). When water begins to boil, turn off heat and let sit covered 10 minutes; remove fish and place on serving plate.

❸ Sprinkle ③ over fish.

❹ Heat ④ until liquid comes to a boil; add ⑤ to thicken and 1T. oil; mix together and pour over fish; serve.

鯧魚⋯⋯⋯ 1 斤

① 酒⋯⋯⋯⋯ 1 大匙
　鹽⋯⋯⋯⋯ 2 小匙
　醬油⋯⋯⋯ 4 大匙
　糖⋯⋯⋯⋯ 1 大匙
　葱⋯⋯ 4 枝 }拍碎
　薑⋯⋯ 4 片

② 茶葉⋯⋯⋯ 半杯
　糖⋯⋯⋯⋯ 2 大匙
　沙拉醬⋯⋯ 4 兩

❶ 鯧魚斜切爲 4 大片，加①料拌醃約 1 小時。
❷ 鐵絲網塗油少許將魚置上。
❸ 烤箱燒至 4 5 0 度，魚放在烤箱上層，把②料置烤盤放烤箱下層，大火烤約 2 5 分鐘，取出塗上麻油，即可排於盤上，吃時沾沙拉醬。
■ 烤魚時，烤箱內將會冒煙。
■ 圍邊用材料：番茄、小黃瓜、泡菜、生菜、沙拉醬。

沙拉烟鯧魚 Smoked Pomfret with Mayonnaise

廣東菜　Cantonese
12人份　12 servings

1　pomfret (about 1⅓ lbs.)

①
1　T.　rice wine
2　t.　salt
4　T.　soy sauce
1　T.　sugar
4　stalks green onion
4　slices ginger root } smashed

②
½　C.　tea leaves
2　T.　sugar
½　C.　mayonnaise

❶ Clean pomfret and cut fish into 4 sections; mix with ① and let sit 1 hour.
❷ Lightly oil or roasting rack; place fish on grill.
❸ Preheat oven to 450°; place fish on grill in oven. Directly underneath grill place ② (contained in a pie pan or plate); bake 25 minutes. Remove fish to serving plate and brush outside lightly with sesame oil; portion mayonnaise onto serving plate and serve.
■ The fumes from the tea and sugar will give the fish a delicious, smoky flavor during baking.
■ Garnish with tomato and cucumber slices, pickled vegetable salad and lettuce.

<table>
<tr><td></td><td>草魚中段⋯⋯⋯⋯1斤半</td><td></td><td>「炸油」⋯⋯⋯⋯⋯⋯6杯</td></tr>
<tr><td></td><td>葱⋯⋯⋯⋯⋯⋯⋯⋯2條</td><td></td><td>醬油⋯⋯⋯⋯⋯⋯3大匙</td></tr>
<tr><td></td><td>薑⋯⋯⋯⋯⋯⋯⋯⋯2片</td><td></td><td>糖⋯⋯⋯⋯⋯⋯⋯2大匙</td></tr>
<tr><td>①</td><td>酒⋯⋯⋯⋯⋯⋯⋯⋯1大匙</td><td>②</td><td>黑醋⋯⋯⋯⋯1½大匙</td></tr>
<tr><td></td><td>醬油⋯⋯⋯⋯⋯⋯3大匙</td><td></td><td>水⋯⋯⋯⋯⋯⋯⋯4大匙</td></tr>
<tr><td></td><td>五香粉⋯⋯⋯⋯半小匙</td><td></td><td></td></tr>
</table>

❶ 草魚切1公分厚薄片，調入①料醃20分鐘。

❷ 「炸油」燒開以中火炸乾(需10分鐘)。

❸ 麻油1大匙燒熱，放入②料及醃魚餘汁，俟燒滾放入魚片，燒至汁收乾即可。

■ 圍邊用材料：生菜。

 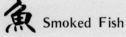 **Smoked Fish**

四川菜　Szechuan
12人份 **12 servings**

<table>
<tr><td></td><td>2　lbs. yellow trout fish</td><td></td><td>6　C.　oil for frying</td></tr>
<tr><td></td><td>2　stalks green onion</td><td></td><td>3　T.　soy sauce</td></tr>
<tr><td>①</td><td>2　slices ginger root</td><td>②</td><td>2　T.　sugar</td></tr>
<tr><td></td><td>1　T.　rice wine</td><td></td><td>1½ T.　vinegar</td></tr>
<tr><td></td><td>3　T.　soy sauce</td><td></td><td>4　T.　water</td></tr>
<tr><td></td><td>½　t.　five spice powder</td><td></td><td></td></tr>
</table>

❶ Slice fish into pieces ⅓ inch thick; mix with ① and let set for 20 minutes.

❷ Heat oil to deep-fry fish over medium heat (about 10 minutes).

❸ Heat 1T. sesame oil; add ② ; wait until it comes to a boil; add fish pieces; cook until fish absorbs sauce; Serve.

■ Garnish with lettuce.

①	②	③
小鯽魚（8公分長）1斤半	葱末……半大匙	醬油…1大匙
薑酒……………1大匙	薑末……半大匙	黑醋…1大匙
白醋……………1大匙	蒜末……半大匙	味精…1小匙
醬油……………2大匙	紅辣椒末半大匙	糖……1小匙
鹽………………半小匙	酒………1大匙	麻油…1小匙
「炸油」…………6杯		太白粉半小匙
		水……1大匙

❶ 小鯽魚去鱗及內臟；再切去頭、尾，並在背二邊各劃一刀，加①料醃２０分鐘後瀝乾。

❷ 「炸油」燒開，投入小鯽魚，中火炸６分鐘連骨都酥脆撈起，留油１大匙，把②料炒香，加酒１大匙，③料及魚炒勻即成。

酥小鯽魚 Crispy Butterfish

四川菜　Szechuan
12人份 12 servings

①	②	③
2 lbs. small butterfish (about 2½ inches long)	½ T. chopped green onion	1 T. soy sauce
1 T. ginger wine	½ T. chopped ginger root	1 T. worcestershire sauce
1 T. vinegar	½ T. chopped garlic	1 t. MSG
2 T. soy sauce	½ T. chopped hot red pepper	1 t. sugar
½ t. salt	1 T. rice wine	1 t. sesame oil
6 C. oil for frying		1½ t. cornstarch
		1 T. water

❶ Clean butterfish; cut off head and tail (discard). Make a diagonal slash in each side of body section; mix fish with ① and let soak 20 minutes; drain.

❷ Heat oil for deep-frying; deep-fry fish over medium heat for 6 minutes until outside skin is crunchy; remove and drain. Remove all but 1T. oil from pan; reheat and add ② ; stir-fry until fragrant and add 1T. rice wine and ③ . Mix until liquid thickens and add fried fish; toss lightly to mix ingredients and remove; serve.

<table>
<tr><td>①{</td><td>黃魚（1條）…1斤半
薑酒………半大匙
醬油………1½大匙
太白粉………3大匙
「炸油」………6杯
里肌肉（切絲）…半杯</td><td>葱絲……2大匙
蒜末……1大匙
冬菇絲……4大匙
熟筍絲……半杯</td><td>③{</td><td>酒…………1大匙
醬油………4大匙
味精………半小匙
糖…………1小匙
胡椒………¼小匙
麻油………1小匙
高湯（或水）…2杯</td><td>④{</td><td>太白粉…1小匙
水………1大匙
薑絲……2大匙</td></tr>
<tr><td>②{</td><td>太白粉………半小匙
水…………半大匙</td><td></td><td></td><td></td><td></td><td></td></tr>
</table>

❶ 用①料塗勻黃魚，醃30分鐘後，沾太白粉，入油鍋炸2分鐘或用煎（免放太白粉），呈金黃色撈起。

❷ 肉絲調②料拌勻。

❸ 油4大匙燒熱，葱、蒜炒香，放進肉絲鏟開，隨入冬菇絲、筍絲略炒，再下酒1大匙，③料及魚燒滾後，用中火燒煮8分鐘，至魚肉熟，並湯汁剩1杯時，將魚盛出，餘汁以④料勾芡，加熱油1大匙，淋在魚上，把薑絲洒上即成。

紅燒黃魚 Red-Cooked Yellow Fish

	1 yellow fish *¹ (2lbs.)	2 T. shredded green onion		1 T. rice wine	④{	1 t. cornstarch
①{	½ T. ginger wine 1½ T. soy sauce	1 T. chopped garlic 4 T. shredded pre-softened		4 T. soy sauce ½ t. MSG		1 T. water 2 T. shredded ginger root
	3 T. cornstarch	Chinese black mushrooms	③{	1 t. sugar		
	6 C. oil for frying	½ C. shredded precooked		¼ t. black pepper		
	½ C. shredded pork loin	bamboo shoot		1 t. sesame oil		
②{	½ t. cornstarch			2 C. stock or water		
	½ T. water					

❶ Rinse fish and drain; rub outside with ① and let sit 30 minutes. Before deep-frying, coat with cornstarch. Heat oil for deep-frying; deep-fry fish over high heat for 2 minutes until golden brown; remove and drain *²

❷ Mix shredded pork loin with ② .

❸ Heat pan and 4T. oil; stir-fry green onion and garlic until fragrant; add pork shreds and mix to separate shreds; add shredded black mushroom and bamboo shoot. Stir-fry together briefly and add 1T. rice wine ③ and fish . When mixture reaches a boil, cook 8 minutes over medium heat until fish is flaky and sauce has reduced to about 1C.; remove fish to serving plate and add ④ to sauce to thicken; add 1T. oil and mix together. Pour sauce over fish and sprinkle shredded ginger on top; serve.

*¹ If yellow fish is unavailable, substitute sea bass, flounder or haddock.

*² You may pan-fry the fish until golden on both sides in 4T. oil; omit coating fish with cornstarch.

草魚尾……2條1斤　　｜醬油…………3大匙　　　太白粉………半大匙
葱（3公分長）…6枝　　｜水……………1½杯　②｜水……………1大匙
薑………………6片　①｜味精…………半小匙　　　麻油…………1小匙
蒜苗……………2枝　　｜糖……………1大匙　　　醋……………半小匙
　　　　　　　　　　　｜胡椒…………¼小匙

❶ 洗淨草魚尾（長約15公分），每條由背部，對剖二片，再直切3條，共計12條備用。

❷ 蒜苗切細絲，泡清水撈出。

❸ 油4大匙燒熱，葱、薑炒香，將魚皮面向鍋底，順序排好（不可零亂），煎20秒後，入酒1大匙調①料，蓋鍋用小火燜煮，10分鐘左右，餘汁剩一半時，以②料勾汁然後翻面，並淋上麻油半小匙，及醋半小匙，並洒入蒜苗即可。

■ 醬油顏色如不夠紅，可加醬色放入①料內。醬色請參照特殊材料說明。

燒划水　Simmered Fish Tails

上海菜　Shanghai
12人份　12 servings

2　fish tails (about 1⅓ lbs.) of grass fish or fresh trout
6　1-inch sections green onion
6　slices ginger root
2　stalks long garlic*

① 3　T.　soy sauce
1½ C.　water
½　t.　MSG
1　T.　sugar
¼　t.　black pepper

② ½　T.　cornstarch
1　T.　water
1　t.　sesame oil
½　t.　vinegar

❶ Clean fish tails and cut each tail in half lengthwise; cut each half into 3 sections (to make 12 sections).

❷ Shred garlic stalk; place briefly in cold water; remove and drain.

❸ Heat pan and 4T. oil; stir-fry onion and ginger until fragrant; add fish sections (skin side down) and fry 20 seconds until golden; add 1T. rice wine and ① ; cover and simmer 10 minutes until liquid has reduced half add ② to thicken sauce and flip fish sections over. Add ½t. sesame oil and vinegar; toss lightly to combine ingredients and remove to serving plate; sprinkle shredded garlic on top and serve.

* If garlic stalk is unavailable, substitute leeks or green onions.

<table>
<tr><td rowspan="6">①</td><td>鯉魚⋯⋯⋯1 條 1 斤半</td><td rowspan="7">②</td><td>酒⋯⋯⋯1 大匙</td><td rowspan="3">③</td><td>太白粉 1 大匙</td></tr>
</table>

鯉魚⋯⋯⋯1 條 1 斤半
「炸油」⋯⋯⋯⋯6 杯
① 葱末⋯⋯⋯1 ½ 大匙
薑末⋯⋯⋯1 ½ 大匙
蒜末⋯⋯⋯1 ½ 大匙
辣豆瓣醬⋯1 ½ 大匙

② 酒⋯⋯⋯1 大匙
鹽⋯⋯⋯半小匙
味精⋯半小匙
醬油⋯1 大匙
糖⋯⋯半大匙
鎮江醋 1 大匙
水⋯⋯⋯2 杯

③ 太白粉 1 大匙
水⋯⋯⋯1 大匙
葱末⋯1 大匙

❶ 魚去鱗及內臟洗淨背肉厚處各劃 2 刀。

❷ 「炸油」燒開,將鯉魚炸約 1 分鐘撈起,留油 3 大匙,將①料炒香隨即入魚及②料,燒煮約 1○分鐘,並以③料太白粉水勾成薄汁,洒下葱末即成。

■ 家庭做法,不炸改用煎的,比較容易做。

豆瓣鯉魚 Braised Carp with Hot Bean Paste

四川菜　Szechuan
12 人份　12 servings

1 whole carp* (about 2lbs.)
6 C. oil for frying
① 1½ T. chopped green onion
1½ T. chopped ginger root
1½ T. chopped garlic
1½ T. hot bean paste
("la do ban jiang")

② 1 T. rice wine
½ t. salt
½ t. MSG
1 T. soy sauce
½ T. sugar
1 T. worcestershire sauce
2 C. water

③ 1 T. cornstarch
1 T. water
1 T. chopped green onion

❶ Clean fish and drain; on one side of fish, make a few diagonal cuts through meat to central bone.

❷ Heat oil for deep-frying; deep-fry fish for about 1 minute; remove and drain. Remove all but 3T. oil from pan; reheat and stir-fry ① until fragrant; add fish (cut side up) and ② ; cover and let simmer for 10 minutes. Add ③ to thicken and chopped green onion; mix lightly and remove to serving plate; serve.

■ In family-style cooking, fish need not be deep-fried; decrease oil to 6T. and fry on both sides until golden brown.

* If carp is unavailable, substitute perch, salmon or sea bass.

①{ 大草魚(中段) 1 斤半
酒‥‥‥‥‥‥半大匙
鹽‥‥‥‥‥‥半小匙 }

②{ 蛋白‥‥‥‥‥ 1 個
太白粉‥‥‥‥半大匙
「炸油」‥‥‥‥‥ 3 杯 }

③{ 葱末 1 大匙
薑末 1 大匙
酒釀1½大匙
(或酒) }

④{ 鹽‥‥‥‥半小匙
糖‥‥‥‥2小匙
太白粉2小匙
高湯‥‥‥ 1 杯 }

❶ 草魚去骨除皮得淨肉 1 0 兩，斜切大薄片以①料拌醃 2 0 分鐘，再拌入②料，將③料、④料各備在碗內。

❷ 「炸油」燒熱，以小火將魚片泡熟撈出，留油 4 大匙，把③料炒香，隨加④料燒開，放入魚片，最後淋上熟油 1 大匙拌勻即起。

■ 家庭做法，魚片不必泡油，可改用開水川燙。

糟溜魚片 Braised Fish Slices in Sauce

北平菜　Peking
12人份 12 servings

①{ 1　lb. mackerel fillets*
½　T. rice wine
½　t.　salt }

②{ 1　egg white
½　T. cornstarch
3　C. oil for frying }

③{ 1　T. chopped green onion
1　T. chopped ginger root
1½ T. fermented rice wine ("jiou niang") or rice wine }

④{ ½　t.　salt
2　t.　sugar
2　t.　cornstarch
1　C. stock }

❶ Diagonally cut fillets into thin slices; mix with ① and let soak 20 minutes; add ② and mix. Prepare mixtures ③ and ④ .

❷ Heat oil for deep-frying; deep-fry fish slices over low heat until color changes; remove and drain. Remove all but 3 T. oil from pan and reheat; stir-fry ③ until fragrant; add ④ and heat until liquid boils; add fish slices and 1T. oil; toss ingredients lightly to mix together; remove and serve.

＊　You may also use sea bass, swordfish or trout.

■　If preparing this dish for family, you may omit deep-frying and cook fish slices in boiling water until color changes.

①	石斑魚肉…半斤	洋葱(小)……1個	番茄醬…3大匙
	鹽………1小匙	「炸油」………3杯	糖………半大匙
	胡椒……¼小匙	葱(3公分長)6枝	麻油……1小匙 ②
	麻油……¼小匙	薑…………6片	太白粉…1小匙
	太白粉…半大匙		水………2大匙

❶ 魚肉用刀劃花紋後，切塊調①料拌勻醃約２０分鐘，洋葱切塊備用。

❷ 「炸油」燒開，以中火將魚肉、洋葱一起落鍋泡油撈起(約１分鐘)，留油１大匙，葱、薑炒香入②料燒開後，下泡熟魚肉及洋葱拌炒均勻加油１大匙即成。

■ 此道是火候菜，宜趁熱吃。

茄汁魚球 Fish Balls in Tomato Sauce

	⅔ lb. grouper fillets*	1 medium-sized onion	3 T. tomato ketchup
①	1 t. salt	3 C. oil for frying	½ T. sugar
	¼ t. black pepper	6 1-inch sections green onion ②	1 t. sesame oil
	¼ t. sesame oil	6 slices ginger root	1 t. cornstarch
	½ T. cornstarch		2 T. water

❶ Score fillets, lightly lengthwise and crosswise; cut into bite-size pieces and mix with ① ; let sit 20 minutes. Cut onion into bite-size pieces.

❷ Heat oil for deep-frying; deep-fry fish pieces and onion pieces over medium heat for 1 minute; remove and drain. Remove all but 1T. oil from pan; reheat and stir-fry green onion and ginger until fragrant; add ② and when liquid comes to a boil, add fish meat and onion; mix together and add 1t. oil. Toss lightly to mix all ingredients and coat fish slices with sauce; remove to serving plate and serve.

* If grouper is unavailable, substitute haddock or flounder.

① 石斑魚肉…半斤　　瘦火腿(4公分長)14條　　｜蕈米醬…半杯
酒………1小匙　　葱(4公分長)……14枝　②｜蛋………2個
鹽……半小匙　　「炸油」…………3杯　　｜鹽……半小匙
味精……¼小匙　　　　　　　　　　　　　　｜味精……¼小匙
糖………半小匙　　　　　　　　　　　　　②｜胡椒……¼小匙
胡椒……¼小匙　　　　　　　　　　　　　　｜麻油…半小匙
麻油…半小匙　　　　　　　　　　　　　　　｜太白粉半大匙
太白粉…1大匙　　　　　　　　　　　　　　｜水……1大匙
蛋黃………半個

❶ 魚肉切14薄片（6公分×4公分），拌上①料調勻。把②料也調勻備用。

❷ 魚片攤開，上置火腿及葱段，捲成魚捲，並沾上太白粉炸至呈金黃色取起。

❸ 油3大匙燒熱，將②料用中火速予拌炒，加油1大匙，再倒進炸好魚捲拌一下即成。

貴妃斑魚捲 Stir-Fried Fish Rolls with Corn

廣東菜　Cantonese
12人份　12 servings

⅔ lb. fillet of haddock or flounder

①
1　t.　rice wine
½　t.　salt
¼　t.　MSG
½　t.　sugar
¼　t.　black pepper
½　t.　sesame oil
1　T.　cornstarch
½　egg yolk

14 matchstick-size pieces Chinese ham
14 1½-inch sections green onion
3　C.　oil for frying

②
½　C.　creamed corn
2　eggs
½　t.　salt
¼　t.　MSG
¼　t.　black pepper
½　t.　sesame oil
½　T.　cornstarch
1　T.　water

❶ Cut fish meat into 14 thin slices (2 x 1½ inches); mix with ① and let sit 20 minutes; beat eggs lightly and mix together ingredients of ② .

❷ In the center of each fish slice, place a piece of Chinese ham and 1 section green onion. Roll up fish slice to enclose filling and coat "fish roll" with cornstarch; repeat for other slices to make 14 rolls. Heat oil until medium hot; deep-fry fish rolls over high heat until golden brown; remove and drain.

❸ Heat pan and 3T. oil; add ② and stir-fry over medium heat until lightly cooked and thick; add 1T. oil and fish rolls; toss lightly to mix ingredients and remove to serving plate; serve.

鱸魚⋯1條1斤4兩
肥肉⋯⋯⋯⋯6兩
熟瘦火腿⋯⋯⋯3兩

① 酒⋯⋯⋯1大匙、麻油⋯⋯1小匙
鹽⋯⋯1小匙、蛋黃⋯⋯⋯1個
糖⋯⋯1小匙、太白粉⋯1大匙
胡椒⋯⋯¼小匙

「炸油」⋯⋯6杯

❶ 鱸魚取肉，肥肉、瘦火腿均切薄片，各計２４片，然後把魚片、肥肉片各加½之①料拌勻備用。
❷ 將肥肉、魚肉、火腿疊成一塊，全部做成２４塊，上下沾好太白粉待煎。
❸ 將魚之中間大骨切除，留魚頭及背脊連尾，洒上太白粉，「炸油」燒沸，炸脆排在盤上成魚狀。
❹ 油半杯燒熱，中火將魚塊下鍋半煎炸，（先由肥肉部份向鍋底）煎至兩面呈金黃色，前後４分
　鐘即可置盤（如圖）。
■ 圍邊用材料：菠蘿、紅辣椒、小黃瓜。

鍋貼鱸魚塊 Deep-Fried Fish Slices with Chinese Ham

廣東菜　Cantonese
12人份　**12 servings**

1 whole perch (about 1⅔lbs.)
6 oz. pork fat
3 oz. precooked Chinese ham

① 1 T. rice wine
1 t. salt
1 t. sugar
¼ t. black pepper
1 t. sesame oil
1 egg yolk
1 T. cornstarch

6 C. oil for frying

❶ Rinse fish and drain; cut fillets from sides of fish, cutting to within one inch of dorsal fin. Cut fillets, pork fat and Chinese ham into 24 slices; mix ½ of ① mixture with fish slices and ½ of ① mixture with pork fat slices; let sit 20 minutes.
❷ Place a piece of pork fat, fish and Chinese ham (in this order) together; group other slices to make 24 sandwiches. Lightly coat "sandwiches" with cornstarch.
❸ Remove central bone from fish, leaving head and tail connected; sprinkle this fish piece with cornstarch. Heat oil for deep-frying; deep-fry fish piece until golden brown and crunchy; remove, drain and place on serving plate.
❹ Reheat pan and ½C. oil until medium hot; fry fish sections (fat side down) over medium heat for about 4 minutes until golden brown; remove, drain and arrange slices around head and tail as illustrated, serve.
■ Garnish with pineapple, cucumber slices and hot red pepper.

大明蝦……1斤	太白粉………¼杯	「炸油」……6杯
薑酒……1大匙	② 雞蛋…………1個	
① 鹽………1小匙	麵包粉……1½杯	
胡椒……¼小匙		

❶ 將蝦去頭及外殼，拭乾水份，切開背部用刀輕輕拍扁調①料醃２０分鐘。

❷ 將②料分別備在盤內。

❸ 將醃好明蝦依太白粉、雞蛋（打勻）、麵包粉，順序兩面沾裹均勻。

❹ 「炸油」燒熱，中火將蝦炸２分鐘至金黃色即可，撈起切塊，盛盤供食。

■ 圍邊用材料：番茄、生菜。

吉列明蝦 Butterfly Shrimp Slices

廣東菜　Cantonese
12人份 **12 servings**

1⅓ lbs. prawns	¼ C. cornstarch	6 C. oil for frying
1 T. ginger wine*	② 1 egg	
① 1 t. salt	1½ C. grated bread crumbs	
¼ t. black pepper		

❶ Remove shells from prawns; make a deep vertical cut along the backside of each prawn. Using the blunt edge of cleaver, pound prawns lightly to tenderize meat; mix with ① and let sit 20 minutes.

❷ Beat egg lightly; portion cornstarch and breadcrumbs to separate plates.

❸ Coat prawns in cornstarch then dip in beaten egg and coat with grated breadcrumbs.

❹ Heat oil for deep-frying; deep-fry prawns over medium heat for 2 minutes until golden brown; remove and drain. Cut into slices and place on serving plate; serve.

* See Helpful Hints for directions for making ginger wine.

■ Garnish with tomato and lettuce.

明蝦（１２條）⋯⋯⋯⋯⋯⋯１斤　　　土司麵包⋯６片　　　「炸油」⋯⋯⋯１０杯

① 　葱⋯⋯⋯⋯２枝、鹽⋯⋯⋯半小匙　　②　蛋白⋯⋯⋯４個　　　火腿末⋯⋯１小匙

　薑⋯⋯⋯⋯２片、酒⋯⋯⋯１小匙　　　麵粉⋯⋯２大匙　　　黑芝麻⋯⋯半小匙

　胡椒⋯⋯¼小匙　　　　　　　　　　　太白粉⋯１大匙　　　香菜菜⋯⋯２４片

❶ 蝦去頭及外殼，僅留尾部之殼，剖開背部挑出腸泥，用刀輕輕拍扁，調入①料拌醃２０分鐘。

❷ 土司去四週硬皮切半總共爲１２片，蛋白四個用打蛋器打至起白泡（約１０分鐘）調入②料拌勻。

❸ 將醃好明蝦用潔巾拭乾水份，每片麵包塗上少許蛋泡，明蝦置上（背部朝下）再把蛋泡糊滿在蝦上，四週用刀抹平，上面用火腿末、香菜、黑芝麻點綴（如圖）。

❹ 「炸油」燒熱，以小火將做好鳳尾明蝦投入（有蝦部份先朝下，熟了再翻過來），起鍋時改用大火前後約２分鐘即可撈出。

■ 使用乾淨豬油，炸出來的顏色潔白好看，如豬油量少可分二次炸。

■ 圍邊用材料：生菜、番茄、葱。

鳳尾明蝦 Prawns with Toast

廣東菜　Cantonese
12人份 **12 servings**

12 prawns (aobut 1½lbs.)

① ⎰ 2 stalks green onion ⎱ smashed
　⎱ 2 slices ginger root ⎰
　¼ t. black pepper
　½ t. salt
　1 t. rice wine

6 slices white bread
4 egg whites

② ⎰ 2 T. flour
　⎱ 1 T. cornstarch

10 C. oil for frying
1 t. chopped precooked ham
½ t. black sesame seeds
24 sprigs of coriander

❶ Remove shells from prawns, leaving tail section intact; devein and rinse; drain. Make a shallow vertical cut along the back side of each prawn. Using the blunt edge of cleaver, pound prawns lightly to flatten meat and tenderize; mix prawns with ① and let sit 20 minutes.

❷ Cut crusts from bread and cut each slice in half (12 pieces); beat egg whites until stiff and form soft peaks; mix with ② until smooth.

❸ Dry prawns; spread each piece of bread with a small amount of egg white mixture; place prawns flat on slices of bread (tail-end up). Add more egg white mixture to cover prawn and use a spoon to smooth mixture evenly over surface; place a sprig of coriander on top and sprinkle sesame seeds and ham as illustrated.

❹ Heat oil until medium hot; place "shrimp toasts" in oil (shrimp side down) and deep-fry about 1 minute over low heat. Turn pieces over and turn heat to high. Deep-fry an additional minute until golden; remove, drain and serve.

■ Garnish with tomato, onion and lettuce.

■ Toasts will look much more attractive if fresh new oil is used for deep-frying.

鱸蝦⋯⋯⋯半斤　①{ 薑酒⋯⋯⋯ 1 小匙
 太白粉⋯⋯半大匙
 「炸油」⋯⋯⋯ 6 杯　②{ 鹽⋯⋯⋯⋯ 1 小匙
 味精⋯⋯⋯半小匙
 蒜末⋯⋯⋯ 2 大匙
 紅辣椒末⋯半大匙

❶ 鱸蝦剪除鬚爪，挑出腸泥，瀝乾水份，加①料拌勻，醃約２０分鐘。

❷ 燒開「炸油」，將鱸蝦用大火炸約１分鐘半撈出。倒淨「炸油」，再放鱸蝦及②料拌勻即可。

■ 家庭小菜，可改用新鮮紅小蝦（價錢便宜）或河蝦，做法與上同。

■ 薑片拍碎加酒擠出的汁叫薑酒。

塩酥蝦 Stir-Fried Shrimp with Garlic

台灣菜　Taiwanese
6人份　6 servings

⅔ lb. medium-sized fresh shrimp　①{ 1 t. ginger wine*
 ½ T. cornstarch
 6 C. oil for frying　②{ 1 t. salt
 ½ t. MSG
 2 T. chopped garlic
 ½ T. chopped hot red pepper

❶ Rinse and cut antennae and all other appendages from shrimp (still in shells); devein and mix with ① ; let sit 20 minutes.

❷ Heat oil for deep-frying; deep-fry shrimp over high heat for 1½ minutes; remove and drain. Remove all oil from pan; add shrimp, ② and stir-fry until fragrant and ingredients are mixed well; remove to serving plate and serve.

* A mixture of rice wine and the juices of smashed ginger root.

■ Prawns may be substituted for shrimp.

明蝦…（１２條）１斤　　┌蒜末…………１大匙　　　┌鹽………半小匙
「炸 油」………６杯　①│薑末…………１大匙　　③│糖………１大匙
　　　　　　　　　　　　│蔥花…………１大匙　　　│水………３大匙
　　　　　　　　　　　　└　　　　　　　　　　　　└太白粉…１小匙
　　　　　　　　　　　┌辣豆瓣醬……１小匙
　　　　　　　　　　②│酒釀（或酒）…１大匙
　　　　　　　　　　　└番茄醬………４大匙

❶ 明蝦剪腳除鬚去腸泥後洗淨。
❷ 「炸 油」燒開，用大火將蝦炸２分鐘至熟撈出，留油２大匙，將①料炒香後，加②料拌炒，並
　 入明蝦及③料燒開，再加熟油１大匙，麻油１大匙，即可起鍋盛盤上。
■ 圍邊用材料：巴西利。

乾燒明蝦 Spicy Stir-Fried Prawns

四川菜　Szechuan
12人份 **12 servings**

12 prawns (aobut 1⅓lbs.)　　┌1　T. chopped garlic　　　　　　　┌½　t.　salt
6　C. oil for frying　　　①│1　T. chopped ginger root　　　③│1　T.　sugar
　　　　　　　　　　　　　└1　T. chopped green onion　　　　│3　T.　water
　　　　　　　　　　　　　┌1　t. hot bean paste ("la do ban jiang")└1　t.　cornstarch
　　　　　　　　　　　②│1　T. fermented rice wine ("jiou niang")*
　　　　　　　　　　　　└4　T. tomato ketchup

❶ Cut antennae and other appendages from prawns; rinse and devein; drain.
❷ Heat oil for deep-frying; deep-fry prawns 2 minutes over high heat; remove and drain.　Remove all
　 but 2T. oil from pan; reheat and stir-fry ① until fragrant; add ② and stir-fry ½ minute; add prawns
　 and ③ and when mixture begins to boil, add 1T. oil and toss lightly to mix ingredients and coat
　 prawns with sauce; remove and portion onto serving plate; serve.
* 　If unavailable, substitute rice wine.

<table>
<tr><td rowspan="5">①</td><td>大明蝦……1斤</td><td>芥蘭菜……1斤半</td><td rowspan="6">②</td><td>鹽………1小匙</td></tr>
<tr><td>薑酒……半大匙</td><td>葱(3公分長)6枝</td><td>味精……半小匙</td></tr>
<tr><td>鹽………⅓小匙</td><td>薑……………6片</td><td>糖………半小匙</td></tr>
<tr><td>蛋白……半只</td><td>「炸油」………3杯</td><td>麻油……1小匙</td></tr>
<tr><td>太白粉…2小匙</td><td></td><td>太白粉…2小匙</td></tr>
<tr><td></td><td></td><td></td><td>水………2大匙</td></tr>
</table>

❶ 大明蝦去殼取肉，去腸泥洗淨後拭乾水份，並在蝦背直劃二刀，調①料拌勻。

❷ 芥蘭菜取嫩莖切段，用6杯燒開的水加鹽2小匙燙煮1分鐘撈起，用清水漂涼待用。

❸ 將油3大匙燒熱，炒芥蘭菜加酒半大匙、鹽、糖各⅓小匙用大火炒半分鐘倒出。

❹ 「炸油」燒熱，將蝦肉泡油約1分鐘撈出。留油1大匙，將葱薑炒香並入蝦及芥蘭菜，再加酒半大匙及②料炒勻，最後淋上半大匙熟油即可。

芥蘭蝦球 Stir-Fried Prawn Balls with Broccoli

廣東菜　Cantonese
12人份　12 servings

<table>
<tr><td rowspan="5">①</td><td>1⅓lbs. prawns</td><td>2　lb. Chinese broccoli*[2]</td><td rowspan="6">②</td><td>1　t.　salt</td></tr>
<tr><td>½　T. ginger wine *[1]</td><td>6　1-inch sections green onion</td><td>½　t.　MSG</td></tr>
<tr><td>⅓　t.　salt</td><td>6　slices ginger root</td><td>½　t.　sugar</td></tr>
<tr><td>½　egg white</td><td>3　C. oil for frying</td><td>1　t.　sesame oil</td></tr>
<tr><td>2　t.　cornstarch</td><td></td><td>2　t.　cornstarch</td></tr>
<tr><td></td><td></td><td></td><td>2　T.　water</td></tr>
</table>

❶ Remove shells from prawns; devein and rinse; drain and make 2 shallow cuts along the back side of each prawn; mix prawns with ① and let sit 20 minutes.

❷ Trim any old leaves from broccoli; cut into 3-inch sections. Heat 6C. water and 2t. salt until boiling; cook broccoli sections 1 minute; remove and place in cold water to cool; drain.

❸ Heat pan and 3T. oil; stir-fry broccoli briefly; add ½T. rice wine, ⅓t. salt and ⅓t. sugar; stir-fry over high heat for 30 seconds; remove.

❹ Heat oil for deep-frying; deeep-fry prawns over medium heat for 1 minute; remove and drain. Remove all but 1T. oil from pan; reheat and stir-fry green onion and ginger until fragrant; add shrimp, broccoli, ½T. rice wine and ② ; mix ingredients together and add ½T. oil. Toss ingredients lightly to mix together and remove to serving plate; serve.

*[1] A mixture of rice wine and the juice of smashed ginger root.

*[2] If Chinese broccoli is unavailable, use American broccoli and cut stalks into ½-inch thick sections.

<table>
<tr><td>① { </td><td>大明蝦……6 條
小蘇打…1 小匙
碱粉……1 小匙
清水………1 杯</td><td>② {</td><td>嫩薑絲…1 大匙
葱絲……2 大匙
紅辣椒絲 1 大匙</td><td>③ {</td><td>鹽………¾小匙
味精……½小匙
糖………¼小匙
水………3 大匙
太白粉…1 小匙</td></tr>
</table>

❶ 大明蝦去頭、殼，並片除淡紅色薄膜洗淨，加入①料醃泡 2 小時後用多量清水漂洗至無碱味並多次換水泡約 1 小時。

❷ 水 5 杯燒開，明蝦煮 1 分半鐘至熟撈起。

❸ ②料盛盤，③料燒開，放入明蝦拌勻，置於②料上即可供食。

玻璃蝦球 "Glassy" Shrimp Balls

廣東菜　Cantonese
6人份　6 servings

① {
6　prawns (about ⅔lb.)
2　t.　baking soda
1　C.　water

② {
1　T.　shredded ginger root
2　T.　shredded green onion
1　T.　shredded hot red pepper

③ {
¾　t.　salt
½　t.　MSG
¼　t.　sugar
3　T.　water
1　t.　cornstarch

❶ Remove shells from prawns; devein and remove all pink outer-skin; rinse, drain and soak in ① 2 hours. Remove and rinse thoroughly to rid prawns of any baking soda. Place prawns in fresh water to cover and let soak 1 hour; drain.

❷ Boil 5C. water and cook prawns for 1½ minutes; remove and drain.

❸ Place ② on serving plate. Heat ③ in a pan (no oil) until boiling; add prawns, and when mixture has thickened, pour over ② . Toss lightly and serve.

蝦仁………半斤		酒………半小匙	「炸油」…6杯
鹽………半小匙		味精……¼小匙	
肥肉………1兩	①	胡椒……¼小匙	
		麻油……半小匙	
		蛋白………1個	
		太白粉…1大匙	

❶ 蝦仁洗淨並拭乾水份，加鹽半小匙搗成蝦泥，肥肉剁碎同盛於大碗內加①料，用手攪動至蝦絨狀（前後約5分鐘）。

❷ 「炸油」略燒熱，離火把攪好之蝦絨用手做成蝦丸狀入鍋，全部做好約14個，再將鍋置爐上，用中火炸呈淡紅色，並漲大時（約3分鐘），趁熱端出供食。

■ 圍邊用材料：小黃瓜、柳丁、紅蘿蔔。

炸蝦丸 Fried Shrimp Balls

台灣菜　Taiwanese
6人份　6 servings

⅔ lb. raw, shelled shrimp		½ t. rice wine	6 C. oil for frying
½ t. salt		¼ t. MSG	
1 oz. pork fat	①	¼ t. black pepper	
		½ t. sesame oil	
		1 egg white	
		1 T. cornstarch	

❶ Clean and devein shrimp; drain. Add ½ t. salt and mix. Using side of cleaver, smash shrimp and chop finely; chop pork fat finely. Mix chopped shrimp, pork fat and ① ; throw ingredients lightly against the inside of the mixing bowl to combine to a smooth paste, (mix for 5 minutes).

❷ Heat oil until medium hot; remove pan from heat and add shrimp balls to oil, one by one. (Taking a portion of shrimp paste in palm of hand, squeeze hand to a fist so that paste is forced out of hole between index finger and thumb. Use a spoon dipped in water to cut paste into sections and shape into 14 balls). Replace pan over medium heat and deep-fry about 3 minutes until balls have expanded and are lightly golden; remove, drain and place on serving plate; serve.

■ Garnish with cucumber, orange and carrot slices.

蝦（２４條）………１斤		酥炸粉	麵粉…………１杯

①
| 蔥…………２枝 |
| 薑…………２片 |
| 酒…………１大匙 |
| 鹽…………１小匙 |

酥
炸
粉
| 麵粉…………１杯 |
| 發粉…………半小匙 |
| 油…………１大匙 |
| 水…………¾杯 |
| 「炸油」…………６杯 |

❶ 蝦去殼留尾，除腸泥，加①料拌醃２０分鐘。

❷ 麵粉、發粉、鹽一齊篩過後，再加油、水調勻即為酥炸粉。

❸ 醃好的蝦，提起蝦尾，在酥炸粉內沾滾一下，「炸油」燒熱，放入用中火炸２分鐘，呈金黃色時取出，置盤上，食時沾椒鹽。

■ 酥炸粉調好後，宜在３０分鐘內炸完。

酥炸蝦 Deep-Fried Butterfly Shrimp

廣東菜　Cantonese
12人份 12 servings

1⅓ lbs. (about 24) fresh shrimp

①
- 2 stalks green onion
- 2 slices ginger root
- 1 T. rice wine
- 1 t. salt

batter
- 1 C. flour
- ½ t. baking powder
- 1 T. oil
- ¾ C. water

6 C. oil for frying

❶ Remove shells from shrimp, leaving tail section intact; remove veins and mix shrimp with ① ; let sit 20 minutes.

❷ Sift flour, baking powder and salt together; add oil and water and beat to a smooth batter.

❸ Heat oil for deep-frying; dip shrimp in batter and drop into hot oil; deep-fry over medium heat for 2 minutes until golden brown; remove, drain and place on serving plate. Serve with 5-spice-powder salt.

■ After batter has been mixed, it should be used within ½ hour.

112

後腿肥肉⋯⋯1斤　　酒⋯⋯1小匙　　蛋白⋯⋯⋯2個
「炸油」⋯⋯⋯6杯　　鹽⋯⋯半小匙　　麵包粉⋯⋯1杯
　蝦仁（切丁）⋯半斤　　味精⋯⋯¼小匙
①　荸薺（切碎）⋯1杯　②　糖⋯⋯⋯2小匙
　葱末⋯⋯⋯⋯半杯　　胡椒⋯⋯¼小匙
　　　　　　　　　　麻油⋯半小匙

❶ 後腿油切成直徑5公分圓形，再切成圓薄片，將每個小薄片，橫刀片開半圓，再以刀尖將另餘半圓在邊緣內片開，成小布袋狀，計24片。

❷ 將①料調入②料拌勻成餡。

❸ 把餡塞入切好之肥肉內，包成小圓球，即為金錢蝦，沾上蛋白（打勻），再沾麵包粉。「炸油」燒熱，以中火把金錢蝦炸至金黃色，約3分鐘撈出置盤。

■ 此道菜為本省名菜，家庭做如肥肉不好片成薄片，可用網油代替。

炸金錢蝦 Fried Golden Shrimp Balls

1⅓ lbs. pork fat (from hind leg)
6　C.　oil for frying
　　⅔　lb. diced, raw, shelled shrimp,
①　1　C.　chopped water chestnuts
　　½　C.　chopped onion

②
1　t.　rice wine
½　t.　salt
¼　t.　MSG
2　t.　sugar
¼　t.　black pepper
½　t.　sesame oil

2　egg whites
1　C.　grated breadcrumbs

❶ Cut pork fat into 2½-inch circles; cut circles into 24 thin slices. Using a sharp knife or cleaver, slice each circle in half as if to create 2 thin circles, stopping short of opposite edge to keep one side connected. This should create a small pocket in each circle. Repeat procedure for all circles.

❷ Mix ingredients of ① and ② together; throw mixture lightly against inside of mixing bowl to combine ingredients. (filling)

❸ Place one portion of filling in the "pocket" of each pork fat circle; press edges to close opening. Beat egg whites until frothy; dip stuffed circles in egg whites and then coat in breadcrumbs.
Heat oil until medium hot; deep-fry stuffed circles for 3 minutes until golden brown; remove, drain and place on serving plate; serve immediately.

■ In family cooking, if it is too difficult to cut pork fat, substitute pork net oil to wrap around filling.

蝦仁⋯⋯⋯半斤	酒⋯⋯⋯⋯半小匙	香腸⋯⋯⋯１２片
蛋白⋯⋯⋯１個	鹽⋯⋯⋯⋯半小匙	香菜⋯⋯⋯１２片
肥肉⋯⋯⋯１兩	味精⋯⋯⋯¼小匙	糯米紙⋯⋯１２張
①	糖⋯⋯⋯⋯¼小匙	蛋黃⋯⋯⋯１個
	胡椒⋯⋯⋯¼小匙	「炸油」⋯⋯⋯６杯
	麻油⋯⋯⋯半小匙	
	太白粉⋯⋯１大匙	

❶ 蝦仁拭乾水份，用刀壓爛剁成泥狀，加蛋白攪拌，入剁爛肥肉及①料繼續攪拌並甩打（前後５分鐘左右），成蝦絨狀分成１２份待用。

❷ 糯米紙一張折疊三角形，底擺香腸一片，香菜一片，並置１份蝦絨，再將糯米紙捲成長方型之蝦捲（類似春捲狀），邊用蛋黃沾黏，做成約１２個蝦捲，以中火炸約１分半鐘至熟撈起盛盤。

紙包酥蝦捲 Paper-Wrapped Fried Shrimp

廣東菜　Cantonese
6人份　　6 servings

⅔ lb. raw, shelled shrimp	½ t. rice wine	12 thin slices pork sausage
1 egg white	½ t. salt	12 sprigs of coriander
1 oz. pork fat	¼ t. MSG	12 sheets glutinous rice paper
	① ¼ t. sugar	1 egg yolk
	¼ t. black pepper	6 C. oil for frying
	½ t. sesame oil	
	1 T. cornstarch	

❶ Rinse and devein shrimp; drain. Using side of cleaver, smash shrimp and chop finely; chop pork fat finely. Mix chopped shrimp with egg white; add chopped pork fat and ① ; beat mixture for 5 minutes and lightly throw against inside of bowl to combine ingredients to a smooth paste. Separate into 12 portions.

❷ Fold each piece of glutinous rice paper diagonally in half to create a triangle. In the middle of each triangle, place a piece of sausage, a sprig of coriander and 1 portion of shrimp paste; fold up paper to enclose filling; rub a little egg yolk in a corner of paper to seal securely (make 12 packages). Heat oil for deep-frying; deep-fry shrimp "packages" over medium heat for about 1½ minutes; remove, drain and place on serving plate; serve.

蝦⋯⋯⋯24條	葱末⋯⋯⋯1大匙	紫菜⋯⋯⋯⋯6張
①{ 薑酒⋯⋯半大匙	酒⋯⋯⋯⋯1小匙	「炸油」⋯⋯⋯6杯
鹽⋯⋯⋯⅓小匙	鹽⋯⋯⋯⅓小匙	椒鹽⋯⋯⋯1大匙
②{ 蝦仁⋯⋯4兩	③{ 味精⋯⋯⋯¼小匙	
肥肉⋯⋯1兩	糖⋯⋯⋯半大匙	
荸薺⋯⋯2兩	胡椒⋯⋯⋯¼小匙	
	麻油⋯⋯⋯¼小匙	
	太白粉⋯⋯半大匙	

❶ 蝦去殼留尾調①料，醃20分鐘。

❷ 將②料剁碎調③料攪拌至有黏性即成餡。

❸ 紫菜1張分切成4小張計24張，每張上放1條蝦、1大匙「餡」包成雞腿狀即成蝦腿。

❹ 「炸油」燒熱，中火炸2分鐘，臨起鍋再改大火炸1分鐘至熟撈起，以椒鹽沾食。

紫菜蝦腿 Shrimp Legs with Nori

台灣菜 Taiwanese
12人份 12 servings

24 shrimp (about 1lb.)

①{ ½ T. ginger wine
⅓ t. salt

②{ 4 oz. raw, shelled shrimp
1 oz. pork fat or suet
2 oz. water chestnuts

③{ 1 T. chopped green onion
1 t. rice wine
⅓ t. salt
¼ t. MSG
½ T. sugar
¼ t. black pepper
¼ t. sesame oil
½ T. cornstarch

6 sheets nori or purple laver seaweed
6 C. oil for frying
1 T. Szechuan peppercorn salt

❶ Rinse shrimp and remove shells, leaving tail end intact; devein and mix with ① ; let soak 20 minutes.

❷ Separately chop ingredients of ② until fine; add ③ and lightly throw mixture against inside of mixing bowl. (filling)

❸ Cut each sheet of nori into 4 pieces; place a shrimp in the middle of each piece of nori, leaving tail end hanging just over edge; add 1T. filling on top of shrimp and fold up nori (as if you are wrapping a package); repeat for all other shrimp.

❹ Heat oil for deep-frying; deep-fry shrimp over medium heat for 2 minutes; turn heat to high and cook an additional minute; remove and drain. Place fried shrimp on serving plate and serve with peppercorn salt.

蝦仁……6兩
① ┌ 鹽……¼小匙
  │ 酒……半小匙
  │ 蛋白……半個
  └ 太白粉2小匙

青豆仁(或毛豆)…半杯
蔥(3公分長)……6枝
薑………6片
「炸油」………3杯

② ┌ 酒……半小匙
  │ 鹽……¼小匙
  │ 味精…¼小匙
  │ 胡椒…¼小匙
  │ 麻油…¼小匙
  │ 水……1大匙
  └ 太白粉半小匙

❶ 洗淨蝦仁拭乾水份調上①料拌勻,醃泡20分鐘。

❷ 青豆煮熟,漂涼撈出。

❸ 「炸油」燒熱,中火將蝦仁泡熟撈出,留油3大匙,蔥、薑炒香,隨即放入蝦仁、青豆及②料拌炒,即可盛出。

■ 配料可依個人喜好選擇。

青豆蝦仁 Stir-Fried Shrimp with Green Peas

四川菜　Szechuan
6人份　6 servings

½ lb. raw, shelled shrimp
① ┌ ¼ t. salt
  │ ½ t. rice wine
  │ ½ egg white
  └ 2 t. cornstarch

½ C. green peas
6 1-inch sections green onion
6 slices ginger root
3 C. oil for frying

② ┌ ½ t. rice wine
  │ ¼ t. salt
  │ ¼ t. MSG
  │ ¼ t. black pepper
  │ ¼ t. sesame oil
  │ 1 T. water
  └ ½ t. cornstarch

❶ Rinse and devein shrimp; drain and mix with ① ; let sit 20 minutes.

❷ Precook peas in boiling water until tender; remove and place in cold water until cool; drain.

❸ Heat oil until medium hot; add shrimp and deep-fry until changed in color; remove and drain.
Remove all but 3T. oil from pan; reheat and stir-fry green onion and ginger until fragrant; add shrimp, peas and ② . Lightly toss mixture to combine ingredients and remove to serving plate; serve.

116

<table>
<tr><td>①</td><td>蝦仁………６兩
鹽………¼小匙
酒………半小匙
蛋白………半個
太白粉…２小匙</td><td>熟筍(切丁)…¼杯
腰果………３兩
「炸油」………３杯
葱(３公分長)６枝
薑………６片</td><td>②</td><td>酒………半小匙
鹽………¼小匙
味精………¼小匙
胡椒………¼小匙
麻油………¼小匙
水………１大匙
太白粉…半小匙</td></tr>
</table>

❶ 蝦仁洗淨，拭乾水份調上①料拌勻，醃泡２０分鐘。

❷ 水３杯燒開，腰果倒入加鹽半小匙，煮約８分鐘撈起瀝乾，「炸油」略燒熱以小火炸約８分鐘撈起，散開盛菜盤內。

❸ 「炸油」燒熱中火將蝦仁泡約３０秒撈起，留油１大匙，葱、薑炒香，倒入蝦仁、筍及②料拌勻，放進腰果加熱油半大匙，一拌即成。

腰果蝦仁 Stir-Fried Shrimp with Cashew Nuts

廣東菜 Cantonese
6人份　6 servings

½ lb. raw, shelled shrimp	¼ C. precooked diced bamboo shoot	½ t. rice wine
¼ t. salt	3 oz. raw cashews	¼ t. salt
½ t. rice wine	3 C. oil for frying	¼ t. MSG
½ egg white	6 1-inch sections green onion	¼ t. black pepper
2 t. cornstarch	6 slices ginger root	¼ t. sesame oil
		1 T. water
		½ t. cornstarch

① (shrimp marinade)　②

❶ Rinse and devein shrimp; drain and mix with ① ; let sit 20 minutes.

❷ Boil 3C. water; add cashews and ½t. salt; cook 8 minutes over medium heat and remove; drain cashews. Heat oil until medium hot; deep-fry cashews about 8 minutes over low heat; remove and drain on absorbent paper.

❸ Reheat oil until medium hot; deep-fry shrimp 30 seconds; remove and drain. Remove all but 1T. oil from pan; reheat and stir-fry green onion and ginger until fragrant; add shrimp, bamboo shoot and ② ; toss ingredients lightly to mix together and add cashews; mix together and remove to serving plate; serve.

①	蝦仁………6兩		熟筍(切小塊)……半杯	②	鹽………¼小匙	
	鹽………¼小匙		熟紅蘿蔔(切小塊)¼杯		味精………¼小匙	
	酒………半小匙		洋菇(切小塊)……¼杯		胡椒………¼小匙	
	蛋白………半個		毛豆………¼杯		麻油………¼小匙	
	太白粉…2小匙		葱(3公分長)……6枝		水………1大匙	
	「炸油」…3杯		薑………6片		太白粉…半小匙	

❶ 蝦仁洗淨，拭乾水份，調上①料拌勻，醃泡２０分鐘。

❷ 「炸油」燒熱，中火將蝦仁及配料，分別泡油３０秒取出，留油１大匙，葱薑炒香，倒進全部
材料及酒１小匙，並入②料炒勻即可。

五彩炒蝦仁 Stir-Fried Shrimp with Assorted Vegetables

廣東菜 Cantonese
6人份 6 servings

①	½ lb. raw, shelled shrimp	½ C. precooked diced bamboo shoot	②
	¼ t. salt	¼ C. diced precooked carrot	
	½ t. rice wine	¼ C. diced mushrooms	
	½ egg white	¼ C. precooked green peas	
	2 t. cornstarch	6 1-inch sections green onion	
	3 C. oil for frying	6 slices ginger root	

② ¼ t. salt / ¼ t. MSG / ¼ t. black pepper / ¼ t. sesame oil / 1 T. water / ½ t. cornstarch

❶ Rinse and devein shrimp; drain; mix with ① and let sit 20 minutes.

❷ Heat oil until medium hot; deep-fry shrimp and vegetables separately about 30 seconds; remove and drain. Reheat pan and 1T. oil; stir-fry green onion and ginger until fragrant; add shrimp and vegetables, 1t. rice wine and ② ; toss lightly to mix all ingredients together; serve.

<table>
<tr><td rowspan="5">①</td><td>蝦仁……半斤</td></tr>
<tr><td>鹽……¼小匙</td></tr>
<tr><td>酒……半小匙</td></tr>
<tr><td>蛋白……半個</td></tr>
<tr><td>太白粉２小匙</td></tr>
</table>

② 蛋黃……………１個
太白粉……１½大匙
「炸油」…………６杯

③ 葱末
薑末
蒜末　各半大匙
紅辣椒末
青椒末………２大匙

④ 糖……１大匙
醋……１大匙
番茄醬１大匙
水……１大匙
鹽……¼小匙

⑤ 太白粉半小匙
水……半大匙

❶ 蝦仁用潔巾拭乾水份，調①料醃約２０分鐘，炸時再加②料（先加蛋黃再加太白粉）拌勻。

❷ 「炸油」燒熱，中火將蝦仁下炸約１分鐘撈起盛盤。

❸ 油２大匙燒熱，中火將③料炒香再將④料倒入燒開，以⑤料太白粉水勾汁淋於炸好的蝦仁上即成。

醋了蝦仁　Stir-Fried Shrimp in Sour Sauce

廣東菜　Cantonese
6人份　6 servings

① ⅔ lb. raw, shelled shrimp
¼ t. salt
½ t. rice wine
½ egg white
2 t. cornstarch

② 1 egg yolk
1½ T. cornstarch
6 C. oil for frying

③ ½ T. chopped green onion
½ T. chopped ginger root
½ T. chopped garlic
½ T. chopped hot red pepper
2 T. chopped green pepper

④ 1 T. sugar
1 T. vinegar
1 T. tomato ketchup
1 T. water
¼ t. salt

⑤ ½ t. cornstarch
½ T. water

❶ Rinse and devein shrimp; drain and mix with ① ; let sit 20 minutes. Before deep-frying, dip shrimp in egg yolk and mix with cornstarch.

❷ Heat oil until medium hot; deep-fry shrimp over medium heat until changed in color (about 1 minute); remove, drain and place on serving plate.

❸ Reheat pan and 2T. oil; stir-fry ③ until fragrant and add ④ . When mixture begins to boil, add ⑤ to thicken; mix together and pour over shrimp; serve.

① 蝦仁………半斤
鹽………¼ 小匙
酒………半小匙
蛋白………半個
太白粉…2 小匙
「炸油」……3 杯

② 水…………3 杯
鹽………1 小匙
味精……半小匙
糖………2 大匙
番茄醬…4 大匙
青豆仁……¼ 杯

③ 太白粉…2 大匙
水………2 大匙
鍋粑………5 兩

❶ 洗淨蝦仁，拭乾水份，調入①料攪勻醃約２０分鐘，鍋粑切成３公分四方塊。

❷ 「炸油」燒熱，中火將蝦仁泡熟(見白)撈出，留１大匙油燒熱隨即放酒１小匙，②料及青豆仁待滾後放入蝦仁，並以③料勾成薄糊狀加１大匙熱油盛於湯碗內。

❸ 「炸油」燒熱，將鍋粑炸約半分鐘，盛於大盤內，馬上就可把燒好的蝦湯沖在鍋粑上即可供食。

■ 蝦湯倒入鍋粑上，可在客人面前做，此時將會冒出煙，且有聲音發出。

鍋粑蝦仁 Stir-Fried Shrimp over Crispy Rice

四川菜　Szechuan
12人份　**12 servings**

① ⅔ lb. raw, shelled shrimp
¼ t. salt
½ t. rice wine
½ egg white
2 t. cornstarch
3 C. oil for frying

② 3 C. water
1 t. salt
½ t. MSG
2 T. sugar
4 T. tomato ketchup
¼ C. green peas

③ 2 T. cornstarch
2 T. water
5 oz. glutinous rice cake*

❶ Rinse and devein shrimp; drain and mix with ① ; let sit 20 minutes. Cut each glutinous rice cake in half.
❷ Heat oil until medium hot; deep-fry shrimp until changed in color; remove and drain. Reheat pan and 1T. oil; add 1t. rice wine and ② ; when mixture begins to boil, add green peas and cook 1 minute; add shrimp and ③ to thicken; mix 1T. oil and remove mixture to a bowl.
❸ Heat oil for deep-frying; deep-fry glutinous rice cakes over high heat about ½ minute until expanded and golden; remove, drain and place on serving plate; pour shrimp mixture over rice cakes and serve immediately.
■ For a dramatic effect for dinner guests, pour shrimp mixture over rice cakes at table. This action creates an impressive noise.
* Glutinous rice cake ("gwo ba") 鍋粑 is a type of dry, puffed rice cake available in packages, which may be purchased at a Chinese grocery store.

鮑魚（１罐）……２４片
冬菇（８朵）……２４片
熟筍片（蝶形）……２４片
生菜（或芥菜）…１２棵
蔥（３公分長）…６枝
薑…………………６片

① {
酒……１大匙
高湯……１杯
蠔油…１大匙
醬油…１小匙
味精…１小匙
糖……半小匙
麻油…１小匙
}

② {
太白粉…半大匙
水………１大匙
}

❶ 生菜修去老葉，加鹽少許炒熟，盛盤四週。

❷ 油４大匙燒熱，將蔥薑炒香，放入酒及①料燒沸，把蔥薑撈出，先放入冬菇燒煮２分鐘，再入筍及鮑魚，再燒沸撈出，順序排在盤內，餘汁以②料勾汁，加熱油１大匙後，淋在鮑魚上即可。

麒麟麻鮑甫　Abalone Slices with Oyster Sauce

廣東菜　Cantonese
12人份 **12 servings**

1 lb. abalone meat (1 can)
8 pre-softened Chinese black mushrooms
1 precooked bamboo shoot
⅔ lb. lettuce
6 1-inch sections green onion
6 slices ginger root

① {
1 T. rice wine
1 C. stock
1 T. oyster sauce
1 t. soy sauce
1 t. MSG
½ t. sugar
1 t. sesame oil
}

② {
½ T. cornstarch
1 T. water
}

❶ Cut abalone, black mushrooms and bamboo shoot into 24 slices each. Heat pan and 4T. oil; stir-fry lettuce and ¼t. salt until vegetable is limp (add a little water if too dry); remove and arrange on serving plate as illustrated.

❷ Heat pan and 4T. oil; stir-fry onion and ginger until fragrant; add rice wine, ① and let liquid come to a boil; strain-out onion and ginger and add black mushroom slices; cook 2 minutes and add bamboo shoot and abalone slices. When liquid begins to boil, remove slices and arrange alternately on serving plate. Reheat liquid and add ② to thicken; add 1T. oil and mix. Pour sauce over slices and serve.

鮑魚‥‥‥‥‥‥半罐
豬腰(大)‥‥‥‥1只
芥蘭菜‥‥‥‥14棵
葱(3公分長)‥6枝
薑‥‥‥‥‥‥‥6片

① 酒‥‥‥‥1小匙
高湯‥‥‥‥1杯
蠔油‥‥‥‥2大匙
醬油‥‥‥‥1大匙
味精‥‥‥半小匙
糖‥‥‥‥半小匙
麻油‥‥‥1小匙

② 太白粉‥‥1大匙
水‥‥‥‥1大匙

❶ 鮑魚切大薄片，豬腰剔除白筋也斜切為大薄片，芥蘭菜去老葉取嫩莖，切約10公分長。
❷ 燒開半鍋水，分別將芥蘭菜、豬腰各燙約20秒鐘撈出，入冷水泡涼，各撈起備用。
❸ 油3大匙燒熱，炒腰片取出。
❹ 油3大匙燒熱，把葱薑炒香，放入芥蘭菜，下酒1小匙及①料燒開，以②料勾汁，放進腰片，鮑魚片，最後淋上熟油1大匙即起。

鮑魚腰片 Stir-Fried Abalone with Kidney

廣東菜 Cantonese
12人份 12 servings

½ can abalone meat (½lb.)
1 pork kidney (½lb.)
14 stalks Chinese broccoli* (⅔lb.)
6 1-inch sections green onion
6 slices ginger root
1 t. rice wine

① 1 C. stock
2 T. oyster sauce
1 T. soy sauce
½ t. MSG
½ t. sugar
1 t. sesame oil

② 1 T. cornstarch
1 T. water

❶ Cut abalone into thin slices; slice pork kidney in half; remove any white membrane and cut into thin slices; trim any dead leaves from broccoli and cut into 3-inch sections.
❷ Heat 6C. water until boiling; precook broccoli sections for 1 minute; remove and blanch kidney sections 20 seconds; remove. Place broccoli and kidney pieces separately in cold water to cool; drain.
❸ Heat pan and 3T. oil; briefly stir-fry kidney and remove.
❹ Reheat pan and 3T. oil; stir-fry onion and ginger until fragrant; add broccoli sections, 1t. rice wine and ①; stir-fry to mix together and when liquid boils, add ② to thicken; add kidney and abalone slices and 1T. oil; toss ingredients lightly to mix and remove to serving plate serve.
* If Chinese broccoli is unavailable, substiture American broccoli or celery cabbage and cut stalks ½ inch thick; use as directed.

鮑魚⋯⋯⋯⋯⋯⋯ 1 罐
鮮草菇（１２兩）⋯ 2 杯
小青江菜⋯⋯⋯ 14 棵
葱（3 公分長）⋯⋯ 6 枝
薑⋯⋯⋯⋯⋯⋯ 6 片

① ｛
酒⋯⋯ 1 小匙
湯⋯⋯⋯ 1 杯
蠔油⋯ 2 大匙
醬油⋯ 1 大匙
味精⋯ 半小匙
糖⋯⋯ 半小匙
麻油⋯ 1 小匙

② ｛
太白粉⋯ 1 大匙
水⋯⋯⋯ 1 大匙

❶ 鮑魚切大薄片，小青江菜去老葉切約１０公分長段備用。

❷ 燒開半鍋水，先將草菇燙３分鐘撈出，再放入小青江菜川燙１分鐘，入冷水泡涼，各撈起備用。

❸ 油３大匙燒熱，放進小青江菜及鹽適量炒熟，取出圍邊。

❹ 油３大匙燒熱，把葱薑炒香，入草菇略炒並下酒１小匙，及①料燒開，以②料勾汁，放進鮑魚片，最後淋上熟油１大匙即起。

鮑魚鮮菇 Stir-Fried Abalone with Straw Mushrooms

廣東菜 Cantonese
12人份 **12 servings**

1 lb. abalone meat
2 C. straw mushrooms (1lb.)
14 stalks green vegetable
6 1-inch sections green onion
6 slices ginger root
1 t. rice wine

① ｛
1 C. stock
2 T. oyster sauce
1 T. soy sauce
½ t. MSG
½ t. sugar
1 t. sesame oil

② ｛
1 T. cornstarch
1 T. water

❶ Cut abalone into paper-thin bite-size slices; remove any old leaves from vegetable and cut into 3-inch sections.

❷ Place straw mushrooms in water to cover and cook 3 minutes; remove and cook vegetable sections for 1 minute; remove and place mushrooms and vegetable sections in cold water to cool; drain.

❸ Heat pan and 3T. oil; stir-fry vegetable sections with ⅓ t. salt for 20 seconds over high heat, remove and arrange sections around edge of serving plate.

❹ Reheat pan and 3T. oil; stir-fry green onion and ginger until fragrant; add straw mushrooms and stir-fry briefly. Add 1t. rice wine and ① ; let mixture come to a boil and add ② to thicken; add abalone and 1t. oil. Toss ingredients lightly to mix together and remove to serving plate; serve.

河鰻‥‥‥‥‥‥1斤
栗子(罐頭)‥‥‥1杯
「炸油」‥‥‥‥‥3杯
葱(3公分長)‥‥6枝
薑‥‥‥‥‥‥‥6片

① 酒‥‥‥‥‥1大匙
水‥‥‥‥‥1½杯
醬油‥‥‥‥3大匙
糖‥‥‥‥‥1大匙
味精‥‥‥半小匙
胡椒‥‥‥¼小匙

② 太白粉‥‥半大匙
水‥‥‥‥半大匙
醋‥‥‥‥半小匙

❶ 河鰻切除頭部及內臟，盛鍋內，用滾水燙半分鐘後，刮除鰻魚身上的黏膜後洗淨，切約3公分長段。

❷ 「炸油」燒開，將瀝乾水份之栗子倒入，用大火炸至金黃色（約1分鐘），取出備用。

❸ 油4大匙燒熱，葱薑炒香，加①料再倒入鰻魚塊，用中火煮約5分鐘，加入炸過之栗子改用小火蓋鍋燜煮15分鐘，至汁剩一半時，用②料勾汁，加醋半小匙，最後澆上熟油1大匙，拌炒即可。

紅燒河鰻 Red-Cooked Eels with Chestnuts

上海菜　Shanghai.
12人份 **12 servings**

1⅓ lbs. fresh eels
1 C. whole chestnuts*
3 C. oil for frying
6 1-inch sections green onion
6 slices ginger root

① 1 T. rice wine
1½ C. water
3 T. soy sauce
1 T. sugar
½ t. MSG
¼ t. black pepper

② ½ T. cornstarch
½ T. water
½ t. vinegar

❶ Cut heads from eels and clean guts from insides; discard. Place eels in pan with boiling water to cover for 30 seconds; remove and rinse any slimy residue from exterior and interior; drain and cut eels into 1-inch sections.

❷ Heat oil for deep-frying; deep-fry chestnuts for 1 minute until golden brown; remove and drain.

❸ Reheat pan and 4T. oil; stir-fry green onion and ginger until fragrant; add ① and eel sections and cook covered for 5 minutes over medium heat. Add chestnuts and turn heat to low; simmer covered for 15 minutes until sauce is near-dry; add ② to thicken, ½t. vinegar and 1T. oil; toss ingredients lightly to mix together and remove to serving plate; serve.

* If using canned chestnuts, drain juice and use as directed. For dried chestnuts, soak in warm water until soft; drain and use as directed.

熟鱔魚肉…6兩　　　　醬油………3大匙　　　　胡椒………¼小匙
「炸油」……3杯　　　　味精………半小匙　　②｛葱花………1大匙
韮菜黃……2兩　　①｛糖…………1小匙　　　　蒜末………2大匙
酒………半大匙　　　　水…………⅓杯　　　　嫩薑絲……2大匙
　　　　　　　　　　　太白粉……半大匙　　　　香菜………2大匙

❶ 鱔魚切7公分長條，韮菜黃切段。

❷ 「炸油」燒熱將鱔魚入油泡1分鐘即撈起，餘油倒出，留油3大匙放進韮菜黃、鱔魚，下酒半
　大匙並調入①料拌炒，即可盛盤，中間挖成凹狀，洒上②料，以3大匙燒開油，澆在葱花、蒜
　末上即成。

■ 盤兩旁可擺嫩薑絲、香菜、一齊拌食。

韮黃炒鱔糊 Stir-Fried Eels with Chives

6　oz. fresh, scaled precooked eels *¹　　3　T. soy sauce　　　　　¼　t　black pepper
3　C. oil for frying　　　　　　　　　½　t. MSG　　　　　　②｛1　T. chopped green onion
2　oz. Chinese leeks *²　　　　　①｛1　t. sugar　　　　　　　　2　T. chopped garlic
½　T. rice wine　　　　　　　　　　⅓　C. water　　　　　　　　2　T. shredded ginger root
　　　　　　　　　　　　　　　　　½　T. cornstarch　　　　　　2　T. coriander

❶ Cut eels into 2½-inch sections; cut Chinese leeks into sections the same size as eels.

❷ Heat oil for deep-frying; deep-fry the eels for 1 minute over medium heat; remove and drain. Remove
all but 3T. oil from pan; reheat and add leek sections, eels, ½T. rice wine, and ① . Stir-fry over high heat
to mix together and remove to serving plate. Make a slight hole or indentation in center of stir-fried
eel; place ② in hole. Heat 3T. oil until very hot and pour over ② ; serve immediately.

■ Garnish with shredded ginger root and coriander; toss lightly to combine ingredients and serve.

*¹ Eels must first be scaled and cleaned (discard heads), then placed in boiling water until meat changes
color and used as directed.

*² If Chinese leeks are unavailable, substitute green onions.

魷魚（乾的泡發）………4條		酒…………………半大匙
「炸油」………………6杯		醬油……3大匙 、 醋………1小匙
干辣椒（切段）…………半杯	①	味精……半小匙 、 太白粉…1小匙
蒜末………………半小匙		糖………1大匙 、 水………2大匙
		麻油……1小匙

❶ 洗淨魷魚，切除尖尾（祇要魷魚身）用刀稍刮去薄皮，每條直剖約四開，在內面切花。（每塊寬約五公分、長四公分）。

❷ 6杯水燒開，將切花之魷魚片下鍋，燙約２０秒，即自行捲花撈出，瀝乾水份。

❸ 「炸油」燒開，將已燙好的魷魚再炸約半分鐘撈出，留油３大匙，將干辣椒炒香，加蒜末並下酒半大匙倒入炸過之魷魚捲及①料拌勻即可。

■ 干辣椒很辣，可由個人之喜愛增減。

宮保魷魚捲 Stir-Fried Squid with Dried Red Peppers

四川菜　Szechuan
12人份 **12 servings**

4	pre-softened dried squid (about 1⅓lbs.)*			3	T.	soy sauce
6	C. oil for frying			½	t.	MSG
½	C. 2-inch sections dried red peppers			1	T.	sugar
½	t. chopped garlic		①	1	t.	sesame oil
½	T. rice wine			1	t.	worcestershire sauce
				1	t.	cornstarch
				2	T.	water

❶ Rinse squid and remove head and tail sections; discard. Cut central body piece into 4 strips; lightly score meat lengthwise and crosswise and cut sections into bite-size pieces (about 2½ x 1½ inches).

❷ Boil 6C. water and cook squid pieces about 20 seconds (pieces will curl up slightly); remove and drain.

❸ Heat oil for deep-frying; deep-fry squid pieces about ½ minute; remove and drain. Remove all but 3T. oil; reheat and stir-fry pepper sections and garlic until fragrant; add ½T. rice wine, squid pieces and ① . Toss lightly to mix ingredients and remove to serving plate; serve.

■ Dried red peppers are usually very hot; use as directed or decrease quantity according to your personal taste.

* Dried squid should be soaked in 1t. baking soda and water to cover until soft; use as directed.

<table>
<tbody>
<tr><td rowspan="4">①</td><td>生魷魚…1斤</td><td>「炸油」………6杯</td><td rowspan="7">②</td><td>鹽……1小匙</td></tr>
<tr><td>熟筍片…半杯</td><td>葱（3公分長）6枝</td><td>味精……半小匙</td></tr>
<tr><td>熟蘿蔔片…¼杯</td><td>薑……………6片</td><td>糖……半小匙</td></tr>
<tr><td>青椒片…¼杯</td><td>蒜頭（拍碎）…1粒</td><td>胡椒……¼小匙</td></tr>
<tr><td></td><td></td><td>麻油……半小匙</td></tr>
<tr><td></td><td></td><td>太白粉1小匙</td></tr>
<tr><td></td><td></td><td>水……1大匙</td></tr>
</tbody>
</table>

❶ 生魷魚，切除尖尾（衹要魷魚身），用刀稍刮去薄皮，每條直剖約2～3開在内面切花。（每塊約5公分×4公分）。

❷ 「炸油」燒熱將魷魚下鍋泡油20秒，即自行捲花撈起，留油4大匙將葱薑蒜炒香，隨即放入①料略炒，再投入已泡熟之魷魚及②料炒拌即成。

■ 在家庭魷魚如要泡油不方便，可用開水先燙熟，再與其他配料炒拌。

生炒魷魚 Stir-Fried Squid with Assorted Vegetables

廣東菜　Cantonese
6人份　6 servings

1⅓ lbs. fresh squid

① ½ C. bite-size slices precooked bamboo shoot
¼ C. bite-size slices precooked carrot
¼ C. bite-size pieces green pepper

6 C. oil for frying
6 1-inch sections green onion
6 slices ginger root
1 clove garlic, smashed

② 1 t. salt
½ t. MSG
½ t. sugar
¼ t. black pepper
½ t. sesame oil
1 t. cornstarch
1 T. water

❶ Remove head and tail from squid; discard. Remove skin and rinse; drain. Cut main section of body into 3 strips; lightly score meat lengthwise and crosswise and cut into bite-size pieces (about 2½ x 1½ inches)

❷ Heat oil for deep-frying; deep-fry squid meat, and ① for 20 seconds; remove and drain. Remove all but 4T. oil from pan; reheat and stir-fry onion, ginger and garlic until fragrant; add squid, ① and ② ; toss lightly to mix all ingredients and remove to serving plate; serve.

■ In family cooking, squid and vegetables need not be deep-fried; precook in boiling water and stir-fry as directed.

| ① 海參…1斤
{葱……2枝
薑……2片
酒…1大匙
水……5杯 | ② 絞肉……4兩
{鹽……半小匙
味精…¼小匙
雞蛋……半個
太白粉1大匙
「炸油」…3杯 | ③ {豆瓣醬…1大匙
蒜末……半大匙
酒………1大匙 | ④ {蠔油…1大匙
味精…半小匙
糖……1小匙
胡椒…¼小匙
麻油…1小匙
高湯………1杯
⑤ {太白粉…1大匙
水………1大匙 |

❶ 海參切大塊，放入①料燒煮5分鐘撈出。

❷ 絞肉調入②料，攪拌甩打後，做成２４個肉丸，「炸油」燒熱，用中火炸２分鐘撈出。

❸ 油４大匙燒熱，把③料炒香，下酒１大匙及④料燒滾後，放入海參、肉丸，用小火燒煮１０分鐘，俟汁快乾時，以⑤料勾汁，加熱油１大匙即成。

肉丸海參 Pork Balls and Sea Cucumbers

	1⅓ lbs. pre-softened sea cucumber* (beche-de-mer)		
① {	2 stalks green onion 2 slices ginger root 1 T. rice wine 5 C. water	② {	4 oz. chopped pork ½ t. salt ¼ t. MSG ½ egg 1 T. cornstarch 3 C. oil for frying
③ {	1 T. black bean paste. ½ T. chopped garlic 1 T. rice wine	④ {	1 T. oyster sauce ½ t. MSG 1 t. sugar ¼ t. black pepper 1 t. sesame oil 1 C. stock ⑤ { 1 T. cornstarch. 1 T. water

❶ Cut sea cucumbers into bite-size pieces; add to ① and cook 5 minutes over medium heat; drain sea cucumbers. (discard liquid).

❷ In a bowl, mix ② with chopped pork and lightly throw mixture against inside of mixing bowl to combine ingredients thoroughly; separate into 14 portions and roll into balls. Heat oil for deep-frying; deep-fry meat balls over medium heat for 2 minutes; remove and drain.

❸ Heat pan and 3T. oil; stir-fry ③ until fragrant; add 1T. rice wine and ④ . When mixture comes to a boil, add sea cucumber and meat balls. Simmer 10 minutes until sauce is near dry; add ⑤ to thicken and 1T. oil; toss ingredients lightly to mix together and remove to serving plate; serve.

* See P. 129 for directions for pre-conditioning sea cucumbers.

<table>
<tr><td rowspan="5">①</td><td>烏參……4只（1斤）</td></tr>
<tr><td>酒………………半大匙</td></tr>
<tr><td>葱………………3枝</td></tr>
<tr><td>薑………………4片</td></tr>
<tr><td>水………………2杯</td></tr>
</table>

葱末……2小匙
薑末……1小匙
蝦子……1½大匙

<table>
<tr><td rowspan="7">②</td><td>味精………¼小匙</td></tr>
<tr><td>糖………半小匙</td></tr>
<tr><td>醬油……2大匙</td></tr>
<tr><td>猪油……1大匙</td></tr>
<tr><td>麻油……半小匙</td></tr>
<tr><td>酒………1小匙</td></tr>
<tr><td>高湯………¾杯</td></tr>
</table>

③ 太白粉……1大匙
水………1大匙

❶ ①料煮約10分鐘撈起（去除腥味）。

❷ 油3大匙燒熱，投葱、薑末炒香、再加入海參（每只切4塊）、蝦子及②料，燜煮約10分鐘，以③料勾成薄汁即成。

蝦子烏參 Stir-Fried Sea Cucumber and Shrimp Eggs

上海菜 Shanghai
6人份 6 servings

<table>
<tr><td rowspan="5">①</td><td>4 sea cucumbers* (bêche-de-mer) (about 1⅓lbs.)</td><td></td></tr>
<tr><td>½ T. rice wine</td><td></td></tr>
<tr><td>3 stalks green onion</td><td></td></tr>
<tr><td>4 slices ginger root</td><td>2 t. chopped green onion</td></tr>
<tr><td>2 C. water</td><td>1 t. chopped ginger root</td></tr>
</table>

1½ T. dried shrimp eggs

<table>
<tr><td rowspan="7">②</td><td>¼ t. MSG</td></tr>
<tr><td>½ t. sugar</td></tr>
<tr><td>2 T. soy sauce</td></tr>
<tr><td>1 T. lard</td></tr>
<tr><td>½ t. sesame oil</td></tr>
<tr><td>1 t. rice wine</td></tr>
<tr><td>¾ C. stock</td></tr>
</table>

③ 1 T. cornstarch
1 T. water

❶ Cut each sea cucumbers into 4 pieces; add to ① and cook 10 minutes over medium heat; remove and drain. (discard liquid)

❷ Heat pan and 3T. oil; stir-fry green onion and ginger until fragrant; add sea cucumber, shrimp eggs and ② ; cook 10 minutes over medium heat. Add ③ to thicken and toss lightly to mix ingredients; remove to serving plate and serve.

* Sea cucumbers are available in dry form in Chinese grocery stores. Must first be pre-conditioned; rinse and place in water to cover; bring water to a boil and lower heat; simmer 5 minutes. Remove pan from heat and when water has cooled, remove sea cucumbers, rinse and place in fresh water to cover; let soak overnight. Place pan with soaking cucumbers over heat and repeat procedure 3 or 4 times until soft. Use as directed in recipe.

①{	海參(大4條)…1斤 葱…………2枝 薑…………2片 酒…………1大匙 水…………4杯	②{	絞肉…………半斤 鹽…………1小匙 味精………半小匙 胡椒………¼小匙 麻油………1小匙 酒…………1大匙 水…………1大匙		太白粉………2大匙 炸扁魚干(碎)2大匙 牙籤…………8枝 酒…………半大匙	③{ ④{	高湯…………3杯 鹽…………半小匙 味精………半小匙 麻油………半小匙 胡椒………¼小匙 太白粉………1小匙 奶水(或水)¼杯

❶ 油1大匙燒熱，將①料之葱薑炒香，下酒及水燒沸，把海參放入煮5分鐘撈出，待冷備用。

❷ 絞肉調入②料攪拌，並拌入太白粉和扁魚干拌勻，成「餡」。

❸ 海參內面洒少許太白粉，再鑲進絞肉抹平後，將牙籤從海參旁橫插穿入餡，直至海參另一旁，每條海參插兩根牙籤。

❹ 油2大匙燒熱，下酒半大匙及③料燒沸，放入海參，慢火燒熟，約25分鐘，湯汁剩1杯時，海參撈出置盤，抽出牙籤，以④料勾汁淋在海參上即成。

■ 將海參鑲好餡，插上牙籤，此乃在燒煮時以免餡掉落。

烏龍睡雪 Braised Stuffed Sea Cucumbers

①{	4　large sea cucumbers (bêche-de-mer)　(1⅓ lbs.)*¹ 2　stalks green onion 2　stalks ginger root 1　T. rice wine 4　C. water	②{	⅔　lb. chopped pork 1　t. salt ½　t. MSG ¼　t. black pepper 1　t. sesame oil 1　T. rice wine 1　T. water		2　T. cornstarch 2　T. chopped, fried 　　dried brillfish*² 8　toothpicks ½　T. rice wine
③{	3　C. stock · ½ t. sesame oil ½　t. salt · ¼ t. black pepper ½　t. MSG			④{	1　t. cornstarch ¼　C. evaporated milk or water

❶ Heat pan and 1T. oil; stir-fry green onion and ginger in ① ; add wine and water and bring to a boil; add sea cucumbers and cook 5 minutes over medium heat; remove sea cucumbers and drain. (discard liquid)

❷ Mix ② with chopped pork; add cornstarch and chopped dried fish; throw mixture lightly against the inside of bowl to combine ingredients thoroughly (filling).

❸ Dust inside of each sea cucumber with cornstarch and stuff with chopped pork filling. Pierce the middle of each sea cucumber with 2 toothpicks to secure the filling inside the sea cucumber.

❹ Reheat pan and 2T. oil; add ½T. rice wine, and ③ ; when mixture begins to boil add stuffed sea cucumbers; cover and simmer 25 minutes over low heat until liquid has reduced to about 1 cup; remove sea cucumbers to serving plate. (discard toothpicks). Heat the remaining liquid and add ④ to thicken. Pour over sea cucumbers and serve.

*¹ For directions for pre-conditioning sea cucumbers, see note on p. 129.

*² Dried brill fish ("bien yu gan") is available at Chinese grocery stores. Deep-fry in oil over low heat until golden brown and remove, drain and chop finely; use as directed.

①	②	③
生蠔⋯⋯⋯1斤 酒⋯2大匙 薑⋯⋯2片 葱⋯⋯2枝 〕擠汁 胡椒¼小匙	鹽⋯⋯⋯¾小匙 麵粉⋯⋯1大匙 太白粉⋯5大匙 蛋⋯⋯⋯1只 麵包粉⋯8大匙 牙籤⋯⋯12枝 「炸油」⋯6杯	辣豆瓣醬1小匙 番茄醬⋯1大匙 黑醋⋯⋯2大匙 麻油⋯⋯1小匙 糖⋯⋯⋯1大匙 醬油⋯⋯1大匙 蒜末⋯⋯半大匙 薑末⋯⋯1大匙

❶ 生蠔洗淨，瀝乾水份，加①料汁醃約20分鐘，炸時加②料調勻。

❷ 醃好生蠔，用牙籤將生蠔穿成12小串，在太白粉裏沾滾，再沾上打勻之蛋汁，最後沾麵包粉大火炸約1分鐘撈起，食時沾上攪勻之③料或椒鹽均可。

■ 圍邊用材料：香菜。

炸生蠔 Deep-Fried Oyster Rolls

1⅓ lbs. fresh shelled oysters	② ¾ t. salt	1 t. hot soybean paste ("la do ban jiang")
① 2 T. rice wine 2 slices ginger root 2 stalks green onion } smashed } Marinade ¼ t. black pepper	1 T. flour 5 T. cornstarch 1 egg, lightly beaten 8 T. grated bread crumbs 12 skewers 6 C. oil for frying	③ 1 T. tomato ketchup 2 T. worcestershire sauce 1 t. sesame oil 1 T. sugar 1 T. soy sauce ½ T. chopped garlic 1 T. chopped ginger root

❶ Carefully rinse oysters and drain; mix with ① and let sit 20 minutes; drain. Before deep-frying mix oysters with ②.

❷ Spear oysters on 12 skewers; coat oysters with cornstarch; dip in beaten egg and then roll in bread crumbs. Heat oil for deep-frying; deep-fry oyster "rolls" for 1 minute over high heat; remove and drain. Place on serving plate and serve with ③ for dipping.

■ Garnish with parsley.

① 生蠔……半斤
葱粒……半杯
薑末…1大匙
蒜末…1大匙
豆豉…2大匙

② 醬油露(或醬油)…3大匙
味精………………半小匙

③ 太白粉…1小匙
水………1大匙

❶ 生蠔洗淨，瀝乾水份，用開水３杯，川燙２０秒鐘呈半熟撈出。

❷ 油４大匙燒熱，大火將①料炒香，並加入生蠔及②料，快炒２０秒至蠔剛熟。燒煮後，如發現很多湯汁，就以③料勾汁，立即盛盤，趁熱供食。

■ 燒蠔時，時間短，煮到剛熟，否則太老縮成很小就不好吃了。

豆豉生蠔 Stir-Fried Oysters with Fermented Black Beans

台灣菜 Taiwanese
6人份 6 servings

⅔ lb. fresh shelled oysters, rinsed and drained

① { ½ C. chopped green onion
1 T. chopped ginger root
1 T. chopped garlic
2 T. fermented black beans

② { 3 T. soy sauce
½ t. MSG

③ { 1 t. cornstarch
1 T. water

❶ Carefully rinse oysters and drain. Boil 3C. water; add oysters and cook 20 seconds; remove and drain.

❷ Heat pan and 4T. oil; stir-fry ① over high heat until fragrant; add oysters and ② stir-fry 20 seconds. Add ③ to thicken, if necessary; remove and serve.

■ Oysters should not be cooked too long, as over cooking will toughen them.

雞蛋⋯⋯6個　　葱薑末(各)⋯1大匙　　　太白粉⋯⋯2小匙
蟹⋯⋯⋯2隻　　酒⋯⋯⋯⋯半大匙　②{ 水⋯⋯⋯⋯1大匙
薑酒⋯1大匙　　　鹽⋯⋯⋯⋯1小匙
「炸油」⋯6杯　　　味精⋯⋯⋯⋯1小匙
　　　　　　①{ 胡椒⋯⋯⋯⋯¼小匙
　　　　　　　　麻油⋯⋯⋯⋯1小匙
　　　　　　　　水⋯⋯⋯⋯⋯半杯

❶ 雞蛋去殼，用筷子調散待用。

❷ 蟹切塊，調上薑酒，醃20分鐘，瀝乾水份。

❸ 燒開「炸油」，入蟹炸約1分鐘取出。餘油倒淨，留油4大匙燒熱，將葱薑末炒香，再入蟹塊
　，放酒半大匙，並下①料燒至水快乾時，以②料勾汁，澆上熟油2大匙，入雞蛋拌炒凝固時，
　即可裝盤供食。

芙蓉炒蟹 Stir-Fried Crab Foo Yung

廣東菜　Cantonese
12人份　**12 servings**

6　eggs
2　small, soft-shelled crabs (about 1⅓ lbs.)
1　T. ginger wine
6　C. oil for frying

1　T. chopped green onion
1　T. chopped ginger root
½　T. rice wine
①{ 1　t. salt
　　1　t. MSG
　　¼　t. black pepper
　　1　t. sesame oil
　　½　C. water

②{ 2　t. cornstarch
　　1　T. water

❶ Beat eggs lightly.
❷ Remove upper shell of crab's body; rinse inside parts, being careful not to dislodge roe; remove any dirty extraneous matter and cut crabs (still in shell) into big pieces; mix with ginger wine and let sit 20 minutes; drain.
❸ Heat oil for deep-frying; deep-fry crab pieces for 1 minute over high heat; remove and drain. Remove all but 4T. oil from pan; reheat and stir-fry green onion and ginger until fragrant; add crab pieces. ½T. rice wine and ① ; let liquid boil and when liquid is almost dry, add ② to thicken; add 2T. oil and beaten eggs. Fry until eggs are lightly cooked, but still soft; remove to serving plate; serve.

<table>
<tr><td rowspan="4">①</td><td>蟹‥‥‥‥‥3隻</td><td rowspan="4">②</td><td>「炸油」‥‥‥‥6杯</td><td rowspan="6">③</td><td>鹽‥‥‥‥‥1小匙</td></tr>
</table>

蟹‥‥‥‥‥3隻		「炸油」‥‥‥‥6杯		鹽‥‥‥‥‥1小匙
① 薑酒‥‥‥1大匙		② 葱薑末(各)1大匙		味精‥‥‥‥1小匙
太白粉‥‥1大匙		蒜末‥‥‥‥半小匙	③	糖‥‥‥‥‥1小匙
青椒‥‥‥‥3個		豆豉‥‥‥‥1大匙		醬油‥‥‥‥1大匙
				麻油‥‥‥‥1小匙
				水‥‥‥‥‥‥半杯

④{ 太白粉‥‥1½小匙
　　水‥‥‥‥‥1大匙

❶ 蟹切塊，以薑酒1大匙拌勻並洒太白粉，青椒切塊待用。

❷ 油3大匙燒熱，放入青椒塊，加水1大匙，鹽半小匙，炒３０秒取出。

❸ 燒開「炸油」，蟹塊用大火炸約1分鐘撈出，留油3大匙，將②料炒香，並入蟹塊，酒1大匙及③料，蓋鍋煮約2分鐘(用大火)，再下④料勾汁，最後澆上熟油1大匙，及青椒塊炒拌即可。

豉椒炒蟹　Stir-Fried Crab with Green Pepper

廣東菜　Cantonese
12人份 12 servings

3　small soft-shelled crabs (about 2 lbs.)	6　C. oil for frying	1　t.　salt
① 1　T. ginger wine	② 1　T. chopped green onion	1　t.　MSG
1　T. cornstarch	1　T. chopped ginger root	③ 1　t.　sugar
3　medium-sized green peppers	½　t. chopped garlic	1　T.　soy sauce
	1　T. fermented black beans	1　t.　sesame oil
		½　C.　water

④{ 1½ t.　cornstarch
　　1　T.　water

❶ Remove upper shell of crab's body; rinse inside parts, being careful not to dislodge roe; remove any dirty extraneous matter and cut crabs (still in shell) into big pieces; mix pieces with 1T. ginger wine from ① and mix with cornstarch; let soak 20 minutes. Remove seeds from green peppers and cut into bite-size pieces.

❷ Heat pan and 3T. oil; stir-fry green peppers with 1T. water and ½t. salt for about 30 seconds over high heat; remove.

❸ Heat oil for deep-frying; deep-fry crab pieces for 1 minute over high heat; remove and drain. Remove all but 3T. oil from pan; reheat and stir-fry ② until fragrant; add 1T. rice wine, crab pieces, and ③ ; cover and cook 2 minutes over high heat; add ④ to thicken and 1T. oil and green pepper; toss lightly to mix ingredients and remove to serving plate; serve.

蟹肉⋯⋯⋯⋯1 杯
熟火腿片⋯⋯¼杯
葱（切片）⋯¼杯

① 蛋白（8個）⋯⋯1 杯
奶水⋯⋯⋯⋯⋯⋯半杯
鹽⋯⋯⋯⋯⋯⋯1 小匙
味精⋯⋯⋯⋯⋯半小匙
太白粉⋯⋯⋯⋯半大匙
水⋯⋯⋯⋯⋯⋯半大匙

炸米粉⋯⋯⋯1 杯

❶ 油2 大匙燒熱，放入蟹肉，加酒半小匙，略炒即起。

❷ 油4 大匙燒熱，隨即倒入調好的①料、火腿片、葱片及蟹肉翻炒約 10 秒鐘，倒在炸好之米粉上即成。

■ 圍邊用材料：香菜。

■ 蟹肉取法：蟹加葱2枝、薑2片，大火蒸熟，切半，蟹蚶拍破將肉挑出。

蟹肉炒鮮奶 Stir-Fried Crab Meat over Fried Rice Noodles

廣東菜 Cantonese
12人份 12 servings

1 C. crab meat*[1]
¼ C. precooked ham, cut to ⅓-inch thin squares
¼ C. minced green onion

①
1 C. egg whites (about 8), lightly beaten
½ C. evaporated milk
1 t. salt
½ t. MSG
½ T. cornstarch
½ T. water

1 C. fried rice noodles*[2]

❶ Lightly break up fried rice noodles and place on serving plate. Heat pan and 2T. oil; add crab meat and ½t. rice wine; stir-fry briefly over high heat and remove.

❷ Reheat pan and 4T. oil; add pre-mixed ① , ham slices, green onion and crab meat; stir-fry 10 seconds over high heat and portion over rice noodles; serve.

*[1] Crab meat may be canned or fresh. If using fresh crab: clean crab and rub exterior with 2 stalks green onion, 2 slices ginger root and 1T. rice wine. Place on a heatproof plate and steam 10~15 minutes over high heat; remove and remove meat from shell: use as directed.

*[2] To fry rice noodles: heat oil for deep-frying; deep-fry rice noodles until golden brown and expanded; remove and drain.

■ Garnish with coriander

|①{|蟹………1 隻
酒……半大匙
葱………2 枝
薑………2 片
青江菜…1 斤| |鮮草菇………1 斤
葱(３公分長)…6 枝
薑…………6 片
酒…………1 小匙|②{|鹽………1 小匙
味精……半小匙
胡椒……¼小匙
麻油……1 小匙
高湯……1 杯|③{|太白粉…1 大匙
水………1 大匙|

❶ 蟹加①料蒸熟（１０分鐘），把肉挑出備用。

❷ 油4 大匙燒熱，將青江菜加少許水及鹽1 小匙炒熟盛起，圍在盤的四周。

❸ 鮮草菇以開水煮約３分鐘撈出。

❹ 油4 大匙燒熱，葱薑炒香後隨下草菇略炒再加酒1 小匙及②料待滾即可倒入蟹肉拌勻，並以③料勾汁盛盤即成。

■ 草菇亦可改用洋菇

蟹肉草菇 Stir-Fried Crab Meat with Straw Mushrooms

廣東菜　Cantonese
12人份 **12 servings**

4　oz. crab meat
1⅓ lbs. green cabbage *¹
2　cans straw mushrooms, drained *²

6　1-inch sections green onion
6　slices ginger root
1　t.　rice wine

①{
1　t.　salt
½　t.　MSG
¼　t.　black pepper
1　t.　sesame oil
1　C.　stock

②{
1　T.　cornstarch
1　T.　water

❶ Heat pan and 4T. oil; stir-fry green cabbage briefly and add 1T. water and 1t. salt; stir-fry vegetable until tender and arrange around outer edge of serving plate.

❷ Cook straw mushrooms 1 minute in boiling water; remove and drain.

❸ Reheat pan and 4T. oil; stir-fry green onion and ginger until fragrant and add straw mushrooms; briefly stir-fry and add 1t. rice wine and ① . Let mixture come to a boil and add crab meat; mix ingredients and add ② to thicken; remove to serving plate and serve.

*¹ If unavailable, substitute celery cabbage or broccoli sections 3-inches long and 1-inch wide.
*² If unavailable, substitute button mushrooms.

蟹………2隻　　　葱（3公分長）…6枝　　③{太白粉…1大匙
酒……1大匙　　　薑…………6片　　　　{水………1大匙
①{葱………2枝　　　酒…………半大匙　　④{蛋白………1個
薑………2片　　　高湯…………3杯　　　{水………2大匙
濕蹄筋…1斤　　　②{鹽…………2小匙
　　　　　　　　　味精…………1小匙
　　　　　　　　　胡椒…………¼小匙
　　　　　　　　　麻油…………1小匙

❶ 蟹加①料拌醃，水開蒸約10分鐘，蒸熟取肉。蹄筋切4公分長段。

❷ 油2大匙燒熱炒葱薑加②料湯汁，放入蹄筋用中火煮5分鐘，加蟹肉並以③料勾汁後，徐徐放入④料最後淋上熟油2大匙盛出即成。

蟹肉燒蹄筋　Stir-Fried Crab Meat with Pork Tendons

廣東菜　Cantonese
12人份　12 servings

2 crabs	6 1-inch sections green onion	③{ 1 T. cornstarch
①{ 1 T. rice wine	6 slices ginger root	1 T. water
2 sections green onion	½ T. rice wine	④{ 1 egg white
2 slices ginger root	②{ 3 C. stock	2 T. water
1⅓ lbs. pre-softened pork tendons	2 t. salt	
	1 t. MSG	
	¼ t. black pepper	
	1 t. sesame oil	

❶ Clean crabs; mix crabs with ① and place on a heatproof plate steam 10 minutes over high heat; remove meat from shells. Cut pork tendons into 1½-inch sections.

❷ Heat pan with 2T. oil, fry green onion and ginger, until fragrant add ②, let the mixture come to a boil, add pork tendons and cook 5 minutes over medium heat; add crab meat and when water boils, add ③ to thicken. Beat ingredients of ④ lightly; slowly add to crab meat mixture, while stirring constantly; add 2T. oil and toss ingredients lightly to mix together; remove to serving plate and serve.

蟹⋯⋯⋯⋯ 3 隻
薑酒⋯⋯ 1 大匙
太白粉⋯⋯ 1 杯
「炸油」⋯⋯ 6 杯

① 糖⋯⋯⋯⋯ 5 大匙
醋⋯⋯⋯⋯ 5 大匙
水⋯⋯⋯⋯ 5 大匙
番茄醬⋯⋯ 3 大匙
鹽⋯⋯⋯⋯ 半小匙
蒜末⋯⋯⋯ 半大匙

② 太白粉⋯⋯ 半大匙
水⋯⋯⋯⋯ 1 大匙

❶ 蟹切塊，用薑酒拌醃 2 0 分鐘，瀝乾水份，沾太白粉。

❷ 「炸油」燒開，大火將蟹炸約 2 分鐘撈起，重將油燒滾，再炸至金黃色撈起。

❸ ①料之糖醋汁燒開，即以②料勾汁，加熟油 1 大匙，倒入炸熟蟹塊，拌勻即可盛入菜盤上。

■ 薑片拍碎加酒擠出的汁叫薑酒。

醋溜肉蟹 Stir-Fried Crab in Sweet and Sour Sauce

廣東菜　Cantonese
12人份 12 servings

3　small, soft-shelled crabs (about 2 lbs.)
1　T. ginger wine
1　C. cornstarch
6　C. oil for frying

① 5　T. sugar
5　T. vinegar
5　T. water
3　T. tomato ketchup
½　t. salt
½　T. chopped garlic

② ½　T. cornstarch
1　T. water

❶ Remove upper shell of crab's body; rinse inside parts, being careful not to dislodge roe; remove any dirty extraneous matter and cut crab, still in shell, into big pieces; mix pieces with ginger wine and let sit 20 minutes; drain. Coat pieces with cornstarch.

❷ Heat oil for deep-frying; deep-fry crab pieces about 2 minutes over high heat; remove. Reheat oil until very hot; deep-fry crab pieces very briefly until golden brown; remove and drain.

❸ Add ① to pan, heat until boiling and add ② to thicken, 1T. oil and crab pieces; toss lightly to coat crab pieces with sauce; remove to serving plate and serve.

田雞腿１２兩   冬菇⋯⋯⋯⋯５朶   醬油⋯１大匙

① 鹽⋯⋯⋯半小匙   ③ 蒜頭(拍破)⋯３個   鹽⋯⋯⋯半小匙

胡椒⋯¼小匙   葱(２公分長)６枝   味精⋯⋯半小匙

太白粉１大匙   薑⋯⋯⋯⋯６片   ④ 糖⋯⋯⋯半小匙

麵筋泡３０個   「炸油」⋯⋯⋯６杯   麻油⋯⋯半小匙

② 開水⋯⋯４杯   酒⋯⋯⋯⋯半大匙   太白粉１小匙

醋⋯⋯１大匙   水⋯⋯⋯⋯⅓杯

❶ 田雞腿去大骨，調①料拌勻，麵筋泡放入②料燒煮５分鐘（以去油味），撈起擠乾水份，切半。冬菇泡軟切片。

❷ 「炸油」燒熱，將田雞中火炸１分鐘撈起，留油３大匙，將③料炒香，隨下冬菇及麵筋略炒，加酒半大匙並入田雞及④料燒煮１分鐘，最後淋熟油１大匙即可。

生筋田雞 Frog's Legs with Fried Gluten Balls

廣東菜 Contonese
12人份 12 servings

1 lb. frog's legs

① ½ t. salt
¼ t. black pepper
1 T. cornstarch
30 fried gluten balls ("mien jin pau")

② 4 C. water
1 T. vinegar

5 Chinese black mushrooms

③ 3 cloves garlic, smashed
6 1-inch sections green onion
6 slices ginger root
6 C. oil for frying
½ T. rice wine

1 T. soy sauce
½ t. salt
½ t. MSG
④ ½ t. sugar
½ t. sesame oil
1 t. cornstarch
⅓ C. water

❶ Debone the frog's legs and cut off feet; mix with ① ; let soak 20 minutes. Heat ② until boiling; cook fried gluten balls 5 minutes (to rid them of oil); remove and drain; cut each into half. Soften Chinese black mushrooms in warm water, remove and discard stems and cut caps into bite-size pieces.

❷ Heat oil for deep-frying; deep-fry frog's legs 1 minute; remove and drain. Remove all but 3 T. oil from pan, reheat and stir-fry ③ until fragrant; add fried gluten balls, rice wine, frog's legs and ④ ; cook 1 minute and add 1 T. oil; toss lightly to mix ingredients and remove; serve.

<table>
<tr><td>豆腐⋯⋯⋯2塊</td><td rowspan="2">酒⋯⋯⋯1大匙</td><td rowspan="2">③</td><td>太白粉1½小匙</td></tr>
</table>

豆腐⋯⋯⋯⋯2塊
① 蒜末⋯⋯⋯1小匙
葱末⋯⋯⋯1大匙
薑末⋯⋯⋯1小匙
絞肉⋯⋯⋯⋯2兩
辣豆瓣醬1大匙

② 酒⋯⋯⋯⋯1大匙
水⋯⋯⋯⋯1杯
味精⋯⋯⋯半小匙
鹽⋯⋯⋯⋯半小匙
醬油⋯⋯⋯1大匙

③ 太白粉1½小匙
水⋯⋯⋯⋯1大匙
蒜苗或葱花少許
花椒粉⋯¼小匙

❶ 豆腐去硬邊切成約1公分小塊。
❷ 把油3大匙燒熱，以中火將①料炒香，續入絞肉及辣豆瓣醬拌炒後，再加②料及豆腐，燒滾即用小火燜煮約3分鐘，以③料勾成薄汁，加熱油半大匙，並洒下蒜苗、花椒粉即成。

麻婆豆腐 Ma-Po's Bean Curd

2　squares bean curd
① 1　t.　chopped garlic
1　T.　chopped green onion
1　t.　chopped ginger root
2　oz. chopped pork
1　T.　hot bean paste ("la do ban jiang")

② 1　T.　rice wine
1　C.　water
½　t.　MSG
½　t.　salt
1　T.　soy sauce

③ 1½ t.　cornstarch
1　T.　water
2　T.　½-inch sections green onion or garlic stalk
¼　t.　Szechuan peppercorn powder*

❶ Remove hard edges dice bean curd.
❷ Heat pan and 3T. oil; stir-fry ① and chopped pork until fragrant, add ② and bean curd, cover and cook 3 minutes, over low heat. Add ③ to thicken and ½T. oil; toss ingredients lightly; remove to serving plate sprinkle green onion or garlic sections and peppercorn powder on top; serve.

*　If unavailable, omit.

<table>
<tr><td>豆腐……1½塊</td><td>冬菇……5片</td><td rowspan="6">②{</td><td>清水……¾杯</td><td>醬油……1大匙</td></tr>
</table>

豆腐……1½塊	冬菇……5片		清水……¾杯	醬油……1大匙
里肌肉……2兩	葱(3公分長)5枝		鹽……半小匙	③{ 太白粉…半大匙
①{ 醬油……1小匙	筍……半枝	②{ 味精……半小匙	水……半大匙
太白粉……1小匙	紅蘿蔔…半枝	糖……半小匙	
麻油……半小匙	芥菜……半棵	麻油……半小匙	
		胡椒……¼小匙	

❶ 豆腐切約18片，里肌肉切薄片拌上①料，冬菇泡軟，筍、紅蘿蔔、芥菜各料煮熟切片（各約7片）。

❷ 油3大匙燒熱，把豆腐煎成兩面均呈金黃色取出，再下3大匙油炒里肌肉及冬菇，見肉顏色變白，隨即放進葱及其他各料，再加②料蓋鍋燒煮，約3分鐘後，加醬油並以③料勾成薄汁，即可食之。

■ 可加味全花瓜（適量），味道更可口。

紅燒豆腐 Red-Cooked Bean Curd with Vegetables

北平菜　　Peking
6人份　6 servings

1½ squares bean curd	5 Chinese black mushrooms	¾ C. water	1 T. soy sauce
2 oz. pork loin	5 1-inch sections green onion	½ t. salt	③{ ½ T. cornstarch
①{ 1 t. soy sauce	½ bamboo shoot	② ½ t. MSG	½ T. water
1 t. cornstarch	½ carrot	½ t. sugar	
½ t. sesame oil	½ stalk mustard cabbage*	½ t. sesame oil	
		¼ t. black pepper	

❶ Cut bean curd into 18 squares; cut pork loin into paper-thin bite-size slices, mix with ① and let sit 20 minutes; Soften black mushrooms in warm water; remove, drain and remove stems; cut caps in half and discard stems. Precook bamboo shoot and carrot in boiling water for 20 minutes; remove and drain. Precook mustard cabbage in boiling water 1 minute; remove, drain and cut into 7 pieces; cut bamboo shoot and carrot into 7 thin slices.

❷ Heat pan and 3T. oil; fry bean curd on both sides until golden brown; remove. Reheat pan and add 3T. oil; stir-fry pork and black mushrooms. When meat changes color, add green onion, precooked vegetables and ②; cover and cook 3 minutes over medium heat. Add soy sauce and ③ to thicken; toss lightly to mix and remove to serving plate; serve.

* If mustard cabbage is unavailable, substitute ½C. snow peas.

豆腐⋯⋯⋯⋯⋯⋯⋯⋯3塊	酒⋯⋯⋯⋯⋯⋯⋯1大匙
麵粉⋯⋯⋯⋯⋯⋯⋯⋯半杯	鹽⋯⋯⋯⋯⋯⋯⋯2小匙
雞蛋(打勻)⋯⋯⋯⋯1個	① 味精⋯⋯⋯⋯⋯1小匙
葱末⋯⋯⋯⋯⋯⋯⋯1大匙	麻油⋯⋯⋯⋯⋯半大匙
薑末⋯⋯⋯⋯⋯⋯⋯1大匙	高湯⋯⋯⋯⋯⋯半杯

❶ 豆腐去硬邊，每塊切成5片(約6公分×2公分×1公分)先沾上麵粉，再沾上打勻蛋液。

❷ 油2大匙燒熱，將豆腐一片片整齊排在鍋底，中火煎約1分鐘，呈金黃色翻面，加油2大匙再煎成金黃色，洒上葱、薑、酒各1大匙並調①料，用叉子，叉透豆腐（使其容易入味），改小火塌至汁收乾即可。

■ 依個人喜好可酌量加入蝦子等料。

鍋塌豆腐 Peking Style Fried Bean Curd

北平菜 Peking
12人份 12 servings

3	squares bean curd	1 T. rice wine
½	C. flour	2 t. salt
1	egg (beaten)	① 1 t. MSG
1	T. chopped green onion	½ T. sesame oil
1	T. chopped ginger root	½ C. stock

❶ Cut bean curd into 2½" x 1" x ½" pieces; coat each piece lightly with flour, then dip into egg.

❷ Heat pan and 2T. oil; arrange bean curd piece by piece evenly at bottom of pan and fry over medium flame for 1 minute; when bean curd is a golden color, turn over, add 2T. oil and fry until golden; add rice wine, scallion, ginger and ① ; pierce bean curd with a fork (to allow liquid to soak through); cook over low flame until liquid is absorbed by bean curd.

豆腐⋯⋯⋯３塊　　鹽⋯⋯⋯¼小匙、胡椒⋯⋯¼小匙　　高湯(或水)⋯１杯　　醬油⋯⋯１大匙
蝦米⋯⋯⋯半兩　①{薑酒⋯１小匙、清水⋯１½大匙　②{鹽⋯⋯⋯⋯半小匙　　③{太白粉⋯１小匙
魚肉⋯⋯⋯１兩　　味精⋯¼小匙　　　　　　　　味精⋯⋯⋯半小匙　　　水⋯⋯⋯半大匙
絞肉⋯⋯⋯２兩

❶ 蝦米略洗與魚肉均剁碎，並與絞肉同盛碗內，入①料攪合後，加太白粉半大匙，調勻成肉餡備
　用。
❷ 豆腐（三寸見方）每塊切四小塊，共計１２小塊，在邊面中間，用刀挖出部份豆腐，內洒太白
　粉，將肉餡塞入並抹平，照此方法，把所有豆腐鑲好待用。
❸ 油四大匙燒熱，把豆腐鑲肉面向鍋底，以中火煎至金黃色，入②料蓋鍋燜熱，隨入醬油１大匙
　，並以③料勾汁，澆上豬油１大匙，及洒入香菜即可。
■ 圍邊用材料：香菜。
■ 鑲好豆腐可煎、可炸、也可蒸。

鑲豆腐 Stuffed Bean Curd

廣東菜　Cantonese
6人份　6 servings

3 squares bean curd			
½ oz. dried shrimp			
1 oz. fish meat			
2 oz. chopped pork			

① {
¼ t. salt
1 t. ginger wine*
¼ t. MSG
¼ t. black pepper
1½ T. water
}

② {
1 C. stock or water
½ t. salt
½ t. MSG
1 T. soy sauce
}

③ {
1 t. cornstarch
½ T. water
}

❶ Lightly rinse dried shrimp; drain and chop finely with fish meat; mix chopped shrimp and fish with chopped pork and add ① ; mix in ½T. cornstarch. Lightly throw mixture against the inside of bowl to combine ingredients thoroughly (filling).

❷ Cut each square of bean curd into 4 pieces (You now have 12 pieces) and cut a hole in the middle of each piece of bean curd; dust with cornstarch, stuff hole with filling; repeat for all squares.

❸ Heat pan and 4T. oil; place stuffed bean curd in pan (meat side down) and fry until golden brown; add ② and cook covered until liquid is nearly evaporated. Add 1T. soy sauce and ③ to thicken; mix and add 1T. oil; remove to serving plate and serve.

■ Garnish with coriander.

* A mixture of rice wine and the juices of smashed ginger root.

<table>
</table>

① ┌ 蝦仁……3兩
  └ 絞肉……3兩

② ┌ 鹽……¼小匙、胡椒……少許
  │ 味精……¼小匙、麻油……¼小匙
  └ 糖……¼小匙、太白粉1小匙

③ ┌ 筍
  │ 紅蘿蔔   切碎
  │ 冬菇   計¼杯
  └ 葱

   豆腐………4塊

④ ┌ 蛋…………1個、麵粉……半杯
  │ 鹽……¼小匙、水………4大匙
  └ 「炸油」……6杯

⑤ ┌ 葱、薑各1小匙、黑醋……1大匙
  │ 番茄醬……1大匙、醬油……1大匙
  └ 糖……1大匙、辣豆瓣醬1小匙

❶ 分別將①料剁碎，調②料再拌入③料成「餡」。

❷ 每塊豆腐橫切除外皮，並片成6大薄片，備盤（塗油）將豆腐1片置上，洒上少許太白粉，塗一層餡加1片豆腐，再洒太白粉及塗餡，如此反覆做豆腐四層，餡三層（2.5公分厚）即成千層豆腐(可做6個)。

❸ 把④料攪拌成蛋糊，塗在千層豆腐表面。

❹ 「炸油」燒熱，把千層豆腐放入以小火炸熟（7分鐘），起鍋前，開大火炸至表面呈金黃色，即撈出切塊，並以調好⑤料沾食。

■ 圍邊用材料：大黃瓜。

千層豆腐 Deep-Fried Layered Bean Curd

台灣菜 Taiwanese
12人份 12 servings

① 3 oz. raw, shelled shrimp
   3 oz. chopped pork

② ¼ t. salt
   ¼ t. MSG
   ¼ t. sugar
   ¼ t. black pepper
   ¼ t. sesame oil
   1 t. cornstarch

③ chopped precooked bamboo shoot
   chopped precooked carrot
   chopped pre-softened Chinese black mushroom
   chopped green onion   } combined ingredients should equal ¼C.

   4 squares bean curd

④ 1 egg
   ¼ t. salt
   ½ C. flour
   4 T. water

6 C. oil for frying

⑤ 1 t. chopped green onion
   1 t. chopped ginger root
   1 T. tomato ketchup
   1 T. sugar
   1 T. worcestershire sauce
   1 T. soy sauce
   1 t. hot bean paste ("la do ban jiang")

❶ Rinse and devein shrimp; separately chop ingredients of ① and add ② ; throw mixture lightly against inside of mixing bowl to combine ingredients; add ③ and mix well. (filling)

❷ Trim the hard edges from the bean curd and discard; slice each bean curd horizontally into 6 slices. Sprinkle a little oil on a plate; place a slice of bean curd on plate and sprinkle a little cornstarch over surface. Add a portion of filling and spread evenly over surface; add another layer of beancurd, sprinkle cornstarch and continue to assemble layers until there are 3 layers of filling and 4 layers of bean curd; (the whole bean curd should be about 1-inch thick). Coat a plate lightly with oil and place finished bean curd on plate; repeat process for 6 other bean curds.

❸ Mix the ingredients of ④ into a batter; slide each stuffed bean curd onto the blade of a cleaver or spatula (to prevent bean curd from splitting); spoon batter on top and sides of bean curd to coat outside.

❹ Heat oil for deep-frying; slide each coated bean curd into the hot oil and deep-fry over low heat for 7 minutes; turn heat to high before removing and cook until golden brown; remove and drain. Cut bean curds into slices and place on serving plate; serve with ⑤ for dipping.

■ Garnish with carrot, cucumber and coriander.

豆腐……………… 2 塊
「炸油」…………… 6 杯
冬菇(泡軟)……… 3 朵
葱(3公分長)… 1 0 枝

① {
高湯…… ¾ 杯
醬油… 1 大匙
蠔油… 1 大匙
味精… ¼ 小匙
糖… ¼ 小匙
}

② {
太白粉… 1 小匙
水…… 2 小匙
麻油…… 1 小匙
}

❶ 冬菇切半，每塊豆腐對切 2 個三角形，每個三角形豆腐再橫切 3 片，共計 1 2 片。

❷ 「炸油」燒開，以大火將豆腐片炸呈金黃色撈出。

❸ 油 4 大匙燒熱，先將葱段及冬菇炒香，隨入①料及豆腐蓋鍋，用小火燒煮 5 分鐘，見餘汁剩一半時，以②料勾汁加上 1 小匙麻油即可。

■ 豆腐可買現成三角形油豆腐。

冬菇扒豆腐 Braised Chinese Mushrooms and Bean Curd

四川菜　Szechuan
6人份　6 servings

2　squares bean curd
6　C. oil for frying
3　pre-softened Chinese black mushrooms
10　1-inch sections green onion

① {
¾　C. stock
1　T. soy sauce
1　T. oyster sauce
¼　t. MSG
¼　t. sugar
}

② {
1　t. cornstarch
2　t. water
}
1　t. sesame oil

❶ Cut Chinese black mushrooms in half; cut bean curd diagonally in half into triangles and then cut each triangle through thickness into 3 slices. (You now have 12 triangular slices)

❷ Heat oil for deep-frying; deep-fry bean curd over high heat until golden brown; remove and drain.

❸ Heat pan and 4T. oil; stir-fry green onion and Chinese black mushrooms until fragrant; add ① and bean curd slices; cover and cook 5 minutes over low heat until the sauce has decreased to about half; add ② to thicken sauce and 1t. sesame oil; toss ingredients lightly and remove to serving plate; serve.

熟筍丁…………¼杯　　毛豆………¼杯　　　辣豆瓣醬…半大匙
熟紅蘿蔔丁……¼杯　　里肌肉……2兩　　②甜麵醬……1大匙
小黃瓜丁………¼杯　①太白粉…半小匙　　　醬油………1大匙
黑豆腐干丁……¼杯　　水………半大匙　　　糖…………半大匙
蝦米…………1大匙　　　　　　　　　　　　味精………¼小匙
花生米…………¼杯

❶ 花生米用温水泡約1小時後去皮，與毛豆同放入開水中煮約5分鐘撈出。里肌肉切丁調①料拌
　勻。

❷ 油4大匙燒熱先將蝦米炒香後倒入肉丁，炒至呈白色時，續將筍、胡蘿蔔、小黃瓜、豆腐干、
　花生米、毛豆等加入拌炒，即全部鏟起。

❸ 油3大匙燒熱，放入②料炒香，隨即加入炒熟各丁，拌炒均勻即起鍋。

八寶辣醬 Eight Treasure Stir-Fried Vegetables

四川菜　Szechuan
6人份　6 servings

¼ C. diced precooked bamboo shoot　¼ C. green peas　　　　　½ T. hot bean paste ("la do ban jiang")
¼ C. diced precooked carrot　　　　2 oz. pork loin　　　　　1 T. sweet bean paste ("tien mien jiang")
¼ C. diced cucumber　　　　　①½ t. cornstarch　　②1 T. soy sauce
¼ C. diced pressed bean curd　　　½ T. water　　　　　　　½ T. sugar
1 T. dried shrimp　　　　　　　　　　　　　　　　　　　¼ t. MSG
¼ C. raw, shelled peanuts

❶ Soak peanuts in warm water for 1 hour; remove, drain and remove skins. Precook peas and peanuts
　about 5 minutes in boiling water; remove and drain. Dice pork loin and mix with ① .

❷ Heat pan and 4T. oil; stir-fry diced pork until it changes color; add bamboo shoot, carrot, cucumber,
　bean curd, dried shrimp, peanuts and peas; stir-fry briefly to heat ingredients and remove.

❸ Reheat pan and 3T. oil; add pre-mixed ② and stir-fry until fragrant; add all other ingredients and mix
　together; remove to serving plate and serve.

豆腐皮…１６張

① 醬油………３大匙、麻油………１大匙
　 鹽…………半小匙、味精………半小匙
　 糖…………１大匙、高湯（或熱水）１杯

紗布（４５公分四方）２張
「炸油」………………半杯

❶ 把①料拌勻後備用。

❷ 將豆腐皮，取一張鋪置在一個長形盤內，塗上約１大匙的①料湯汁，再鋪蓋上第二張，也塗上湯汁，如此將８張豆腐皮均鋪蓋上並塗勻①料，從左右兩邊向中間摺疊成四方形，並捲成約２０公分×５公分長條狀，用紗布包好；另將其他８張豆腐皮，照上述方法，同樣做好。（把湯汁用完，盡量使豆腐皮濕潤）蒸１０分鐘取出，拿掉紗布。

❸ 「炸油」（或麻油）半杯燒熱，投入素雞，小火兩面煎３０秒，呈金黃色時鏟出，切斜塊，整齊裝入盤內即成。

素雞 Vegetarian Chicken Loaves

上海菜　Shanghai
12人份 **12 servings**

16 sheets bean curd skin

① 3　T. soy sauce • ½ t. salt • 1 T. sugar
　 1　T. sesame oil • ½ t. MSG
　 1　C. hot stock or hot water

2　12-inch squares gauze wrapping
½　C. oil or sesame oil

❶ Mix ingredients of ① until sugar has dissolved; separate to 2 portions.
❷ Place 1 bean curd sheet in a flat pan; spread 1T. of ① mixture across surface; place a second bean curd sheet on top of the first with opposite sides together, so that the round edge of the second bean curd is matched with the straight edge of the first bean curd sheet. Add 1T. of ① mixture and spread over sheet; repeat process for 8 more sheets, continuing to rotate each sheet and add ① . Fold sheets to a 8½ x 1½-inch oblong loaf; wrap in gauze or cheesecloth and place in steamer; repeat procedure to make another loaf. Pour any remaining ① mixture over leaves so that they are completely saturated; steam 10 minutes over high heat and remove loaves from gauze; let cool. (bean curd loaves)
❸ Heat oil until medium hot; fry loaves for 30 seconds over low heat until golden brown on all sides; remove to cutting board and slice. Place slices on serving plate and serve.
■ Garnish with turnip slices and coriander.

<table>
<tr><td>絞肉⋯⋯3 兩</td><td rowspan="2">②{</td><td>洋蔥(切碎)⋯¼杯</td><td rowspan="2">③{</td><td>蛋⋯⋯⋯1 個</td></tr>
<tr><td>蝦仁⋯⋯1 兩</td><td>炸扁魚(壓碎)¼兩</td><td>麵粉⋯3 大匙</td></tr>
</table>

① 胡椒⋯⅛小匙、糖⋯⋯¼小匙
鹽⋯⋯¼小匙、麻油⋯¼小匙
味精⋯⅛小匙、太白粉半大匙

茄子(細)⋯⋯1 條
韮菜⋯⋯⋯⋯2 條

豆腐皮⋯1 張
紫菜⋯⋯1 張
「炸油」⋯6 杯

❶ 絞肉、蝦仁剁爛，調入①料拌勻，並用打，加入②料分成二份。

❷ 茄子，整條炸軟（約 1 分鐘）撈出，撕成 2 條，韮菜也在油內燙熟（也可用水煮）。

❸ 豆腐皮、紫菜各切二半（豆腐皮修成長方形），每張豆腐皮糊上③料攪勻之蛋糊後，舖上紫菜，再塗蛋糊及肉餡，將茄子與韮菜放在當中捲成長條狀，中火炸四分鐘至呈金黃色撈起，切塊後即以花椒鹽(乾淨鍋，將鹽 2 大匙炒熱，呈微黃時加 1 小匙花椒粉或五香粉拌勻而成)沾食。

■ 圍邊用材料：香菜、番茄。

腐皮茄子 Eggplant Rolls with Chopped Pork

台灣菜 Taiwanese
6人份 6 servings

3 oz. chopped pork
1 oz. raw, shelled shrimp

①{
⅛ t. black pepper
¼ t. salt
⅛ t. MSG
¼ t. sugar
¼ t. sesame oil
½ T. cornstarch

②{
¼ C. chopped onion
1 T. chopped, brill fish ("bien u gan") *1

2 slices eggplant, 4 inches long and ⅓-inch thick
2 stalks Chinese chives *2 or leeks

③{
1 egg
3 T. flour

1 sheet bean curd skin
1 sheet nori or purple laver
6 C. oil for frying

❶ Rinse and devein shrimp; drain. Separately chop pork and shrimp finely; add ① and throw mixture lightly against the inside of bowl to combine ingredients to a smooth paste; add ② and mix together; separate into 2 portions. (filling).

❷ Heat oil for deep-frying; deep-fry the eggplant slices for ① minutes until soft; drain. Deep-fry chives in oil for 5 seconds; remove and drain.

❸ Cut bean curd skin in half and trim each half to a square; cut nori sheet in half. Spread some of ③ across surface of bean curd skin; place nori sheet on top and spread more of ③ over surface. Spread 1 portion of filling across closer half of nori sheet. Lay 1 section eggplant and 1 stalk Chinese chive across filling in center and roll up tightly; repeat for other roll. Heat oil for deep-frying and deep-fry rolls over medium heat for 4 minutes until golden brown; remove, drain and cut rolls into bite-size sections. Place pieces on serving plate and serve with 5-spice salt for dipping.

■ Garnish with coriander and tomato slices

*1 Dried brill fish is available at any Chinese grocery store. First fry in oil over low heat until golden; remove, drain and chop finely, then use as directed. If unavailable, omit.

*2 Green onions may be substituted for Chinese chives.

	百頁………8张	②	葱末…半小匙	③	蒸百頁餘汁 } ¾杯
①	小蘇打…1 小匙		薑末…半小匙		高湯
	清水………2 杯		鹽……¼ 小匙		冬菇…………3 朵
	蝦仁………2 兩		味精……少許		熟筍絲……¼ 杯
	絞肉………3 兩		麻油…半大匙		鹽…………¼ 小匙
				④	太白粉……1 小匙
					水…………2 小匙

❶ 百頁以①料浸泡２０分鐘後，用清水沖洗多次備用。

❷ 蝦仁剁碎，與絞肉同調②料拌勻成肉餡分成８份。冬菇泡軟、切細絲備用。

百頁攤開，將１份肉餡在中間抹成８公分長、２公分寬，並包成春捲狀，全部做好，放入蒸鍋大火蒸約１０分鐘，餘汁倒出，百頁捲擺在盤上。

❸ 將③料燒開，以④料勾汁，澆上麻油１小匙，淋在百頁捲上即成。

三鮮百頁捲 Stuffed Bean Curd Rolls

上海菜　Shanghai
6人份　6 servings

	8 bean curd sheets ("bai ye")	②	½ t. chopped green onion	③	steaming liquid } ¾C.
①	1 t. baking soda		½ t. chopped ginger root		stock
	2 C. water		¼ t. salt		3 Chinese black mushrooms
	2 oz. raw, shelled shrimp		¼ t. MSG		¼ precooked shredded bamboo shoot
	3 oz. chopped pork		½ T. sesame oil		¼ t. salt
				④	1 t. cornstarch
					2 t. water

❶ Place bean curd sheets in ① and soak 20 minutes until soft; remove and rinse lightly in water until sheets are rid of any baking soda solution.

❷ Rinse and devein shrimp; drain and chop finely; mix with chopped pork and ② . Lightly throw mixture against inside of mixing bowl to combine ingredients (filling); separate filling into 8 portions. Soften Chinese black mushrooms in warm water; remove, drain. Remove stems (discard) and shred caps. On each bean curd sheet, place one portion of filling diagonally across sheet; fold up bean curd sheet to enclose filling and form a roll. Lightly oil a heatproof plate; place folded rolls on plate and place in steamer; steam 10 minutes over high heat; remove steamed rolls and place on serving plate, (retain liquid and use in ③ . If not enough, add stock to equal ¾C.)

❸ Place ③ in a pan (no oil) and bring liquid to a boil; add ④ to thicken and 1t. sesame oil; stir-lightly and pour over steamed rolls; serve.

素腸⋯⋯⋯⋯2朵　　五花肉⋯⋯⋯⋯2兩
素腸⋯⋯⋯⋯5條　　嫩薑絲⋯⋯⋯⋯半杯

① 醬油⋯⋯⋯1½大匙
　 鹽⋯⋯⋯⋯⋯半小匙
　 味精⋯⋯⋯⋯半小匙
　 胡椒⋯⋯⋯⋯¼小匙
　 麻油⋯⋯⋯⋯1小匙

❶ 素腸撕成細絲，冬菇泡軟、五花肉均切成細絲。
❷ 將油3大匙燒熱，先把肉絲爆香，續入冬菇、素腸炒熟，最後加嫩薑絲 及①料，拌炒即可盛盤

■ 素腸在豆腐攤有售。

冬菇素腸 Stir-Fried Chinese Mushrooms with "Su-Tsang"

<table>
<tr><td></td><td>台灣菜
6人份</td><td>Taiwanese
6 servings</td></tr>
</table>

2　Chinese black mushrooms　　2　oz. fresh bacon
5　rolls "su-tsang"*　　　　　½　C. shredded ginger root

① 1½ T, soy sauce
　 ½　t. salt
　 ½　t. MSG
　 ¼　t. black pepper
　 1　t. sesame oil

❶ Shred "su-tsang" and soften black mushrooms in warm water; remove stems (discard) and shred caps. Cut bacon into shreds.
❷ Heat pan and 3T. oil; stir-fry bacon until it changes color and add black mushroom and "su-tsang" shreds; stir-fry over high heat until fragrant; add shredded ginger and ① . Lightly toss ingredients to mix together and remove to serving plate; serve.
* "Su-tsang" are long, thin rolls made of wheat gluten and may be purchased at a Chinese grocery store.

烤麩⋯⋯⋯⋯⋯4個
「炸油」⋯⋯⋯⋯3杯
葱(3公分長)⋯6枝
薑⋯⋯⋯⋯⋯6片

① {
冬菇(泡軟切半)⋯¼杯
金針(泡軟打結)⋯¼杯
木耳(泡軟略切)⋯半杯
筍(煮熟切片)⋯⋯半杯
豆腐干(切片)⋯⋯1杯
}

② {
酒⋯⋯⋯半大匙
水⋯⋯⋯⋯2杯
醬油⋯⋯⋯3大匙
味精⋯⋯⋯1小匙
糖⋯⋯⋯2小匙
胡椒⋯¼小匙
麻油⋯半大匙
}

❶ 烤麩切0.5公分薄片，「炸油」燒熱，大火將烤麩炸呈金黃色撈出，放入開水內煮約3分鐘，擠乾水份。

❷ 油4大匙燒熱，將葱薑炒香，隨入①料略炒，再加酒、②料及烤麩小火燒煮10分鐘即可。

■ 烤麩在豆腐攤買。

冬菇烤麩 Stir-Fried "Kau-fu" with Assorted Vegetables 上海菜 Shanghai 12人份 12 servings

4 sections "kau fu"*
3 C. oil for frying
6 1-inch sections green onion
6 slices ginger root

① {
¼ C. pre-softened Chinese black mushrooms, halved
¼ C. pre-softened tiger lilies, tied into knots
½ C. pre-softened wood ears, halved
½ C. precooked sliced bamboo shoot
1 C. sliced pressed bean curd
}

② {
½ T. rice wine
2 C. water
3 T. soy sauce
1 t. MSG
2 t. sugar
¼ t. black pepper
½ T. sesame oil
}

❶ Cut "kau fu" into ¼-inch slices. Heat oil for deep-frying; deep-fry "kau fu" until golden brown; remove and drain. Cook "kau fu" 3 minutes in boiling water to remove excess oil; remove and drain.

❷ Heat pan and 4T. oil; stir-fry green onion and ginger until fragrant; add ① and stir-fry 1 minute over high heat; add rice wine, ② and "kau fu" slices. Turn heat to low and cook 10 minutes until liquid is almost dry; remove to serving plate and serve.

* "Kau fu" is a spongy-type of ingredient made from wheat gluten, which may be stored for a long time. It may be purchased at a Chinese grocery store where bean curd is sold.

①
- 絞肉…4兩
- 蝦仁…2兩
- 冬菇…2朵
- 蛋……3個

②
- 鹽……半小匙、麻油……半小匙
- 糖……¼小匙、水……1大匙
- 味精…¼小匙、太白粉…半大匙
- 胡椒…¼小匙

③
- 高湯………半杯
- 鹽……¼小匙
- 味精……¼小匙
- 麻油……¼小匙
- 胡椒……¼小匙

④
- 太白粉…1小匙
- 水………1小匙

❶ ①料之蝦仁切碎，冬菇泡軟切細絲連同絞肉置碗內，加入②料拌合成餡，分成12個圓形肉丸備用。

❷ 蛋打勻；鍋燒熱，用布或紙沾油擦鍋，蛋分兩次下鍋（用小火），慢煎成蛋皮，切成細絲。

❸ 將肉丸滾上蛋絲成球狀，置抹油之蒸盤大火蒸約10分鐘取出置盤。

❹ 油1大匙燒熱，加酒¼小匙及③料，燒開以④料勾成薄汁澆在蛋球上即成。

■ 圍邊用材料：青菜（用油加適量鹽炒熟）。

東坡绣球 Shredded Egg Balls

廣東菜 Cantonese
6人份 6 servings

①
- 4 oz. chopped pork
- 2 oz. raw, shelled shrimp
- 2 Chinese black mushrooms
- 3 eggs

②
- ½ t. salt
- ¼ t. sugar
- ¼ t. MSG
- ¼ t. black pepper
- ½ t. sesame oil
- 1 T. water
- ½ T. cornstarch

③
- ½ C. stock
- ¼ t. salt
- ¼ t. MSG
- ¼ t. sesame oil
- ¼ t. black pepper

④
- 1 t. cornstarch
- 1 t. water

❶ Rinse and devein shrimp; chop finely. Soften black mushrooms in warm water; remove, drain and remove stems (discard); shred caps. Mix ingredients of ① and ② ; throw lightly against inside of mixing bowl to thoroughly combine ingredients. (filling) Divide filling into 12 pieces and roll pieces into balls.

❷ Lightly beat eggs; heat pan until medium hot; coat surface of pan lightly with oil; add half of eggs and tilt pan so that egg spreads evenly and thinly over bottom of pan. Cook over medium heat until "egg sheet" is firm; flip over and brown lightly on opposite side; remove to cutting board and shred; repeat for other half of egg mixture.

❸ Coat meatballs with shredded egg; lightly coat a heatproof plate with oil. Place shredded egg balls on plate and place in steamer; steam over high heat for 10 minutes; remove balls to serving plate.

❹ Heat pan and 1T. oil; add ¼t. rice wine and ③ . When mixture begins to boil, add ④ to thicken; pour over shredded egg balls, Reheat pan and 4T. Oil.

■ stir-fry spinach and ¼t. salt until spinach is limp; remove and arrange around shredded egg balls; serve.

蛋‥‥‥‥‥‥3個
絞肉‥‥‥2½兩

① 味精‥‥‥‥¼小匙
醬油‥‥‥‥1小匙
胡椒‥‥‥‥¼小匙
麻油‥‥‥‥¼小匙
太白粉‥‥‥1小匙
葱薑末各‥‥¼小匙

② 酒‥‥‥‥‥1小匙
水‥‥‥‥‥¾杯
醬油‥‥‥‥1大匙
鹽‥‥‥‥‥¼小匙
糖‥‥‥‥‥¼小匙
味精‥‥‥‥半小匙

❶ 先將蛋盛在大碗裏調散。將絞肉調上①料拌成肉餡。

❷ 鍋燒熱塗少許油在鍋面（用小火）舀一大匙蛋汁在鍋裏，鍋子轉動使成直徑７公分之圓形蛋皮，包上１小匙肉餡再將蛋皮合攏成半圓形即成蛋餃，按照上法全部做好，大約可做１２～１５個。

❸ 乾淨鍋放入煎好的蛋餃及②料，蓋鍋，把蛋餃裏面的肉燒熟，見汁將收乾，即可起鍋。

蛋餃子 Golden Egg Dumplings

北平菜 Peking
6人份 6 servings

3 eggs
2½ oz. chopped pork

① ¼ t. MSG
1 t. soy sauce
¼ t. black pepper
¼ t. sesame oil
1 t. cornstarch
¼ t. chopped green onion
¼ t. chopped ginger root

② 1 t. rice wine
¾ C. water
1 T. soy sauce
¼ t. salt
¼ t. sugar
½ t. MSG

❶ Lightly beat eggs; mix chopped pork with ① . (filling)

❷ Heat a lightly oiled pan; spoon 1T. egg into pan and rotate pan to form a 2½-inch pancake; place 1t. filling in middle and fold egg pancake over in half; cook over low heat until all sides are golden; remove and repeat to make 12-15 dumplings.

❸ Place ② in a pan with egg dumplings; cover and cook over medium heat until liquid is almost dry (about 5 minutes); remove to serving plate and serve.

鹹鴨蛋⋯⋯⋯⋯⋯3個　　鹽⋯⋯⋯⋯⋯⋯⋯半小匙
皮蛋⋯⋯⋯⋯⋯⋯3個　①　猪油（或麻油）⋯⋯1大匙
雞蛋⋯⋯⋯⋯⋯⋯3個　　味精⋯⋯⋯⋯⋯⋯$\frac{1}{4}$小匙
　　　　　　　　　　　清水⋯⋯⋯⋯⋯⋯⋯3大匙

❶ 將鹹鴨蛋煮熟，連同皮蛋均切1公分四方小丁。

❷ 雞蛋加①料，用筷子攪勻，再把鹹蛋、皮蛋，放入攪拌，即倒在方型便當盒中（四週先塗少許油），用蒸鍋中火蒸約２０分鐘，蒸熟取出候冷，切塊排於菜盤即可。

■ 如在便當盒內放置玻璃紙（二面抹油）可使蒸好之三色蛋較容易倒出。

■ 圍邊用材料：香菜。

三色蛋 Three-Color Egg Slices

北平菜　　Peking
12人份　12 servings

3　salty eggs
3　preserved ("thousand year old") eggs　　　① ½　t.　salt
3　chicken eggs　　　　　　　　　　　　　　　　1　T.　lard or sesame oil
　　　　　　　　　　　　　　　　　　　　　　　　¼　t.　MSG
　　　　　　　　　　　　　　　　　　　　　　　　3　T.　water

❶ Cook salty eggs in boiling water about 10 minutes until hard-boiled; remove shells from salty eggs and preserved eggs and dice into ½-inch cubes.

❷ Beat chicken eggs lightly and add ① ; mix lightly and add other diced eggs; mix again. Lightly oil a 6 x 4 inch square mold or box*, pour egg mixture into mold and place in steamer. Steam over medium heat for about 20 minutes until eggs are firm; remove mold from steamer and let cool; invert onto cutting board and slice. Place slices on serving plate and serve.

*　A lightly oiled piece of heavy-duty cellophane may be used to line greased mold to facilitate removal of egg mold.

■ Garnish with coriander.

雞蛋…………4 個　　　　油…………半杯

① ┌ 鹽…………半小匙
　│ 味精…………¼ 小匙
　│ 麵粉…………1 小匙
　└ 水…………半大匙

❶ 雞蛋打散，調①料拌勻備用。

❷ 油半杯燒熱，倒入打勻蛋汁，改小火蓋嚴烘３分鐘（轉動鍋子，使蛋烘均勻）呈金黃色，餘油倒出翻面蓋嚴再烘３分鐘，呈金黃色取出即成。

白油烘蛋 Golden Omelet

四川菜　Szechuan
6人份　6 servings

4　eggs　　　　½ C. oil
① ┌ ½ t. salt
　│ ¼ t. MSG
　│ 1 t. flour
　└ ½ T. water

❶ Scramble eggs; mix ① thoroughly with eggs.
❷ Heat ½C. oil; pour in egg mixture, cover pan and cook over low heat 3 minutes (tip pan so that egg mixture is distributed evenly). When egg is golden, flip over and cook another 3 minutes; Serve.

①	雞蛋…１０個 鹽…1½ 小匙 味精…1 小匙 糖…1 小匙 胡椒…¼ 小匙 麻油…1 小匙	②	蝦仁……………1 杯 「炸油」…………1 杯 熟筍絲…………1 杯 叉燒肉絲………半杯 韮黃（３公分長）…1 杯	③	水…………1 杯 鹽………半小匙 味精……¼ 小匙 太白粉 1½ 小匙

❶ 蝦仁拭乾水份，泡油３０秒取出。

❷ 雞蛋調①料（打散）並與蝦仁及②料拌合。

❸ 油５大匙燒熱倒入拌好的材料炒拌按扁成圓餅狀，兩面煎呈金黃色並倒入③料燒沸即成。

■ 圍邊用材料：香菜。

美蓉炒蛋 Egg Foo Yung

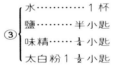

廣東菜 Cantonese
12人份 **12 servings**

①	10 eggs 1½ t. salt 1 t. MSG 1 t. sugar ¼ t. black pepper 1 t. sesame oil	②	1 C. raw, shelled shrimp 1 C. oil for frying 1 C. shredded precooked bamboo shoot ½ C. shredded roasted pork 1 C. 1-inch sections Chinese chives*	③	1 C. water ½ t. salt ¼ t. MSG 1½ t. cornstarch

❶ Devein shrimp; rinse and drain. Heat oil until medium hot and deep-fry shrimp over medium heat until changed in color; remove and drain.

❷ Lightly beat eggs; add ① and mix; add precooked shrimp, ② , and stir lightly.

❸ Heat pan and 5T. oil; add egg mixture and lightly stir-fry over medium heat until mixture has begun to solidify; flatten lightly to form a big pancake. Continue to cook until golden brown. Flip over to uncooked side and cook until golden; add ③ and when sauce has thickened, toss lightly to coat pancake; remove to serving plate and serve.

* If Chinese chives are unavailable, substitute green onion or leeks.

■ Garnish with coriander

雞蛋⋯⋯⋯⋯⋯5個　　　　「炸油」⋯⋯⋯⋯⋯半杯

① 鹽⋯⋯⋯⋯⋯⋯ 1 小匙　　　洋葱(切絲)⋯⋯ 1½ 杯

味精⋯⋯⋯⋯⋯半小匙

胡椒⋯⋯⋯⋯⋯¼小匙

麻油⋯⋯⋯⋯⋯半小匙

❶ 雞蛋加①料打勻備用。

❷ 油半杯燒熱，將洋葱炒軟，放入打好蛋液炒至剛剛凝固不可過老即成。

■ 圍邊用材料：香菜。

洋葱炒蛋 Stir-Fried Eggs with Onion Shreds

5 eggs

① 1 t. salt
½ t. MSG
¼ t. black pepper
½ t. sesame oil

½ C. oil for frying
1½ c. shredded onion

❶ Add ① to eggs and beat lightly.

❷ Heat pan and ½C. oil; stir-fry onion until soft; add egg mixture and stir-fry until eggs become slightly scrambled, but are still soft (do not overcook). Remove eggs to serving plate and serve.

■ Garnish with coriander.

鵪蛋⋯⋯⋯8個	蝦仁⋯⋯⋯6兩	① 酒⋯⋯⋯⋯半小匙、麻油⋯⋯⋯半小匙
土司⋯⋯⋯5片		鹽⋯⋯⋯⋯半小匙、蛋白⋯⋯⋯半個
火腿末⋯1大匙		味精⋯⋯¼小匙、太白粉⋯⋯1大匙
黑芝麻⋯1大匙		胡椒⋯⋯⋯¼小匙
香菜⋯⋯15片		「炸油」⋯⋯⋯⋯⋯⋯⋯⋯6杯

❶ 鵪蛋水煮（5分鐘）去殼，切半，每片土司去除硬邊，切3片修成4公分×4公分菱形。

❷ 蝦仁洗淨並拭乾水份，用刀壓成蝦泥，盛於大碗內加①料，用手攪動至蝦絨狀（前後約5分鐘）。

❸ 取1片土司抹上薄薄一層蝦絨，中間放半個鵪蛋，四週再以蝦絨小心抹平，上置1片香菜，用筷子分別沾上黑芝麻與火腿點綴其上備用。

❹ 「炸油」燒熱，中火炸土司鵪蛋至熟（1分鐘），控制火候，以免表面炸焦。

土司鵪蛋 Shrimp Toast with Quail Eggs

四川菜　Szechuan
12人份 12 servings

8 quail eggs
5 slices white bread
1 T. chopped ham
1 T. black sesame seeds
15 sprigs of coriander

6 oz. raw, shelled shrimp

①
½ t. rice wine
½ t. salt
¼ t. MSG
¼ t. black pepper
½ t. sesame oil
½ egg white
1 T. cornstarch
6 C. oil for frying

❶ Cook eggs about 5 minutes until hard-boiled; remove shells and cut each egg in half; remove crusts from bread (discard) and cut each slice into 3 sections; trim each section into a diamond shape.

❷ Rinse and devein shrimp; chop finely and mix with ① ; lightly throw mixture against inside of bowl about 5 minutes to form a smooth paste.

❸ Spread a portion of shrimp paste on a piece of bread; place half of a quail egg on shrimp paste. Add a little more shrimp paste around edges of egg to secure it to bread and smooth surface. Dip the tip of a chopstick in chopped ham and then place ham on shrimp paste; repeat process for sesame seeds. Place one section of coriander beside ham and sesame seeds.

❹ Heat oil until medium hot; deep-fry shrimp paste slices about 1 minute until golden brown; remove, drain and place on serving plate; serve.

■ To prevent bread from picking up impurities during deep-frying, deep-fry in clean oil.

<table>
<tr><td>鵪蛋·············24個</td><td>醬油············2大匙</td></tr>
</table>

① {
鵪蛋·············24個
豆腐皮············4張
蛋··············1個
太白粉···········3大匙
「炸油」···········6杯
}

② {
醬油············2大匙
糖·············1大匙
鎮江醋··········1大匙
麻油············半大匙
太白粉··········半小匙
水·············2大匙
}

❶ 鵪蛋煮熟去殼，每張豆腐皮分切為6小張，①料調成麵糊。

❷ 將豆腐皮塗勻麵糊，包上1個鵪蛋，依此法全部包好備用。

❸ 「炸油」燒熱，中火將包好鵪蛋炸2分鐘呈金黃色撈出，②料燒滾，供沾食用。

虎皮鵪蛋 Wrapped Quail Eggs

江浙菜 Shanghai
12人份 12 servings

① {
24 quail eggs
4 sheets bean curd skin
1 egg
3 T. cornstarch
6 C. oil for frying
}

② {
2 T. soy sauce
1 T. sugar
1 T. vinegar
½ T. sesame oil
½ t. cornstarch
2 T. water
}

❶ Cook eggs until hard-boiled; remove shells; slice bean curd skin into 6 small sheets; mix ① into a paste.

❷ Spread paste evenly on bean curd sheets; wrap each egg in sheet so that it is totally covered.

❸ Heat oil; over a medium flame, deep-fry eggs until golden (about 2 minutes); remove heat ② to boiling; pour mixture is a small bowl for dipping and serve with eggs.

鶉蛋⋯⋯⋯⋯⋯2打　　酒⋯⋯半大匙
醬油⋯⋯⋯⋯⋯2大匙　①{水⋯⋯⋯半杯、糖⋯⋯1小匙　②{太白粉⋯半大匙
小青江菜⋯⋯12棵　　鹽⋯⋯⅓小匙、胡椒⋯¼小匙　　水⋯⋯⋯半大匙
洋菇⋯⋯⋯⋯⋯2杯　　味精⋯半小匙、醬油⋯3大匙
「炸油」⋯⋯⋯⋯3杯
葱(3公分長)⋯6枝

❶ 鶉蛋煮約5分鐘去殼趁熱入醬油2大匙，沾勻待用。

❷ 青江菜取嫩莖，用開水煮約1分鐘，撈出漂涼，洋菇燙開水半分鐘。

❸ 「炸油」燒開，鶉蛋炸至金黃色撈出，留油3大匙，將青江菜加鹽1小匙略炒盛盤。

❹ 油4大匙燒熱，將葱炒香，隨加洋菇略炒，下酒半大匙及①料燒煮約2分鐘，放入鶉蛋並以②料勾汁，最後淋上熟油1大匙即可。

洋菇扒鶉蛋 Braised Mushrooms with Quail Eggs

廣東菜　Cantonese
12人份　12 servings

2 dozen quail eggs
2 T. soy sauce
12 stalks green cabbage (1⅓ lbs)*
2 C. canned button mushrooms
3 C. oil for frying
6 1-inch sections green onion

½ T. rice wine
½ C. water
①{
⅓ t. salt
½ t. MSG
1 t. sugar
¼ t. black pepper
3 T. soy sauce

②{
½ T. cornstarch
½ T. water

❶ Cook quail eggs in boiling water for 5 minutes until hard-boiled, remove, drain and remove shells; mix with 2T. soy sauce while still warm.

❷ Remove any old leaves from green cabbage and discard; cut cabbage into 4-inch sections. Precook in boiling water for 1 minute; remove and precook mushrooms in water for ½ minute; remove and place vegetables in cold water to cool; remove and drain.

❸ Heat oil for deep-frying and deep-fry quail eggs over high heat until golden brown; remove and drain. Remove all but 3T. oil from pan and reheat; stir-fry green cabbage sections with ⅓ t. salt over high heat for 30 secodns, remove and arrange on serving plate as illustrated.

❹ Reheat pan and 4T. oil; stir-fry green onion until fragrant and add mushrooms, ½T. rice wine, and ① ; cook 2 minutes over high heat and add quail eggs and ② to thicken.　Add 1T. oil and toss lightly to mix ingredients; remove to serving plate and serve.

* If green cabbage is unavailable, substitute celery cabbage or broccoli, cut into sections ½-inch thick.

絞肉········2 兩
粉絲········2 把

① 葱末········2 小匙
　 薑末········1 小匙
　 辣豆瓣醬···半大匙

② 鹽·········¾ 小匙
　 味精········¼ 小匙
　 醬油········2 大匙
　 糖·········1 小匙
　 太白粉·····1 小匙
　 高湯·········2 杯

❶ 粉絲用剪刀略剪，以開水燙軟撈起備用。

❷ 油4大匙燒熱，將絞肉炒約2分鐘，加入①料拌炒，並下粉絲及②料，改小火燜煮約8分鐘即成。

■ 圍邊用材料：香菜。

螞蟻上樹 Stir-Fried Bean Threads with Chopped Pork

四川菜　Szechuan
12人份 **12 servings**

2　oz. chopped pork
2　packages bean threads

① 2　t.　chopped green onion
　 1　t.　chopped ginger root
　 ½　T.　hot bean paste ("la do ban jiang")

② ¾　t.　salt
　 ¼　t.　MSG
　 2　T.　soy sauce
　 1　t.　sugar
　 1　t.　cornstarch
　 2　C.　stock or water

❶ Cut bean threads into 8-inch sections; soften in warm water and drain.
❷ Heat pan and 4T. oil; stir-fry chopped pork for 2 minutes and add ① ; stir-fry until fragrant and add bean threads and ② ; cover and simmer over low heat for about 8 minutes; remove to serving plate and serve.
■ Garnish with coriander.

干貝⋯⋯⋯⋯⋯⋯⋯⋯⋯⋯半兩
紅蘿蔔球⋯⋯⋯⋯⋯⋯⋯⎫
白蘿蔔球⋯⋯⋯⋯⋯⋯⋯⎬ 淨重１０兩
菜心球(或小黃瓜球)⋯⋯⎭ （約２½杯）

① ⎰ 鹽⋯⋯⋯⋯⋯⋯⋯⋯⋯１小匙
⎱ 味精⋯⋯⋯⋯⋯⋯⋯¼小匙
糖⋯⋯⋯⋯⋯⋯⋯⋯半小匙
高湯⋯⋯⋯⋯⋯⋯⋯⋯２杯

② ⎰ 太白粉⋯⋯⋯⋯⋯１½小匙
⎱ 水⋯⋯⋯⋯⋯⋯⋯⋯１大匙

❶ 洗淨干貝，加温水半杯，置蒸鍋內，蒸約半小時取出，撕成細絲備用。

❷ 紅、白蘿蔔、菜心去皮，分別切成一寸見方之小塊，再削修成圓球狀（或用挖圓器挖成球狀）
。先將紅、白蘿蔔球，入滾水內煮至半軟（７分鐘），撈出漂涼，再把菜心球，加鹽同煮（４
分鐘），半軟亦撈出漂涼。

❸ 鍋入①料及紅、白蘿蔔球、菜心球，燒煮入味撈出，置於菜盤內，餘汁再入干貝連蒸汁，以②
料勾汁，淋於菜上即可。

■ 此菜宜宴客，如家常將干貝改用蝦米，做法同上。

干貝三色球 Scallops with Tri-Colored Balls

北平菜　　Peking
6人份　　6 servings

½ oz. dried scallops *[1]
½ lb. carrots
½ lb. turnips *[2]
½ lb. cucumbers

① ⎰ 1 t.　salt
⎱ ¼ t.　MSG
½ t.　sugar
2 C.　stock

② ⎰ 1½ t.　cornstarch
⎱ 1 T.　water

❶ Rinse dried scallops; drain and place in ½C. warm water; place in steamer and steam 30 minutes over medium heat until soft; shred.

❷ Remove the skin from carrot, turnip and cucumber; cut each into 1-inch cubes; trim cubes to balls or use a melon scoop to make balls. (combined balls should equal about 2½C.) Cook turnip and carrot balls in 6C. boiling water for 7 minutes; drain and place in cold water to cool. Place cucumber balls in boiling water with 2t. salt and cook 4 minutes; remove and place in cold water; drain.

❸ In a pan, place ① and vegetable balls; cook 10 minutes over low heat; remove balls to serving plate. Reheat liquid and add ② to thicken and shredded scallops; pour over vegetable balls and serve.

*[1] In family cooking, dried shrimp may be substituted.

*[2] If turnips are unavailable, substitute icicle radish.

小菜心···1斤半　　｜高湯··········4杯　②｜太白粉······2小匙
玉米筍······2罐　①｜鹽·········1½小匙　　｜水·········2小匙
草菇········2罐　　｜味精······1小匙　　雞油········1大匙
番茄(小)···3個

❶ 小菜心去老葉燙熟，番茄用沸水略燙去皮，各放入冷水內泡涼撈出，然後番茄每只對開成4塊。

❷ 鍋放入多的①料燒滾，依序分別投入小菜心、玉米筍、草菇、番茄，分別撈出。取大盤，整齊的排上小菜心和玉米筍，再把番茄排成如圖狀，最後置草菇於中央，煮菜湯汁不要。

❸ 另剩餘①料燒滾，②料勾成薄汁，澆在四色素菜上，淋上雞油，即成。

四色素菜 "Four Kinds of Vegetables" Plate

四川菜　Szechuan
12人份　12 servings

2 lbs. heart of green vegetables*
1—2 lbs. can baby corn shoots
1—2 lbs. can straw mushrooms
3 medium-sized tomatoes

① 4 C. stock
　1½ t. salt
　1 t. MSG

② 2 t. cornstarch
　2 t. water
　1 T. melted chicken fat

❶ Remove any old leaves from heart of green vegetables; precook stalks in boiling water for 1 minute; remove and drain. Blanch tomatoes in boiling water and remove skin and seeds; place green vegetable and tomatoes in cold water to cool; drain. Cut each tomato into 4 sections.

❷ Place ⅔ of ① in a pan and heat until boiling; add heart of green vegetables, corn shoots and mushrooms and cook 2 minutes; remove and cook tomatoes 2 minutes in same liquid; remove and discard liquid. Arrange all vegetables on serving plate as illustrated.

❸ Heat the remaining ⅓ of ① until boiling; add ② to thicken slightly and pour over vegetables; sprinkle melted chicken fat on top and serve.

* "Syau tsai syin" is the pictured Chinese vegetable which may be purchased at a Chinese grocery store. If unavailable, substitute celery cabbage and cut into sections about 3-inches long and ½-inch thick.

包心菜（或大白菜）… 1 斤

① 干辣椒……半杯
花椒粒… 1 〇粒
薑末……半大匙

② 太白粉…半小匙
味精……¼小匙
醬油……¾大匙
酒………半小匙
麻油……半大匙
糖………半大匙
鎮江醋…半大匙

❶ 包心菜切塊，干辣椒切2公分長段。
❷ 油4大匙燒熱，用大火炒包心菜，約1分鐘取出，瀝乾水份。
❸ 油4大匙燒熱，將①料炒香，再入包心菜及②料炒勻即可。

搶白菜 Stir-Fried Cabbage with Szechuan Peppers

四川菜　Szechuan
12人份 **12 servings**

1⅓ lbs. Chinese cabbage

① ½ C. dried hot red peppers
10 Szechuan peppercorns
½ T. chopped ginger root

② ½ t. cornstarch
¼ t. MSG
¾ T. soy sauce
½ t. rice wine
½ T. sesame oil
½ T. sugar
½ T. vinegar

❶ Rinse cabbage and cut into 2-inch squares; cut dried peppers into ½-inch sections.
❷ Heat pan and 4T. oil; stir-fry cabbage over high heat until soft (about 1 minute); remove and drain.
❸ Reheat pan and 4T. oil; stir-fry ① until fragrant and add cabbage and ② ; stir-fry briefly to mix ingredients and remove to serving plate; serve.

白菜………1斤　　薑…………2片　　酒…………半大匙

冬菇………3朵　　　高湯…………半杯

火腿………6片　① 鹽…………1½小匙

蝦米……2大匙　　　味精………半小匙

　　　　　　　② 太白粉……半大匙

　　　　　　　　　水…………半大匙

　　　　　　　　　雞油………半小匙

❶ 白菜洗淨切大塊；放入6杯滾水內燒煮3分鐘，撈起，瀝乾水份，蝦米泡水10分鐘備用。

❷ 油2大匙燒熱，將薑、冬菇、火腿、蝦米炒香，續將白菜略炒再加酒及①料待滾，以②料勾成薄汁，加入雞油即成。

雞油白菜 Stir-Fried Cabbage in Chicken Sauce

上海菜　Shanghai
6人份　6 servings

1⅓lbs. Chinese cabbage

2 slices ginger root
3 pre-softened Chinese black mushrooms
6 thin slices precooked Chinese ham
2 T. dried shrimp

　　　½ T. rice wine
① ½ C. stock
　 1½ t. salt
　 ½ t. MSG
② ½ T. cornstarch
　 ½ T. water
　　　½ t. melted chicken fat

❶ Rinse cabbage and cut into bite-size pieces (about 2-inch squares). Boil 6C. water and add cabbage pieces; cook 3 minutes and remove; drain. Soak dried shrimp in warm water for 10 minutes; remove and drain.

❷ Heat pan and 2T. oil; stir-fry ginger root, black mushrooms, ham and dried shrimp until fragrant; add cabbage and briefly stir-fry; add rice wine and ① . When liquid comes to a boil, add ② to thicken and melted chicken fat; toss lightly to combine ingredients and remove to serving plate and serve.

■ Chinese black mushrooms and ham may be omitted and replaced by dried shrimp.

大白菜……2斤　　奶油(或猪油)5大匙　　②{ 白菜餘汁2½杯
瘦肉(切片)4兩　洋葱(切碎)……半杯　　　　 奶水………半杯
　　①{ 鹽………2小匙　麵粉…………5大匙
味精……半小匙
糖………1小匙
水…………2杯

❶ 大白菜洗淨切粗塊，用開水川燙（由莖部先下）至軟撈起。

❷ 將油4大匙燒熱，先炒肉片，隨即倒進白菜略炒調入①料，中火煮約10分鐘撈起瀝乾，放入烤模內餘汁留用。

❸ 奶油燒熱，先把洋葱炒軟，再將麵粉炒香，並加②料炒勻成麵糊，倒在白菜上面，入烤箱以350度烤20分鐘即成。

奶油焗菜胆 Baked Cabbage and Butter

3 lbs. Chinese cabbage
4 oz. pork loin
①{ 2 t. salt
½ t. MSG
1 t. sugar
2 C. water

5 T. butter or lard
½ C. chopped onion
5 T. flour

②{ 2½ C. retained cabbage soup
½ C. evaporated milk

❶ Cut pork loin into paper-thin bite-size pieces; rinse cabbage lightly; drain and cut into bite-size pieces. Precook cabbage pieces in boiling water until soft (add stalk pieces of cabbage first); remove and drain.

❷ Heat pan and 4T. oil; stir-fry pork loin until it changes color; add cabbage and stir-fry briefly over high heat; add ① and turn heat to medium and cook 10 minutes; remove and drain off liquid to a bowl (retain). Place cabbage in a casserole.

❸ Heat pan and butter; saute onion until soft; add flour and stir-fry over low heat until fragrant; add ② and mix; pour over cabbage, preheat oven to 350° F; bake cabbage casserole for 20 minutes; remove and serve.

菜花……1 斤
水……4 杯
酒……半大匙
① { 高湯……2 杯
鹽……1 小匙
味精…半小匙

② { 高湯………半杯
鹽………1 小匙
味精……半小匙

③ { 太白粉…半大匙
水………1 大匙

奶水………¼ 杯
熟火腿末1 大匙

❶ 菜花切小朶塊狀，水燒開煮 2 分鐘瀝乾水份。

❷ 油 3 大匙燒熱，下酒半大匙及①料，將菜花中火燒煮 5 分鐘蓋鍋，至汁快收乾，花向底，盛於中碗內，反扣菜盤中。

❸ 油 1 大匙燒熱將②料燒開，以③料勾汁，再加奶水攪勻，加熱油半大匙，淋於菜花上，上洒火腿末即成。

奶油菜花 Stir-Fried Cauliflower in Milk Sauce

廣東菜　Cantonese
6人份　6 servings

1⅓ lbs. cauliflower
4　C. water
½　T. rice wine
① { 2　C. stock
1　t. salt
½　t. MSG

② { ½　C. stock
1　t. salt
½　t. MSG
③ { ½　T. cornstarch
1　T. water

¼　C. evaporated milk
1　T. chopped precooked ham

❶ Rinse and drain cauliflower; separate flowerets into bite-size sections. Heat water until boiling and add cauliflower sections; cook 2 minutes; remove and drain.

❷ Heat pan and 3 T. oil; add rice wine and ① . When liquid boils, add cauliflower sections and cook 5 minutes over medium heat (liquid should be almost dry); remove and arrange cauliflower sections (flower-side down) to line the bottom of a medium-size bowl; pack lightly and invert onto a serving plate.

❸ Heat pan and 1 T. oil; add ② and heat until boiling; add ③ to thicken and slowly add evaporated milk, stirring constantly; add ½ T. oil and pour over cauliflower mold; sprinkle chopped ham on top and serve.

緑豆芽‥‥‥‥‥‥ 1 斤　　　鹽‥‥‥‥‥‥ 1 小匙
青椒絲‥‥‥‥‥‥ ¼ 杯　①　糖‥‥‥‥‥‥ 半小匙
花椒粒‥‥‥‥‥‥ 1 小匙　　味精‥‥‥‥‥‥ 半小匙
　　　　　　　　　　　　　　醋‥‥‥‥‥‥ 2 小匙

❶ 緑豆芽摘去芽及根洗淨，泡在水裏，用時撈乾。

❷ 油3大匙燒熱用中火炒花椒，炒到有香味時把花椒粒挑出不要，再放入緑豆芽、青椒絲、及①
料用大火爆炒均勻，即可裝入菜盤內。

■ 此道菜，青椒絲有無都可，緑豆芽需摘去芽及根，吃起來才清脆可口。

醋烹豆芽 Stir-Fried Bean·Sprouts and Vinegar　　　北平菜　Peking
　　　　　　　　　　　　　　　　　　　　　　　　　　　　　　6人份　**6 servings**

1⅓lbs. (3C.) bean sprouts　　　　1　t.　salt
¼　C. shredded green pepper　①　½　t.　sugar
1　t.　Szechuan peppercorns　　　½　t.　MSG
　　　　　　　　　　　　　　　　　2　t.　vinegar

❶ Remove discolored ends from bean sprouts and rinse; place in cold water to keep fresh; before using drain.

❷ Heat pan and 3T. oil; stir-fry Szechuan peppercorns over medium heat until fragrant; remove peppercorns (leaving oil) and discard. Add bean sprouts, green pepper and ① ; stir-fry over high heat until ingredients are heated through and remove to serving plate; serve.

■ Green pepper may be omitted; however, the ends of the bean sprouts should be removed to improve taste and appearance of dish.

①	雞肉	⋯⋯⋯半斤		綠豆芽	⋯⋯6兩		
	鹽	⋯⋯⋯半小匙		「炸油」	⋯⋯3杯		
	酒	⋯⋯⋯1小匙					
	蛋白	⋯⋯⋯1個					
	太白粉	⋯2小匙					

	②	
酒	⋯⋯⋯	1 小匙
鹽	⋯⋯⋯	半小匙
味精	⋯⋯⋯	¼ 小匙
糖	⋯⋯⋯	¼ 小匙
胡椒	⋯⋯⋯	¼ 小匙
麻油	⋯⋯⋯	¼ 小匙
水	⋯⋯⋯	1½ 大匙
太白粉	⋯⋯⋯	1 小匙

❶ 雞肉除筋切細絲，調①料攪拌後，加太白粉2小匙攪勻。

❷ 綠豆芽摘去頭尾，留白莖部。

❸ 「炸油」3杯燒開，用中火將雞絲，泡油1分鐘撈起，餘油倒出，留油1大匙，先放入綠豆芽略炒再加雞絲及②料炒勻即可。

豆芽雞丝 Stir-Fried Chicken Shreds with Bean Sprouts 北平菜 6人份　Peking 6 servings

①	⅔ lb. chicken meat		½ lb. (1½C.) bean sprouts	②	1 t. rice wine
	½ t. salt		3 C. oil for frying		½ t. salt
	1 t. rice wine				¼ t. MSG
	1 egg white				¼ t. sugar
	2 t. cornstarch				¼· t. black pepper
					¼ t. sesame oil
					1½ T. water
					1 t. cornstarch

❶ Cut chicken meat into shreds and mix with ① ; let sit 20 minutes. Mix with 2t. cornstarch.

❷ Remove discolored ends from bean sprouts and rinse; place in cold water to keep fresh; before cooking, drain.

❸ Heat 3C. oil for deep-frying; deep-fry chicken shreds about 1 minute over medium heat until color changes (stir to separate shreds); remove and drain. Remove all but 1T. oil from pan; stir-fry bean sprouts briefly and add chicken shreds and ② ; stir-fry to mix together and remove to serving plate; serve.

熟筍片……1½杯　　　┌湯…………半杯　　②┌太白粉……半小匙
季菜…………2兩　　①│鹽………半小匙　　　│水…………1小匙
豬油…………1杯　　　│味精……¼小匙　　　└雞油………2大匙
　　　　　　　　　　　└糖………¼小匙

❶ 季菜去老葉，切約1公分長。

❷ 豬油1杯燒滾，慢火把筍片泡半分鐘，盛起，留2大匙油，炒季菜放入①料及筍片，並以②料
　勾汁，淋上熟油1大匙，即置菜盤，再淋雞油2大匙即可。

■ 如無季菜，可用西洋菜或豆苗來代替。

季菜冬筍 Stir-Fried Bamboo Shoots

上海菜　Shanghai
6人份　6 servings

1½ C. precooked sliced bamboo shoot
2 oz. green vegetable*
1 C. oil

①┌ ½ C. stock
　│ ½ t. salt
　│ ¼ t. MSG
　└ ¼ t. sugar

②┌ ½ t. cornstarch
　│ 1 t. water
　　2 T. melted chicken fat

❶ Trim any old leaves from green vegetable; rinse, drain and cut into ½-inch pieces.

❷ Heat pan and 1C. oil; stir-fry the bamboo shoot slices about ½ minute over low heat; remove and drain. Remove
all but 2T. oil from pan; reheat and add green vegetable sections; stir-fry briefly and add ① and bamboo
shoot slices. When liquid boils, add ② to thicken and 1T. oil. Toss ingredients lightly to mix together
and remove to serving plate. Pour melted chicken fat on top and serve.

* The pictured Chinese vegetable is called "chi tsai" and may be purchased at a Chinese grocery store. If
unavailable, substitute watercress.

鵝筍尖（萵苣）…1斤半

①	高湯…………………2杯	②	高湯………………1杯	
	鹽……………1½小匙		鹽…………半小匙	
	味精…………半小匙		味精…………¼小匙	
			酒…………半小匙	
			太白粉………半小匙	

❶ 鵝筍尖去老葉，修去老皮。

❷ 燒開①料，放入鵝筍尖燒煮約5分鐘，置於盤上，湯汁不用，另將②料邊攪動燒沸，加熱油1大匙，即可淋於鵝筍上，趁熱供食。

上湯鵝筍尖 Fresh Asparagus with Sauce

上海菜 6人份　　Shanghai 6 servings

	2 lbs. fresh asparagus		1 C. stock	
①	2 C. stock	②	½ t. salt	
	1½ t. salt		¼ t. MSG.	
	½ t. MSG		½ t. rice wine	
			½ t. cornstarch	

❶ Remove hard ends from asparagus and rinse asparagus lightly; drain.

❷ Place ① in a pan and heat until boiling; add asparagus and cook 5 minutes; remove and place asparagus on serving plate (discard liquid). Heat ② until thick, stirring constantly, and add 1T. oil; mix together and pour over asparagus; serve.

絲瓜……2條（2斤）　　　酒…………半大匙　　　③{太白粉……1小匙
①{水……………3杯　　②{高湯………1½杯　　　　{水…………1大匙
{鹽…………半大匙　　　{鹽…………1小匙
　　　　　　　　　　　　{味精………半小匙

❶ 絲瓜去皮，盡量保留綠部份去子，切成菱形，在①料內燒煮3分鐘撈出。
❷ 油2大匙燒熱略炒絲瓜，下酒及②料燒煮5分鐘後，以③料勾汁即成。
■ 如果此菜改用黃瓜或節瓜時，②料內之高湯及燒煮時間要增加。

上湯絲瓜 Stir-Fried Cucumber

廣東菜　Cantonese
6人份　6 servings

2 cucumbers (about 2⅔lbs.)　　½ T. rice wine　　③{1 t. cornstarch
①{3 C. water　　②{2 C. stock　　　　　{1 T. water
{½ T. salt　　　{1 t. salt
　　　　　　　{½ t. MSG

❶ Remove the skin from the cucumbers (thinly pare skin to retain green-colored meat); remove seeds and cut meat into bite-size pieces. Add pieces to ① and cook 3 minutes over medium heat; remove and drain.
❷ Heat pan and 2T. oil; stir-fry cucumber pieces briefly; add rice wine and ② and cook 10 minutes; add ③ to thicken and remove to serving plate; serve.

172

冬瓜（１５公分×１５公分×６公分）１塊

① { 高湯…………８杯
鹽…………２小匙
干貝…………３個
鴨腎…………２個
雞肉（切丁）…半杯
「炸油」………３杯 }

② { 洋菇（切丁）…半杯
火腿（切丁）…¼杯
冬菇（切丁）…¼杯
濕蹄筋（切丁）…¼杯
蓮子…………¼杯 }

③ { 酒…………半大匙
高湯……１杯
鹽……１小匙
味精…半小匙
麻油…半小匙 } 兩份

④ { 太白粉…２小匙
水…………２小匙 } 兩份
火腿末………１大匙

❶ 冬瓜削皮保留綠部份四角稍修圓，以①料煮約４０分鐘，煮冬瓜湯汁不要。干貝加水¼杯蒸爛撕成細絲備用。

❷ 鴨腎切除白筋切丁，油３杯燒熱先將鴨腎及雞肉丁泡熟撈出，留油３大匙把②料放入略炒，加酒半大匙及③料燒煮１分鐘，再入干貝及泡熟鴨腎及雞丁，以④料勾汁盛起（餡）。

❸ 煮好冬瓜皮部份朝下，挖成凹形，先將餡放入，再把挖出之冬瓜覆蓋，放於中型碗內蒸３０分鐘至冬瓜完全熟爛取出，倒出餘汁反扣在大盤內。

❹ ③料及蒸冬瓜餘汁燒開以④料勾汁淋在冬瓜上，上洒火腿末即成。

白玉藏珍 Winter Melon Surprise

廣東菜 Cantonese
12人 12 servings

1 section winter melon (about 6 x 6 x 2 inches thick)

① { 8 C. stock
2 t. salt
3 dried scallops
2 duck gizzards
½ C. diced chicken meat
3 C. oil for frying }

② { ½ C. diced onion
¼ C. diced ham
¼ C. diced pre-softened Chinese black mushrooms
¼ C. diced pork tendons
¼ C. pre-softened lotus seeds
½ T. rice wine }

③ { 1 C. stock
1 t. salt
½ t. MSG
½ t. sesame oil } Double and place in separate bowls

④ { 2 t. cornstarch
2 t. water } Double and place in separate bowls
1 T. chopped Chinese ham

❶ Remove the skin from the winter melon (being careful not to cut too deep so as to leave green-colored melon meat); round and smooth the corners of the melon section with a knife; place melon section with ① in a pan and cook 40 minutes covered over medium heat; remove and drain melon section. (discard liquid). Rinse dried scallops and place in a bowl with ¼C. water; steam ½ hour over high heat; remove, drain and shred.

❷ Cut away white membrane of gizzards and discard; dice gizzards finely. Heat 3C. oil for deep-frying; deep-fry diced gizzards and chicken until changed in color and remove; drain. Remove all but 3T. oil from pan and reheat; stir-fry ② briefly and add ½T. rice wine and one portion of ③; cook 1 minute and add shredded scallops, gizzards, and chicken meat; add one portion of ④ to thicken. (filling)

❸ On the underside of the winter melon, lightly cut a hole in which to place filling. Stuff this hole with the filling and replace the cut-out melon pieces on top. Place stuffed melon in a medium-sized bowl and place in steamer; steam 30 minutes over medium heat until tender. Drain off liquid and add to second portion of ③; invert melon into serving bowl and demold.

❹ Heat second portion of ③ until boiling; add second portion of ④ to thicken and pour over stuffed winter melon; sprinkle chopped ham on top and serve.

173

茄子‥‥‥‥‥‥1斤　　辣豆瓣醬‥2小匙　　酒‥‥‥‥‥1小匙
「炸油」‥‥‥3杯　　葱末‥‥‥‥2大匙　　醬油‥‥‥‥1小匙
絞肉‥‥‥‥‥4兩　① 薑末‥‥‥‥1大匙　　鹽‥‥‥‥‥半小匙
　　　　　　　　　　蒜末‥‥‥‥1大匙　②糖‥‥‥‥‥1小匙
　　　　　　　　　　　　　　　　　　　味精‥‥‥‥半小匙
　　　　　　　　　　　　　　　　　　　醋‥‥‥‥‥1小匙
　　　　　　　　　　　　　　　　　　　水‥‥‥‥‥⅓杯

❶ 茄子去皮，切約７公分長段，然後對剖二開或四開。

❷ 燒開「炸油」，把茄子炸熟(約３分鐘)，茄子水份多，「炸油」不超出炒鍋之６分滿為宜。

❸ 將油３大匙燒熱，把絞肉炒香如油太多，倒出部份，隨入①料炒３０秒後，入茄子及②料炒勻即可。

魚香茄子 Fish-Flavored Eggplant

四川菜　Szechuan
6人份　6 servings

1⅓lbs. eggplant
3　C. oil for frying
4　oz. chopped pork

①
2　t. hot bean paste ("la do ban jiang")
2　T. chopped green onion
1　T. chopped ginger root
1　T. chopped garlic

②
1　t. rice wine
1　t. soy sauce
½　t. salt
1　t. sugar
½　t. MSG
1　t. worcestershire sauce
⅓　C. water

❶ Remove ends from eggplant and cut into 2½-inch sections; cut each section into 2 to 4 slices.

❷ Heat oil for deep-frying; deep-fry eggplant slices for 3 minutes until soft; remove and drain.

❸ Heat pan and 3T. oil; stir-fry chopped pork until it changes color (if there is too much oil, remove some) ; add ① and stir-fry 30 seconds until fragrant. Add eggplant and ② ; toss ingredients lightly to mix together and remove; serve.

四季豆…12兩	蝦米（切碎）…2大匙	
絞肉………1兩	榨菜（切碎）…4大匙	
	「炸油」…………3杯	

① 醬油………半大匙
糖…………半小匙
味精………¼小匙
水…………半大匙
葱末………半大匙
麻油………半小匙

❶ 四季豆去兩頭及筋洗淨，切約8公分長備用。

❷ 燒開「炸油」，將四季豆以中火炸約5分鐘撈出，留油3大匙，將絞肉炒香並加蝦米及榨菜末同炒30秒後，倒入四季豆、酒1小匙，並調上①料炒乾，洒葱末，最後澆上麻油半小匙炒勻即可。

干扁四季豆 Dry-Cooked String Beans

四川菜　Szechuan
6人份　6 servings

1 lb. string beans	2 T. chopped dried shrimp	
1 oz. chopped pork	4 T. chopped Szechuan pickled mustard green	
	3 C. oil for frying	

① ½ T. soy sauce
½ t. sugar
¼ t. MSG
½ T. water
½ T. chopped green onion
½ t. sesame oil

❶ Remove ends from string beans and pull away any "veiny" strings; rinse and drain; cut into 3-inch sections.

❷ Heat oil for deep-frying; deep-fry string beans over medium heat for 5 minutes; remove and drain. Remove all but 3T. oil from pan and reheat; stir-fry chopped pork until it changes color and add dried shrimp and Szechuan pickled mustard green and stir-fry 30 seconds. Add string beans, 1t. rice wine and ①; stir-fry until sauce is dry and add chopped green onion and ½t. sesame oil; toss lightly to combine ingredients and remove to serving plate; serve.

熟筍塊······３杯
「炸油」······６杯

① 甜麵醬······２大匙
醬油·········２大匙
糖·········１大匙
味精·········１小匙
酒·········半大匙
清水·········半杯

② 豌豆苗·········半斤
鹽·········半小匙
味精·········¼小匙

❶ 「炸油」燒開，將筍塊大火炸約２分鐘，呈金黃色撈起，留油３大匙，將①料炒香，繼入筍及清水半杯，用中火燒煮３分鐘，至汁收乾，再加麻油１大匙盛盤。

❷ 油４大匙燒熱，放進豌豆苗及②料炒熟，瀝乾水份，置於盤子的兩端即可。

■ 如無豌豆苗，可用其他青菜代替，①料宜事先調勻。

醬燒筍 Saucy Stir-Fried Bamboo Shoots

四川菜　Szechuan
12人份　12 servings

3　small precooked bamboo shoots (about 1⅓ lbs.)
6　C. oil for frying

① 2　T. sweet bean paste
2　T. soy sauce
1　T. sugar
1　t. MSG
½　T. rice wine
½　C. water

② ⅔ lb. green vegetable*
½　t. salt
¼　t. MSG

❶ Cross-cut bamboo shoot into bite-size pieces (about 3 cups). Heat oil for deep-frying; deep-fry bamboo shoot 2 minutes over medium heat until golden brown; remove and drain. Remove all but 3T. oil from pan; stir-fry pre-mixed ① until fragrant; add bamboo shoot and ½C. water; cook over medium heat about 3 minutes until near-dry. Add 1T. sesame oil and toss ingredients lightly to mix together; place bamboo shoot on center of serving plate.

❷ Heat pan and 4T. oil; stir-fry vegetable and ② 30 seconds. Portion to both sides of serving plate, surrounding bamboo shoot; serve.

* ''Dou miau'', which is the pictured Chinese vegetable, is the stalk and leaves of the mustard plant. It may be purchased at a Chinese grocery store, however, if unavailable, substitute spinach.

冬菇……１２朵
冬筍……２斤半
「炸油」……３杯

① ｛ 蠔油……２大匙
醬油……１大匙
糖………１小匙
味精……半小匙
麻油……１小匙
水………１½杯

② ｛ 太白粉…１小匙
水………２小匙

青江菜……１斤

❶ 冬菇泡軟去蒂，筍去殼切塊（計３杯），青江菜對切兩半燙熟，放入冷水內漂涼瀝乾備用。

❷ 油３大匙燒熱放入青江菜、鹽１小匙、味精半小匙炒均勻盛出。

❸ 「炸油」燒熱，將筍塊下炸２分鐘撈出，留油２大匙炒冬菇，續入筍及①料燒煮８分鐘，至汁剩一半時以②料勾汁，淋上熟油１大匙，置於盤內，以青江菜圍邊。

蠔油双冬 Stir-Fried Mushrooms & Bamboo Shoots with Oyster Sauce

廣東菜 Cantonese
12人份 12 servings

12 Chinese black mushrooms
3⅓ lbs. bamboo shoots
3 C. oil for frying

① ｛ 2 T. oyster sauce
1 T. soy sauce
1 t. sugar
½ t. MSG
1 t. sesame oil
1½ C. water

② ｛ 1 t. cornstarch
2 t. water

1⅓ lbs. green cabbage

❶ Soak mushrooms until soft; cut off stems; slice bamboo shoots (about 3 cups); cut green cabbage in half, lengthwise; precook in boiling water; plunge cabbage into cold water then remove and drain.

❷ Heat 3 T. oil; stir-fry green cabbage, 1t. salt and ½t. MSG; mix thoroughly; remove and set aside.

❸ Heat oil; deep-fry bamboo shoots for 2 minutes; remove bamboo shoots and all oil but 2T.; stir-fry Chinese black mushrooms; add bamboo shoots and ① ; simmer for 8 minutes; thicken sauce with ② ; sprinkle 1T. hot oil over top. Transfer to a serving dish; arrange green cabbage around vegetables.

冬菇（直徑３公分）……１２朵
①酒………１小匙、糖……半小匙
醬油…１½大匙、高湯……半杯
味精……１小匙、豬油…１大匙

洋菇………………………１杯
②鹽…………………………半小匙
味精…………………………¼小匙
高湯…………………………半杯
青江菜（或小芥菜）…１斤半

③太白粉…２小匙
水………１大匙
奶水………¼杯

❶ 青江菜對切兩半，燙熟，放入冷水內漂涼，瀝乾。油４大匙燒熱，將青江菜加鹽１小匙略炒圍邊。

❷ 冬菇洗淨，泡軟去蒂，加①料蒸２０分鐘，放入炒鍋以½③料勾芡加１大匙熟油拌勻，置盤（如圖）。

❸ 洋菇去蒂放入開水內川燙，撈出，與②料燒煮並以½③料勾芡，再加奶水及１大匙熟油拌勻置盤。

扒金銀菇 Gold and Silver Mushrooms

廣東菜 Cantonese
12人份 12 servings

①
12 Chinese black mushrooms
1 t. rice wine
1½ T. soy sauce
1 t. MSG
½ t. sugar
½ C. stock
1 T. shortening or lard

②
1 C. button mushrooms
½ t. salt
¼ t. MSG
½ C. stock
2 lbs. green cabbage
or mustard greens

③
2 t. cornstarch
1 T. water
¼ C. milk

❶ Cut green cabbage in half; precook in boiling water; plunge in cold water; remove and drain. Heat 4T. oil, briefly stir-fry cabbage and 1t. salt.

❷ Wash Chinese black mushrooms; soak until soft, remove stems; mix with ① and steam 20 minutes. stir-fry in pan using ½ ③ to thicken; add 1T. hot oil and mix thoroughly; remove and place in serving dish as pictured.

❸ Remove stems from button mushrooms; precook in boiling water; remove; simmer with ② using ½ ③ to thicken; add milk and 1T. hot oil; mix thoroughly and place in serving dish.

麵筋泡…20粒　　青江菜(半斤)…3棵　　酒………1大匙　　③{太白粉…1小匙
腐竹……1兩半　　熟筍片………半杯　　水………2杯　　　　　水………1大匙
「炸油」……3杯　①{熟紅蘿蔔片……¼杯　　醬油……4大匙
　　　　　　　　濕木耳………1杯　②{味精……1小匙
　　　　　　　　冬菇………¼杯　　　糖………1大匙
　　　　　　　　素腸……1條切片　　胡椒……¼小匙
　　　　　　　　葱(3公分長)…6枝　　麻油……1小匙
　　　　　　　　薑………6片　　　　醋………1大匙

❶ 「炸油」燒熱，中火將腐竹炸1分鐘，呈金黃色撈起。

❷ 青江菜，剖開四瓣，將水5杯燒沸，燙熟撈起（2分鐘），隨入麵筋泡、腐竹燒煮3分鐘撈起
　，腐竹切4公分長段備用。

❸ 油3大匙燒熱，葱薑炒香，下酒1大匙及②料，繼入①料、麵筋泡及腐竹，中火燒煮5分鐘，餘
　汁快收乾時，以③料勾汁後，加熱油1大匙即成。

■ 麵筋泡、腐竹在豆腐攤或雜貨店買。

羅漢素菜 Stir-Fried Vegetarian Dish

廣東菜　Cantonese
12人份　12 servings

20 fried gluten balls ("mien jin pau")*[1]
1½ oz. bean curd sticks ("fu dzu")
3 C. oil for frying

①
- 3 stalks green cabbage (about ⅔lb.)*[2]
- ½ C. precooked sliced bamboo shoot
- ¼ C. precooked sliced carrot
- 1 C. softened wood ears, cut in half
- ¼ C. pre-softened, sliced Chinese black mushrooms
- 1 roll sliced "su-tsang"*[1]
- 6 1-inch sections green onion
- 6 slices ginger root

②
- 1 T. rice wine
- 2 C. water
- 4 T. soy sauce
- 1 t. MSG
- 1 T. sugar
- ¼ t. black pepper
- 1 t. sesame oil
- 1 T. vinegar

③
- 1 t. cornstarch
- 1 T. water

❶ Heat oil for deep-frying; deep-fry bean curd sticks about 1 minute over medium heat until golden brown; remove and drain.

❷ Cut each stalk of green cabbage into 4 sections. Heat 5C. water until boiling; add green cabbage sections and cook 2 minutes; remove, drain and place in cold water until cool; drain. Cook fried gluten balls and bean curd sticks in boiling water 3 minutes to remove excess oil; remove and drain. Cut bean curd sticks into 1½-inch sections.

❸ Heat pan and 3T. oil; stir-fry green onion and ginger until fragrant. Add 1T. rice wine ②, ①, fried gluten balls and bean curd sticks sections; cook over medium heat for 5 minutes until soup is almost dry. Add ③ to thicken and 1T. oil and toss lightly to mix all ingredients; remove to serving plate and serve.

*[1] Fried gluten balls and "su tsang" are both ingredients made from wheat gluten. They may be stored for a long period of time and may be purchased in dry-form at a Chinese grocery store.

*[2] If unavailable, substitute broccoli and cut into bite-size pieces; use as directed above.

雞胸肉 ……………………………半斤
薑酒 ……1 大匙、麻油 ……1 小匙
① 鹽 ……半小匙、蛋白 ………2 個
味精 …… ¼ 小匙、太白粉 …2 小匙
胡椒 …… ¼ 小匙

小菜心 ……1 ○棵
冬菇 (泡軟) …1 個
火腿末 ……1 大匙

② 高湯 ………1 杯
鹽 …… ⅓ 小匙
味精 …… ⅓ 小匙

③ 太白粉 …1 小匙
水 ……1 小匙

❶ 雞胸肉去皮捶成泥,調上①料。

❷ 水8杯燒開將小菜心煮約1分鐘撈出,以冷水漂涼,每一棵對切成半,拭乾水份。

❸ 在小菜心切口及冬菇背面各洒上少許太白粉,並鑲上雞肉泥,及洒火腿末,以大火蒸約5分鐘,取出盛在盤上(如圖)。

❹ ②料燒開以③料勾成汁,淋在菜心和冬菇上。

■ 為求美觀,最後可洒上少許雞油。

■ 薑片拍碎加酒擠出的汁叫薑酒。

鑲萬年青 Chinese Black Mushrooms Stuffed with Chicken

四川菜　Szechuan
12人份 **12 servings**

	⅔ lb. chicken breast meat	10 hearts green vegetable*		1 C. stock
	1 T. ginger wine	1 pre-softened Chinese black mushroom	②	⅓ t. salt
	½ t. salt	1 T. chopped precooked ham		⅓ t. MSG
①	¼ t. MSG		③	1 t. cornstarch
	¼ t. black pepper • 2 egg whites			1 t. water
	1 t. sesame oil • 2 t. cornstarch			

❶ Chop chicken meat very finely and add ① ; lightly throw mixture against the inside of bowl to combine ingredients to a smooth paste; separate into 21 portions.

❷ Boil 8C. water and add vegetable hearts; cook for 1 minute and remove; place in cold water until cool; remove, drain and cut each stalk in half.

❸ Lightly dust the cut side of each stalk half with cornstarch; shape filling portions into balls and place one in the base of each vegetable stalk. Stuff mushroom cap with one portion of filling; sprinkle chopped ham on top of filling. Place stuffed stalks and mushroom cap on a heatproof plate and steam 5 minutes over high heat; remove and arrange on serving plate as illustrated.

❹ Place ② in a pan and bring to a boil; add ③ to thicken and pour over stuffed stalks and mushroom.

■ You may sprinkle a little chicken fat over stuffed stalks and mushroom to improve appearance and enhance flavor.

* "Syau tsai syin" is the pictured Chinese vegetable which may be purchased at a Chinese grocery store. If unavailable, substitute celery cabbage and use as directed.

小冬菇２４朶
①
猪油…半大匙、鹽…$\frac{1}{4}$小匙
醬油…半大匙、水…２大匙
糖……$\frac{1}{4}$小匙、葱……１條
酒……半小匙、薑……１片

蝦仁…半斤
蛋白…半只
肥肉…１兩

②
酒………１小匙
鹽………半小匙
味精……$\frac{1}{4}$小匙
胡椒……$\frac{1}{4}$小匙
麻油……半小匙
太白粉…１小匙

瘦火腿末１大匙
香菜葉…２４片
③
高湯………半杯
鹽………$\frac{1}{4}$小匙
麻油……$\frac{1}{4}$小匙
④
太白粉…半小匙
水………１小匙

芥蘭菜…１４棵
（或其他青菜）

❶ 冬菇泡軟，剪去蒂，加①料，蒸約２０分鐘。芥蘭菜在滾水內燙熟撈出，放入冷水內漂涼，瀝乾水份。

❷ 蝦仁洗淨拭乾水份，拍碎剁爛成蝦絨，盛碗內加蛋白半只，再加剁爛肥肉及②料用手攪動至蝦絨狀(前後約５分鐘)。

❸ 蒸熟冬菇，每朶內面沾少許乾太白粉，再鑲進蝦絨抹平，上面洒少許火腿末及香菜，置於擦過油之蒸盤，蒸約６分鐘後裝在盤內，另將③料燒開，加④料勾汁淋於冬菇上面。

❹ 油４大匙燒熱，把芥蘭菜入鍋略炒，下酒半大匙，鹽$\frac{1}{3}$小匙，糖$\frac{1}{3}$小匙，炒熟圍邊即可。

海棠百花菇 Stuffed Mushrooms with Shrimp Paste

廣東菜 Cantonese
12人份 12 servings

24 Chinese black mushrooms
①
½ T. lard or sesame oil
½ T. soy sauce
¼ t. sugar
½ t. rice wine
¼ t. salt
2 T. water
1 stalk green onion
1 slice ginger root

⅔ lb. raw, shelled shrimp
½ egg white
1 oz. chopped pork fat
②
1 t. rice wine
½ t. salt
¼ t. MSG
¼ t. black pepper
½ t. sesame oil
1 t. cornstarch

1 T. chopped precooked ham
24 sprigs of coriander
③
½ C. stock
¼ t. salt
¼ t. sesame oil
④
½ t. cornstarch
1 t. water
14 stalks Chinese broccoli* (about 1lb.)

❶ Soften black mushrooms in warm water; drain and remove stems (discard); mix ① with mushroom caps and steam 20 minutes over medium heat; drain and add liquid to ③. Cut broccoli stalks into 3-inch sections; precook in boiling water for 1 minute; remove and place in cold water to cool; remove and drain.

❷ Rinse and devein shrimp; drain and chop finely; add egg white, chopped pork fat and ②. Throw mixture lightly against inside of bowl to combine ingredients (about 5 minutes).

❸ Sprinkle the flat side of each mushroom cap with cornstarch and spread a portion of shrimp paste over the surface of each mushroom cap; smooth filling with the underside of a spoon. Place 1 sprig of coriander on the shrimp paste and sprinkle with chopped ham. Place each finished mushroom on a heatproof plate and steam 5 minutes over high heat. Remove mushrooms and place on serving plate. Heat ③ in a pan until boiling; add ④ to thicken and pour over stuffed mushrooms.

❹ Heat pan and 4T. oil; briefly stir-fry broccoli sections; add ½T. rice wine, ⅓t. salt, ⅓t. sugar and stir-fry together; remove and arrange broccoli sections around serving plate; serve.

* If chinese broccoli is unavailable, substitute American broccoli and cut cut stalk into ½-inch sections.

苦瓜(瘦長)……半斤			蒜末……1小匙		紅辣椒……1條

苦瓜(瘦長)……半斤
絞肉……………6兩

① 蒜末……1小匙
　鹽………半小匙
　味精……半小匙
　麻油……1小匙
　太白粉…半大匙

　紅辣椒……1條
　豆豉……1大匙
② 鹽………半小匙
　糖………半小匙
　水………半杯

❶ 苦瓜去頭尾切約1公分厚，去子，半鍋水燒開，加鹽半小匙，苦瓜倒入，煮約3分鐘撈起，放入冷水中漂涼，紅辣椒切小粒。

❷ 絞肉調入①料拌勻即成肉餡。

❸ 苦瓜瀝乾水份，在內邊抹上少許太白粉用肉餡填滿。

❹ 油半杯燒熱，中火將鑲好苦瓜下鍋二面煎熟約3分鐘。

❺ 油2大匙燒熱，豆豉、紅辣椒下鍋炒香，再將苦瓜倒入，加②料中火煮約3分鐘，即可將苦瓜盛菜盤內。

豆豉鑲苦瓜 Stuffed Bitter Gourd with Fermented Black Beans

湖南菜　Hunan
6人份　6 servings

⅔ lb. bitter gourd *
6 oz. chopped pork

① 1 t. chopped garlic
　½ t. salt
　½ t. MSG
　1 t. sesame oil
　½ T. cornstarch

　1 hot red pepper
　1 T. fermented black beans
② ½ t. salt
　½ t. sugar
　½ C. water

❶ Remove ends and stem from bitter gourd; cut into slices ⅓-inch thick and remove seeds (discard). Place in boiling water to cover with ½t. salt and cook 3 minutes; remove and place in cold water to cool; drain. Shred hot red pepper.

❷ Add ① to chopped pork and lightly throw mixture against inside of bowl to thoroughly combine ingredients. (filling)

❸ Lightly dry bitter gourd and sprinkle cavities with cornstarch; stuff with filling.

❹ Heat pan and ½C. oil until medium hot; fry stuffed bitter gourd on both sides until meat is golden brown and vegetable is tender. (about 3 minutes); remove.

❺ Reheat pan and 2T. oil; stir-fry fermented black beans and hot red pepper until fragrant; add bitter gourd slices and ② . Cook 3 minutes over medium heat and remove to serving plate; serve.

* If unavailable, substitute squash or zucchini.

青椒（大）…4個	①	鹽 …………… 半小匙	③	醬油 ……… 1 大匙
絞肉 ……… 6 兩		糖 …………… 半小匙		鹽 ………… ¼ 小匙
蝦仁 ……… 2 兩		胡椒 ……… ¼ 小匙		味精 ……… ¼ 小匙
蝦米 ……… 半兩		太白粉 …… 1 大匙		糖 ………… ¼ 小匙
	②	豆豉…1 大匙		水 …………… 半杯
		蒜頭 …… 2 粒 } 剁爛		
		薑 ……… 2 片		

❶ 洗淨蝦仁拭乾水份，蝦米泡軟，均用刀剁碎，與絞肉盛於碗內調上①料攪拌，並甩打（有膠狀），做成肉餡。

❷ 每個青椒切開成三大塊，修去邊成直徑6公分之圓形‧內面洒少許乾太白粉，將肉餡添入抹平。

❸ 油6大匙燒熱，將青椒有肉餡部份向鍋底煎約1分鐘，呈金黃色，將鑲青椒鏟於一旁，炒香②料，隨入③料蓋鍋燜煮8分鐘即可盛盤供食。

鑲青椒 Stuffed Green Peppers

廣東菜　Cantonese
6人份　6 servings

4	large green peppers	①	½ t. salt	③	1 T. soy sauce
6	oz. chopped pork		½ t. sugar		¼ t. salt
2	oz. raw, shelled shrimp		¼ t. black pepper		¼ t. MSG
½	oz. dried shrimp		1 T. cornstarch		¼ t. sugar
		②	1 T. chopped fermented black beans		½ C. water
			2 cloves garlic, chopped		
			2 slices ginger root, chopped		

❶ Rinse dried shrimp and soften in warm water; drain. Separately chop dried shrimp, fresh shrimp and chopped pork until fine; add ① to chopped shrimp and throw mixture lightly against inside of mixing bowl to combine thoroughly. (filling)

❷ Cut each green pepper into three sections and remove seeds; trim each section of green pepper to a 2-inch circle and sprinkle inside of green pepper with cornstarch; fill cavity of green pepper with filling and smooth filling surface with the underside of spoon.

❸ Heat pan and 6T. oil; place stuffed green peppers in pan (meat-side down) and fry 1 minute until golden brown. Push green peppers to the side of pan and add ② ; stir-fry until fragrant and add ③ , returning peppers to the center of pan. Cover and cook 8 minutes over low heat until liquid is almost dry; remove to serving plate and serve.

<table>
<tr><td>①</td><td>發好魚翅⋯⋯⋯6兩
發好魚皮⋯⋯⋯6兩
葱（3公分長）⋯6枝
薑⋯⋯⋯⋯⋯⋯6片</td></tr>
</table>

①{
發好魚翅⋯⋯⋯6兩
發好魚皮⋯⋯⋯6兩
葱（3公分長）⋯6枝
薑⋯⋯⋯⋯⋯⋯6片

②{
筍絲⋯⋯⋯⋯⋯1杯
冬菇（泡軟切絲）¼杯
里肌肉絲⋯⋯⋯半杯
火腿絲⋯⋯⋯⋯2大匙

③{
酒⋯⋯⋯⋯1大匙
高湯⋯⋯⋯⋯4杯
醬油⋯⋯⋯⋯3大匙
鹽⋯⋯⋯⋯半小匙
味精⋯⋯⋯半小匙
糖⋯⋯⋯⋯半小匙
麻油⋯⋯⋯半小匙

④{
太白粉⋯3大匙
水⋯⋯⋯3大匙

醋⋯⋯⋯⋯1大匙
胡椒⋯⋯⋯¼小匙
火腿絲⋯⋯1大匙

❶ 魚翅撕成細絲，魚皮切絲，油1大匙燒熱將①料炒香，加酒1大匙，清水4杯，待滾揀去葱薑，隨把魚翅、魚皮放入煮約5分鐘，撈起備用。

❷ 將③料燒沸再加入②料及魚翅、魚皮，煮約6分鐘，見魚翅已軟以④料勾汁最後加醋及胡椒，上洒火腿絲以增美觀。

■ 如魚翅太硬可加鹽、味精各半小匙，高湯2杯，預先用蒸鍋蒸爛。

三丝鱼翅 Three-Flavor Shredded Soup

北平菜　Peking
12人份 12 servings

6 oz. pre-softened shark's fin *[1]
6 oz. pre-softened fish skin *[1]
①{
6 1-inch sections green onion
6 slices ginger root

②{
1 C. shredded bamboo shoot
¼ C. shredded pre-softened black mushroom
½ C. shredded pork loin
2 T. shredded Chinese ham *[2]

③{
1 T. rice wine
4 C. stock
3 T. soy sauce
½ t. salt
½ t. MSG
½ t. sugar
½ t. sesame oil

④{
3 T. cornstarch
3 T. water
1 T. vinegar
¼ t. black pepper
1 T. shredded Chinese ham

❶ Shred shark's fin and fish skin. Heat pan and 1T. oil and stir-fry ① until fragrant; add 1T. rice wine and 4C. water; cook 2 minutes and remove onion and ginger; add shark's fin and fish skin and cook 5 minutes; remove and drain. (discard liquid).

❷ Heat ③ until boiling and add ingredients of ② plus shark's fin and fish skin; cook about 6 minutes over medium heat and add ④ to thicken. Add vinegar, pepper and stir; remove to serving bowl and sprinkle shredded ham on top.

*[1] See "Helpful Hints" for directions for pre-softening shark's fin and fish skin.
*[2] You may substitute and vary the shredded ingredients according to your preference.

<table>
<tr><td>雞……1 隻 1 斤半</td><td rowspan="6">② { 酒……1 大匙
醬油…3 大匙
味精…1 小匙
糖……半小匙
高湯……4 杯</td><td>③ { 筍絲………1 杯
冬菇絲…2 大匙
火腿絲…2 大匙</td></tr>
</table>

雞……1 隻 1 斤半
醬油………2 大匙
「炸油」……6 杯
發好魚翅……4 兩
發好魚皮……4 兩
① { 葱（3 公分長）5 枝
薑……………5 片

② { 酒……1 大匙
醬油…3 大匙
味精…1 小匙
糖……半小匙
高湯……4 杯

③ { 筍絲………1 杯
冬菇絲…2 大匙
火腿絲…2 大匙
④ { 太白粉…3 大匙
水………3 大匙
醋………1 大匙
胡椒……¼ 小匙

❶ 醬油 2 大匙抹勻雞身，入油鍋以大火炸呈金黃色撈起。

❷ 魚翅撕成細絲，魚皮切絲，油 1 大匙燒熱，將①料炒香加酒 1 大匙，水 4 杯待滾，揀去葱、薑隨把魚翅魚皮放入煮約 5 分鐘，撈起備用。

❸ ②料燒開，將雞、魚翅、魚皮及③料放入煮約 3 0 分鐘，見雞熟透，先把雞撈起，盛大湯碗內，剩餘以④料勾汁加 1 大匙醋，並洒胡椒粉即可，淋在雞上趁熱供食。

魚翅燒雞 Braised Chicken with Shark's Fin

台灣菜　Taiwanese
12 人份　12 servings

1 whole chicken (about 2 lbs.)
2 T. soy sauce
6 C. oil for frying
4 oz. pre-softened shark's fin
4 oz. pre-softened fish skin
① { 5 1-inch sections green onion
5 slices ginger root

② { 1 T. rice wine
3 T. soy sauce
1 t. MSG
½ t. sugar
4 C. stock

③ { 1 C. shredded precooked bamboo shoot
2 T. shredded Chinese black mushroom
2 T. shredded Chinese ham

④ { 3 T. cornstarch
3 T. water
1 T. vinegar
¼ t. black pepper

❶ Rub exterior of chicken with 2T. soy sauce. Heat oil for deep-frying; deep-fry chicken over high heat until golden brown; remove and drain.

❷ Shred pre-softened shark's fin and fish skin. Heat pan and 1T. oil; stir-fry ① until fragrant; add 1T. rice wine and 4C. water. When liquid comes to a boil, remove onion and ginger; add shark's fin and fish skin shreds; cook 5 minutes and remove; drain (discard liquid).

❸ In a large pot or casserole, bring ② to a boil; add chicken, shark's fin, fish skin and ③. Cook 30 minutes covered, over medium heat. (Chicken should be very tender). Remove chicken to serving casserole; heat soup until boiling; add ④ to thicken, vinegar and black pepper. Pour soup over chicken and serve.

<table>
<tr><td>

熟鴨肉絲‥‥‥‥‥‥‥‥半杯
① ┌ 筍絲‥‥‥‥‥‥‥‥‥半杯
　　│ 冬菇（泡軟切絲）
　　│ 木耳（泡軟切絲）
　　│ 海參（泡軟切絲）　　各¼杯
　　│ 豬皮（水煮１０分鐘
　　└　　　切絲）

</td><td>

② ┌ 高湯‥‥‥‥‥‥‥‥‥６杯
　　│ 醬油‥‥‥‥‥‥‥‥２大匙
　　│ 鹽‥‥‥‥‥‥‥‥‥１小匙
　　│ 味精‥‥‥‥‥‥‥‥半小匙
　　│ 麻油‥‥‥‥‥‥‥‥１小匙
　　└ 胡椒‥‥‥‥‥‥‥‥¼小匙
③ ┌ 太白粉‥‥‥‥‥‥‥２大匙
　　└ 水‥‥‥‥‥‥‥‥‥２大匙

</td></tr>
</table>

❶ 將②料燒沸，放入①料及鴨絲煮２分鐘，再以③料勾汁即成。

 燴 鴨 絲 Shredded Duckling
and Assorted Vegetable Soup　　　　廣東菜　Cantonese
12人份 **12 servings**

½　C.　shredded precooked duckling meat
① ┌ ½　C.　shredded bamboo shoot
　│ ¼　C.　shredded pre-softened Chinese black mushroom
　│ ¼　C.　shredded pre-softened wood ears
　│ ¼　C.　shredded pre-softened sea cucumber (bêche-de-mer)
　└ ¼　C.　shredded pre-softened pork skin

② ┌ 6　C.　stock
　│ 2　T.　soy sauce
　│ 1　t.　salt
　│ ½　t.　MSG
　│ 1　t.　sesame oil
　└ ¼　t.　black pepper
③ ┌ 2　T.　cornstarch
　└ 2　T.　water

❶ Heat ② until boiling; add ingredients of ① and shredded duckling meat. Cook 2 minutes over medium heat; add ③ to thicken and pour into soup serving bowl; serve.

<table>
<tbody>
<tr><td rowspan="5">①</td><td>魷魚絲‥‥‥‥⅓杯</td></tr>
<tr><td>海參絲‥‥‥‥⅓杯</td></tr>
<tr><td>木耳絲‥‥‥‥⅓杯</td></tr>
<tr><td>豆腐絲‥‥‥‥⅓杯</td></tr>
<tr><td>雞血絲‥‥‥‥⅓杯</td></tr>
</tbody>
</table>

冬菇絲　　　各2大匙
火腿絲 }

② 里肌肉…2兩
醬油…1小匙
太白粉1小匙
麻油…半小匙

③ 水‥‥‥‥6杯
鹽‥‥‥2小匙
味精‥‥1小匙
糖‥‥‥1小匙

④ 太白粉3大匙
水‥‥‥3大匙
雞蛋‥‥2個

⑤ 醬油‥2大匙
醋‥‥‥3大匙
麻油‥1小匙
胡椒‥1小匙
香菜‥1大匙
葱絲‥2大匙
薑絲‥2大匙

❶ 將①料在滾水內川燙撈起。蛋打勻備用。

❷ 里肌肉切絲，調②料。

❸ ⑤料調在湯碗裡。

❹ 將③料燒開，下①料及冬菇、火腿絲待滾，放入肉絲，再以④料勾成薄汁後把蛋徐徐放入湯內，用鍋鏟攪勻倒入盛有⑤料之湯碗內即成。

■ 家庭做使用材料可簡化，如僅用豆腐、雞血、肉、蛋等亦可。

酸辣湯 Hot and Sour Soup

<table>
<tbody>
<tr><td rowspan="7">①</td><td>⅓ C. shredded squid</td></tr>
<tr><td>⅓ C. shredded sea weed</td></tr>
<tr><td>⅓ C. shredded pre-softened wood ears</td></tr>
<tr><td>⅓ C. shredded bean curd</td></tr>
<tr><td>⅓ C. shredded chicken blood*</td></tr>
<tr><td>2 T. shredded pre-softened Chinese black mushrooms</td></tr>
<tr><td>2 T. shredded precooked Chinese ham</td></tr>
</tbody>
</table>

2 oz. pork loin

② 1 t. soy sauce
1 t. cornstarch
½ t. sesame oil

③ 6 C. water
2 t. salt
1 t. MSG
1 t. sugar

④ 3 T. cornstarch
3 T. water

2 eggs

⑤ 2 T. soy sauce
3 T. vinegar
1 t. sesame oil
1 t. black pepper
1 T. chopped coriander
2 T. shredded green onion
2 T. shredded ginger root

❶ Blanch ingredients of ① in boiling water and remove; beat eggs lightly.

❷ Shred pork loin and mix with ② .

❸ Place ingredients of ⑤ in a soup bowl.

❹ Heat ③ until boiling; add ingredients of ① , Chinese black mushrooms, and Chinese ham; when liquid boils again, add shredded pork loin. Stir to separate pork shreds and add ④ to thicken. Trun off heat and add eggs slowly in a thin stream; stir lightly and pour into soup bowl with ⑤ ; mix and serve.

■ Family-style Hot and Sour Soup may be made using only shredded bean curd, softened wood ears, pork loin and eggs.

* May be omitted.

黄魚……半條半斤	高湯………………6 杯	太白粉……3 大匙
① 鹽…………¾小匙	② 營養豆腐(切小片)…1 條	③ 水…………3 大匙
酒…………1 小匙	熟筍片………………半杯	④ 蛋白………1 個
薑…………1 片	洋菇片………………半杯	水…………1 大匙
葱…………1 枝	鹽…………………2 小匙	
	味精………………1 小匙	

❶ 黄魚去鱗及內臟，調①料拌醃後蒸熟，趁熱把魚肉全部拆出，魚骨不要。

❷ ②料各料切小片，蛋白加水 1 大匙打勻成蛋白水。

❸ 油 1 大匙燒熱，加酒半大匙及②料待滾，魚肉連蒸汁傾下，即以③料勾成薄汁熄火徐徐倒入④
　料攪拌，最後加麻油、胡椒各少許盛湯碗內即可供食。

■ 宴客時可用火腿、蹄筋、干貝等珍貴配料。

黃魚羹 Yellow Fish Soup

廣東菜　Cantonese
12人份　12 servings

½ yellow fish*(about ⅔ lb.)	6　C. stock	3　T. cornstarch
① ¾ t. salt	② 1　square bean curd	③ 3　T. water
1 t. rice wine	½　small precooked bamboo shoot	④ 1　egg white
1 slice ginger root	½　C. button mushrooms	1　T. water
1 stalk green onion	2　t. salt	
	1　t. MSG	

❶ Clean fish half and mix with ① ; place in steamer and steam 10 minutes over high heat until tender; remove fish meat and shred. (discard bones and skin, but retain liquid)

❷ Cut bean curd into ½-inch slices; slice bamboo shoot and mushrooms into paper-thin ⅓-inch squares; beat ④ lightly.

❸ Heat pan and 1T. oil; add ½T. rice wine and ② . When mixture begins to boil, add fish meat and retained liquid; add ③ to thicken and mix. Turn off heat and add ④ slowly in a thin stream; add ½t. sesame oil and a dash of black pepper; mix lightly and serve.

* If yellow fish is unavailable, substitute sea bass or flounder.

■ Chinese ham and dried scallops may also be added for extra flavor.

瘦肉……………２兩	②{ 水…………３杯 冬菇絲…２大匙 筍絲………半杯	⑤{ 醬油…半大匙 黑醋…１小匙 胡椒…¼小匙 麻油…¼小匙 香菜……少許
①{ 醬油………１小匙 太白粉………１小匙 麻油………¼小匙 炸香紅葱頭…１大匙 魚漿……………１兩	③{ 鹽………１小匙 味精……半小匙 糖……半小匙 ④{ 水……２大匙 太白粉…２大匙	

❶ 瘦肉切薄片，調①料，醃約２０分鐘後，與炸香紅葱頭及魚漿攪勻。

❷ ②料燒開，投入肉片並調③料，隨即以④料太白粉水勾汁，最後調上⑤料並洒香菜即成。

■ 配料可改白蘿蔔、大黃瓜、花菜或白菜等。

肉　羹 Meat Slices with Fish Paste in Broth

台灣菜　Taiwanese
6人份　6 servings

2 oz. pork loin	3 C. water	4{ 2 T. water 2 T. cornstarch
①{ 1 t. soy sauce 1 t. cornstarch ¼ t. sesame oil	②{ 2 T. shredded pre-softened Chinese black mushroom ½ C. shredded, precooked bamboo shoot *2	½ T. soy sauce 1 t. worcestershire sauce
1 T. chopped, sauteed shallots *1 1 oz. fish paste	③{ 1 t. salt ½ t. MSG ½ t. sugar	⑤{ ¼ t. black pepper ¼ t. sesame oil

few sprigs chopped coriander

❶ Slice pork loin into paper-thin bite-size pieces; mix with ① and soak 20 minutes. Add chopped sauteed shallots and mix; add fish paste and mix ingredients.

❷ Heat ② in a pan. When mixture begins to boil, add pork slices, one by one, making sure that each piece is thoroughly coated with fish paste; add ③ and ④ to thicken. Add ⑤ , chopped coriander and stir; pour into soup bowl and serve.

*1 Shallots must first be minced and sauteed lightly in oil until brown; remove and use as directed.

*2 Shredded turnip, cucumber or cabbage may be substituted for bamboo shoot.

① 蘆筍‧‧‧‧‧‧‧‧‧‧‧‧‧‧ 1 罐
　高湯‧‧‧‧‧‧‧‧‧‧‧‧‧‧ 4 杯
　酒‧‧‧‧‧‧‧‧‧‧‧‧‧‧‧‧ 半大匙
　鹽‧‧‧‧‧‧‧‧‧‧‧‧‧‧ 1½小匙
　味精‧‧‧‧‧‧‧‧‧‧‧‧‧‧ 1 小匙

② 太白粉‧‧‧‧‧‧‧‧‧‧‧‧ 3 大匙
　水‧‧‧‧‧‧‧‧‧‧‧‧‧‧‧‧ 3 大匙

③ 蛋白‧‧‧‧‧‧‧‧‧‧‧‧‧‧ 2 個
　水‧‧‧‧‧‧‧‧‧‧‧‧‧‧‧‧ 2 大匙

❶ 蘆筍切2公分長段，連蘆筍汁放入①料內燒開，改小火，以②料勾成薄糊狀熄火，隨即徐徐倒入調勻之③料，並以鍋鏟攪動，使其散開，趁熱供食。

蘆筍濃湯 Fluffy Asparagus Soup

① 1 lb. 3 oz. can asparagus with liquid
4 C. stock
½ T. rice wine
1½ t. salt
1 t. MSG

② 3 T. cornstarch
3 T. water

③ 2 egg whites
2 T. water

❶ Drain asparagus (retain liquid) and cut into ½-inch sections. Heat ① , asparagus sections and retained liquid until boiling over low heat; add ② to thicken and turn off heat. Lightly beat ③ and slowly add to soup in a thin stream; mix lightly and serve.

① ⎰ 粟米……1 罐
　　高湯……4 杯
　　鹽……1 小匙
　　味精…半小匙

② ⎰ 太白粉……4 大匙
　　水…………4 大匙

③ ⎰ 青豆仁……1 杯
　　高湯………2 杯
　　鹽………半小匙
　　味精……¼ 小匙

❶ 將①料燒開後，以 ⅔ 之②料，勾成薄糊狀，盛於大湯碗內。

❷ 將③料用果汁機打細後，燒開以 ⅓ ②料勾成薄糊狀，加在粟米湯上，做成太極花樣（如圖狀）。

太極青雲 Green Peas and Corn Soup

廣東菜　Cantonese
6人份　6 servings

① ⎰ 1　lb. 1 can creamed corn (about 2C.)
　　4　C. stock
　　1　t. salt
　　½　t. MSG

② ⎰ 4　T. cornstarch
　　4　T. water

③ ⎰ 1　C. green peas
　　2　C. stock
　　½　t. salt
　　¼　t. MSG

❶ Heat ① until boiling; using ⅔ of ② mixture. Slowly add to thicken; pour into serving bowl.

❷ Place ③ mixture in a blender and blend at high speed until mixture is very fine; pour into a saucepan and heat until boiling; use remaining ⅓ of ② to thicken; slowly pour into one side of serving bowl. Already containing corn mixture. Using a spoon, coax liquid into the illustrated design; serve.

虱目魚⋯⋯⋯1條12兩

① 當歸⋯⋯⋯⋯⋯1錢半
水⋯⋯⋯⋯⋯⋯6杯
鹽⋯⋯⋯⋯⋯⋯2小匙
味精⋯⋯⋯⋯⋯1小匙
酒⋯⋯⋯⋯⋯⋯1大匙
薑⋯⋯⋯⋯⋯⋯2片

❶ 虱目魚洗淨，斜切成塊，置碗內，加①料，燉約30分鐘即成。

當歸虱目魚 Fresh Fish and Dang Guei Broth

1　whole pickerel (about 1lb.)

① 1/6 oz. "dang guei" (4—5 pieces)*
6　C. water
2　t.　salt
1　t.　MSG
1　T.　rice wine
2　slices ginger root

❶ Clean fish and cut into 1-inch thick sections; mix with ① and place in steamer; steam about 30 minutes over medium heat; pour into soup bowl and serve.

* "Dang guei" is a type of dry, pungent herb used for flavoring. It is very beneficial nutritionally and is available at any Chinese herbal drug store.

牛肉(煮湯用)１斤	番茄……２個	③	鹽……４小匙
馬鈴薯………２個	洋葱……１個		味精…２小匙
①{ 紅蘿蔔(大)…１條	②{ 醬油…１大匙		
包心菜(中)…半個	酒……１大匙		

❶ 牛肉、馬鈴薯、紅蘿蔔、包心菜切塊，番茄、洋葱切小丁備用。

❷ 牛肉在開水內川燙撈起，盛入快鍋加水１５杯中火煮３０分鐘，至牛肉８分爛。

❸ 油４大匙燒熱，將洋葱炒軟隨入番茄略炒，加②料炒香即與①、③料同入牛肉鍋內蓋鍋，中火
煮１５分鐘即可。

羅 宋 湯 Beef Soup a la Lo Sung

1⅓ lbs. beef (for soup)	2 tomatoes	③{	4 t. salt
①{ 2 potatoes	1 onion		2 t. MSG
1 carrot (large)	②{ 1 T. soy sauce		
½ Chinese celery cabbage	1 T. rice wine		

❶ Cut beef, potatoes, carrot, Chinese celery cabbage into large cubes and dice tomatoes and onions.

❷ Scald the beef in boiling water and remove, then place into a pressure cooker, add 15C. water; cook
for 30 min., until the beef is 80% cooked.

❸ Heat 4T. oil and fry onions until softened, then add tomatoes and stir-fry briefly. Pour in ②. Put
this mixture, together with ① and ③ into pressure cooker and cook over moderate heat for 15 min.

雞……半隻1斤	麻油………4大匙		水…………2杯半
	老薑…………6片	①	糖…………1小匙
	酒…………1杯		鹽…………1小匙

❶ 將雞切塊備用。

❷ 麻油燒熱薑片下鍋炒香，即將雞塊倒入炒1分鐘，加酒1杯待滾，即入①料大火燒開改小火煮約20分鐘即成。

麻油雞湯 Sesame Chicken Soup

台灣菜　Taiwanese
6人份　6 servings

½ chicken (about 1½lbs.)	4 T. sesame oil		2½ C. water
	6 slices ginger root	①	1 t. sugar
	1 C. rice wine		1 t. salt

❶ Rinse chicken and drain; cut (through bones) into bite-size pieces.

❷ Heat pan and sesame oil; stir-fry ginger root until fragrant and add chicken pieces; stir-fry 1 minute and add rice wine. When mixture begins to boil, add ① . Turn heat to low and simmer covered for 20 minutes; pour into serving bowl and serve.

雞‥‥‥‥‥‥1 隻　　味全花瓜‥‥‥半杯　　｜水‥‥‥‥‥‥6 杯

花瓜汁‥‥‥3 大匙　　｜鹽‥‥‥‥‥‥半小匙

①｜酒‥‥‥‥‥‥半大匙

｜葱‥‥‥‥‥‥2 枝

｜薑‥‥‥‥‥‥2 片

❶ 雞以熱水燙洗後，盛入燉盅內加入①料，燉約３０分鐘，再把花瓜連同花瓜汁再燉１０分鐘即可。

■ 雞經燙洗後，燉出的湯汁較清。

1　whole chicken (about 2⅔lbs.) *[1]　　½　C.　Wei-Chuan pickled cucumbers　　6　C.　water

3　T.　pickled cucumber marinade　　½　t.　salt

①　½　T.　rice wine

2　stalks green onion

2　slices　ginger root

❶ Clean chicken and place in soup pot or heatproof casserole; add ① and steam *[2] 30 minutes; add pickled cucumbers and marinade and steam an additional 10 minutes; remove and serve.

*[1]　See note on chicken on P. 196.

*[2]　See note on steaming on P. 196.

雞‥‥‥‥‥‥‥‥‥‥‥1 隻　　　清水‥‥‥‥‥‥‥‥‥4 杯
冬菇（小）‥‥‥‥‥1 2 朵　　　酒‥‥‥‥‥‥‥‥‥‥1 大匙
　　　　　　　　　　　①鹽‥‥‥‥‥‥‥‥‥1 ½ 小匙
　　　　　　　　　　　　　葱‥‥‥‥‥‥‥‥‥‥2 枝
　　　　　　　　　　　　　薑‥‥‥‥‥‥‥‥‥‥2 片
　　　　　　　　　　　　　味精‥‥‥‥‥‥‥‥‥½ 小匙

❶ 雞以熱水燙洗後，裝入燉盅內加①料燉約３０分鐘。
❷ 冬菇洗淨泡軟與味精加進燉雞內，繼續燉２０分鐘即可。

冬菇燉雞 Stewed Chicken with Chinese Black Mushrooms

台灣菜　Taiwanese
12人份　12 servings

1 whole chicken*¹ (about 2⅔ lbs.)
12 small Chinese black mushrooms

① 4 C. water
1 T. rice wine
1½ t. salt
2 stalks green onion
2 slices ginger root
½ t. MSG

❶ Clean chicken and place in soup pot or casserole; add ① and steam*² 30 minutes over medium heat.
❷ Soften black mushrooms in warm water; drain and remove stems (discard). Add mushroom caps to soup with ½t. MSG; cover and steam an additional 20 minutes; remove and serve.
*¹ The chicken may be cooked whole as directed or cut into bite-size pieces before cooking.
*² This soup may be cooked directly on stove over medium heat or steamed in a steamer as directed above.

冬菇‥‥‥‥‥‥‥‥ 1 兩 　　　高湯‥‥‥‥‥‥‥‥ 6杯
雞腳‥‥‥‥‥‥‥‥ ２４隻 　酒‥‥‥‥‥‥‥‥ 半大匙
　　　　　　　　　①〈鹽‥‥‥‥‥‥‥‥ ２小匙
　　　　　　　　　　　葱‥‥‥‥‥‥‥‥ ２枝
　　　　　　　　　　　薑‥‥‥‥‥‥‥‥ ２大片

❶ 冬菇泡軟，去蒂待用。

❷ 雞腳尖及中間大骨去掉，入開水川燙１分鐘撈出，用清水洗淨，盛燉鍋內加①料，蒸約３０分
　　鐘後，放入冬菇繼續燉約２０分鐘，即可供食。

鳳足冬菇 Black Mushroom and Chicken-Foot Soup

廣東菜 Cantonese
12人份 12 servings

12 Chinese black mushrooms
24 chicken feet

① {
6　C. stock
½　T. rice wine
2　t. salt
2　stalks green onion
2　slices ginger root
}

❶ Soften black mushrooms in warm water; drain and remove stems (discard).

❷ Remove nails and main bone from chicken feet; cook feet in boiling water for 1 minute to clean; rinse again. Place chicken feet and ① in a pan and steam 30 minutes over medium heat; add black mushroom caps and steam and additional 20 minutes; serve.

■ See note on steaming on P. 196.

<table>
<tr><td>①{</td><td>雞翼‥‥‥‥１６隻
冬菇（泡軟）‥‥３朵
瘦火腿‥‥‥‥１兩
熟筍‥‥‥‥‥１枝
里肌肉‥‥‥‥２兩</td><td>②{</td><td>醬油‥‥‥‥１½小匙
味精‥‥‥‥¼小匙
太白粉‥‥‥１小匙</td><td>③{</td><td>洋菇‥‥‥‥半杯
大黃瓜‥‥‥１條
高湯‥‥‥‥半杯
酒‥‥‥‥‥１小匙
鹽‥‥‥‥‥半小匙
味精‥‥‥‥¼小匙</td><td>④{</td><td>高湯‥‥‥‥‥４杯
鹽‥‥‥‥‥１小匙
味精‥‥‥‥半小匙
麻油‥‥‥‥半小匙</td></tr>
</table>

❶ 將①料切成長條（０.５公分×０.５公分×３公分）各１６條。里肌肉去白筋切薄片調②料拌勻，洋菇整粒劃刀、大黃瓜切滾刀塊，分別放入開水內燙熟撈出。

❷ 水６杯燒開，雞翼放入煮５分鐘撈起待冷，由二節彎處切開，翼尖留用，翼身取出大骨（皮勿破）其空隙處塞入①料各１枝，整齊的擺三排在蒸碗底，上置肉片，黃瓜及翼尖加③料，蒸約１５分鐘取出，上蓋一只盤子，將湯汁濾出加在④料內，隨即反扣在大湯碗內，四週擺入洋菇，淋上燒開④料即成。

■ 如無火腿可用鹹菜代替。

川翼洋菇 Stuffed Chicken Wing Soup

16 chicken wings

①{
3 pre-softened Chinese black mushrooms
1 oz. precooked Chinese ham
1 precooked bamboo shoot
2 oz. pork loin

②{
1½ t. soy sauce
¼ t. MSG
1 t. cornstarch

③{
½ C. button mushrooms
1 large cucumber
½ C. stock
1 t. rice wine
½ t. salt
¼ t. MSG

④{
4 C. stock
1 t. salt
½ t. MSG
½ t. sesame oil

❶ Cut each ingredient of ① into 16 matchstick-sized pieces about 1½-inches long. Slice pork loin into thin, bite-size pieces and mix with ② ; lightly score the tops of mushroom caps and cross-cut the cucumber into, bite-size pieces. Separately cook the pork loin and button mushrooms in boiling water 1 minute; remove and cook the cucumber in boiling water for 3 minutes; remove and drain.

❷ Boil 6C. water and add chicken wings; cook 5 minutes and remove; let cool. Make 2 light cuts on the underside of each wing at each end of the main bone; cut each wing in two at the elbow and remove the main bone. Insert 1 stick of each ingredient of ① into the hole left by the main bone. In a medium-sized soup bowl, arrange the stuffed wings sections in 3 rows to line sides of bowl; place pork loin, cucumber pieces and wing elbows on top and pack securely. Add ③ and place in steamer; steam 15 minutes over medium heat; remove and drain liquid from bowl (add to ④) and invert chicken wings into soup serving bowl; place mushrooms on sides. Heat ④ until boiling and pour into soup serving bowl; serve.

			①	
鶉蛋⋯⋯⋯ 1 打	熟筍⋯⋯⋯⋯⋯⋯ 1 枝		高湯⋯⋯⋯ 6 杯	
香菜⋯⋯ 1 2 片	熟紅蘿蔔⋯⋯⋯⋯ 1 條		酒⋯⋯⋯ 半大匙	
火腿末⋯ 1 大匙	洋菇⋯⋯⋯⋯⋯⋯ 半罐		鹽⋯⋯⋯ 2 小匙	
	熟火腿⋯⋯⋯⋯⋯ 2 兩		味精⋯⋯ 1 小匙	
	油菜或白菜⋯⋯ 1 2 兩			

❶ 備湯匙或小碟，在其底塗上油，每 1 只湯匙打 1 個鶉蛋，上面放 1 片香菜及少量火腿末，慢火蒸約 3 分鐘。

❷ 筍及紅蘿蔔切成花片，洋菇、火腿切片，油菜取其嫩莖。

❸ 先用滾水川燙油菜，將筍、紅蘿蔔、洋菇、火腿、鶉蛋依順序燙熱放在大碗裡。

❹ ①料燒滾，倒在盛好鶉蛋碗中即成。

洋菇鶉蛋湯 Mushroom and Quail Egg Soup

廣東菜　Cantonese
12人份　**12 servings**

			①	
1 dozen quail eggs *[1]	1 precooked bamboo shoot		6 C. stock	
12 sprigs of coriander	1 precooked carrot		½ T. rice wine	
1 T. chopped precooked ham	½ C. button mushrooms		2 t. salt	
	2 oz. precooked Chinese ham		1 t. MSG	
	1 lb. rape *[2]			

❶ Lightly coat 12 egg cups or molds of an egg poacher with oil; break an egg into each and sprinkle coriander and ham on top; steam or poach eggs for 3 minutes over low heat; remove from steamer and when eggs are cool, remove.

❷ Slice bamboo shoot and carrot into thin bite-size pieces. Cut Chinese ham into thin slices and remove any old leaves from rape and trim stalks; cut into 4-inch sections.

❸ Cook rape in boiling water for 1 minute; remove and place in soup serving bowl. Place bamboo slices, carrots, mushrooms, rape sections and eggs in boiling water and cook until heated through; remove and place in soup serving bowl.

❹ Heat ① until boiling and pour into soup bowl; serve.

*[1] If quail eggs are unavailable, substitute chicken eggs and increase poaching time to 7 minutes.

*[2] Rape ("you tsai") is the pictured Chinese vegetable and may be purchased at a Chinese grocery store. If unavailable, substitute spinach.

蝦仁⋯⋯⋯6兩		草菇⋯⋯⋯⋯1杯
肥肉⋯⋯⋯1兩	酒⋯⋯⋯⋯半小匙	酒⋯⋯⋯⋯半大匙
	鹽⋯⋯⋯⋯半小匙	高湯⋯⋯⋯⋯6杯
	味精⋯⋯⋯半小匙	鹽⋯⋯⋯⋯2小匙
①	胡椒⋯⋯⋯¼小匙	② 味精⋯⋯⋯2小匙
	麻油⋯⋯⋯半小匙	葱（3公分長）6枝
	蛋白⋯⋯⋯⋯1個	
	太白粉⋯⋯1大匙	

❶ 蝦仁拭乾水份，用刀壓成蝦泥，盛於大碗內加肥肉（剁碎）及①料，用手攪動至蝦絨狀（前後約5分鐘）。

❷ 草菇用開水煮3分鐘，撈起。

❸ 將蝦絨1個1個擠成蝦丸，放入②料內，俟全部做好後，以中火燒沸煮2分鐘，再放入草菇，即以大火燒開，盛湯碗內，再洒葱段即成。

鮮菇蝦丸湯 Shrimp Balls in Mushroom Soup

廣東菜 Cantonese
12人份 12 servings

6 oz. raw, shelled shrimp		1 C. straw mushrooms
1 oz. pork fat	½ t. rice wine	½ T. rice wine
	½ t. salt	6 C. stock
	½ t. MSG	2 t. salt
①	¼ t. black pepper	② 2 t. MSG
	½ t. sesame oil	6 1-inch sections green onion
	1 egg white	
	1 T. cornstarch	

❶ Rinse and devein shrimp; drain and smash with the side of cleaver; chop finely. Chop pork fat finely and mix with chopped shrimp and ① ; throw ingredients lightly against inside of mixing bowl to thoroughly combine. (shrimp paste).

❷ Cook straw mushrooms in boiling water for 1 minute; remove and drain.

❸ Shape shrimp paste into balls and place in ② ; heat mixture over medium heat and cook 2 minutes; add straw mushrooms and turn heat to high. When liquid boils, add green onion sections and remove to serving bowl; serve.

粉蚌（1斤）…24個		鹽………1小匙、胡椒………¼小匙		鹽………半小匙
蝦仁……………2兩		味精……半小匙、冬菇末……1大匙	②	味精………¼小匙
荸薺……………1兩	①	酒………半大匙、洋火腿末……1大匙		胡椒………¼小匙
絞肉……………4兩		麻油……半小匙、太白粉……1大匙		嫩薑絲…1大匙

❶ 蝦仁拭乾水份，與荸薺均剁碎。

❷ 粉蚌用清水5杯煮（淹蓋殼面），見蚌殼口微開時，即熄火候冷，蚌湯留用。

❸ 將蚌肉取出，與絞肉、蝦絨、荸薺末及①料攪勻，做成肉餡，鑲入蚌殼內抹平、大火蒸熟（約5分鐘左右）取置容器內。

❹ 將蚌湯燒開調②料，倒入容器內，上面洒薑絲，即可供食。

■ 此道菜可當湯，可當菜，依各人喜好將湯增減。

清蒸粉蚌 Stuffed Clams in Broth

台灣菜 Taiwanese
12人份 12 servings

24 clams (about 1⅓lbs.)
2 oz. raw, shelled shrimp
1 oz. water chestnuts
4 oz. chopped pork

①
1 t. salt
½ t. MSG
½ T. rice wine
½ t. sesame oil
¼ t. black pepper
1 T. chopped pre-softened Chinese black mushrooms
1 T. chopped Chinese ham
1 T. cornstarch

②
½ t. salt
¼ t. MSG
¼ t. black pepper
1 T. shredded ginger root

❶ Rinse and devein shrimp; drain and separately chop shrimp and water chestnuts finely.

❷ Rinse clams and place in 5C. water; cook until clams open slightly; drain clams and retain broth.

❸ Remove meat from clams and chop meat finely (keep 24 of the shells and discard the rest); mix clam meat with chopped pork, shrimp, water chestnuts and ① thoroughly. (filling). Place 1 portion filling in each clam shell and smooth top with the underside of a spoon; place stuffed clams on a heatproof plate and steam 5 minutes over high heat; remove and place in serving bowl.

❹ Heat retained clam broth until boiling and add ② ; mix lightly and pour into serving bowl; sprinkle shredded ginger on top and serve.

<table>
<tr><td rowspan="8">①</td><td>蝦仁（４８條）…半斤</td></tr>
<tr><td>酒……………１小匙</td></tr>
<tr><td>鹽……………½小匙</td></tr>
<tr><td>味精…………½小匙</td></tr>
<tr><td>胡椒…………½小匙</td></tr>
<tr><td>蛋白…………半個</td></tr>
<tr><td>太白粉………２大匙</td></tr>
</table>

蝦仁（剁碎）………４兩
肥肉（剁碎）………半兩
② 紅蘿蔔（切碎）…２大匙
荸薺（切碎）………２大匙
葱（切碎）…………１大匙

高湯………４杯
菜心………１條
③ 鹽…………１小匙
味精………半小匙
胡椒………¼小匙
酒…………１小匙

❶ 將蝦去殼，從蝦背切開（兩端不要切斷）調½的①料醃約２０分鐘。

❷ 將剩餘①料調入②料內，拌勻成餡。

❸ 每１條蝦攤開成片狀，二片中間（切口朝外）夾上餡可做２４個，置蒸盤（抹油）蒸約５分鐘取起放在湯碗內。

❹ 菜心切塊，放入高湯內煮熟，調③料，並倒入蒸好的蝦煮沸即可。

清湯合蝦 Stuffed Shrimp and Cucumber Soup

48 raw, shelled shrimp (about ⅔ lb.)

① 1 t. rice wine
¼ t. salt
¼ t. MSG
¼ t. black pepper
½ egg white
2 T. cornstarch

② 4 oz. raw, shelled shrimp, chopped finely
½ oz. pork fat, chopped finely
2 T. chopped precooked carrot
2 T. chopped water chestnuts
1 T. chopped green onion

4 C. stock
1 medium-sized cucumber

③ 1 t. salt
½ t. MSG
¼ t. black pepper
1 t. rice wine

❶ Rinse and devein shrimp; drain and slit each shrimp's mid-section in half, leaving halves connected at tail and head; mix shrimp with ½ of ① and let sit 20 minutes.

❷ Mix the other half of ① with ② ; lightly throw mixture against the inside of bowl to thoroughly combine ingredients, (filling). Separate filling into 24 portions.

❸ Open the "flaps" of each shrimp and stuff a portion of filling in middle; smooth edges with a spoon and place each stuffed shrimp on a lightly-oiled heatproof plate. Place in steamer and steam 5 minutes over medium heat.

❹ Peel skin from cucumber and roll-cut into bite-size pieces and cook in 4C. stock for about 5 minutes until tender; add stuffed shrimp and ③ ; stir and pour into serving bowl; serve.

蝦仁⋯⋯⋯⋯⋯⋯⋯⋯⋯6兩
肥肉⋯⋯⋯⋯⋯⋯⋯⋯⋯1兩
① 酒⋯⋯⋯半小匙、麻油⋯⋯半小匙
鹽⋯⋯⋯半小匙、蛋白⋯⋯1個
味精⋯⋯⋯¼小匙、太白粉⋯1大匙
胡椒⋯⋯⋯¼小匙

雞蛋⋯⋯⋯1個
② 太白粉⋯半小匙
水⋯⋯⋯1小匙
紫菜⋯⋯⋯2張

菜心（或黃瓜）⋯⋯1條
鹽⋯⋯⋯⋯2小匙
味精⋯⋯⋯1小匙
③ 胡椒⋯⋯¼小匙
麻油⋯⋯⋯1小匙
高湯⋯⋯⋯6杯

❶ 蝦仁洗淨並拭乾水份，用刀面壓成蝦泥，肥肉剁碎同盛於大碗內加①料，用手攪動至蝦絨狀（前後約5分鐘）。

❷ 雞蛋1個（將拌蝦仁剩餘蛋黃一起拌入）打散為避免煎破加入②料調勻。

❸ 鍋平均燒熱，用布或紙沾上油，塗擦在鍋面，把調好的蛋液倒入，將鍋轉動（使蛋液流成直徑30公分圓形）用小火烙至凝固，見蛋皮邊乾時，翻面略烙，即成蛋皮，切半，與紫菜各修成20公分×10公分各計2張。

❹ 蛋皮攤開，將¼份蝦絨抹平，上舖紫菜，再塗上一層蝦絨，由兩端捲起成如意形，接口處用蝦絨黏合，蒸7分鐘至熟，斜切1公分厚備用。

❺ 菜心煮熟，切滾刀塊，連同如意捲置於湯碗，注入燒開③料即可。

■ 為求美觀，做如意捲時，可酌量加入紅蘿蔔絲、綠蔥或香菇絲等。

清湯如意捲 Egg & Shrimp Rolls in Broth

台灣菜 Taiwanese
12人份 12 servings

½ lb. raw, shelled shrimp
1 oz. pork fat or suet
① { ½ t. rice wine • ½ t. sesame oil
½ t. salt • 1 egg white
¼ t. MSG • 1 T. cornstarch
¼ t. black pepper

1 egg
② { ½ t. cornstarch
1 t. water
2 sheets nori or purple laver seaweed

1 medium-size cucumber
③ { 2 t. salt
1 t. MSG
¼ t. black pepper
1 t. sesame oil
6 C. stock

❶ Rinse and devein shrimp; drain and smash with the side of cleaver; chop finely. Chop pork fat finely and mix with chopped shrimp and ① ; throw ingredients lightly against inside of mixing bowl to thoroughly combine (filling). Peel cucumber and roll-cut into bite-size pieces.

❷ Beat egg lightly (you may add the remaining egg yolk from ①); mix with ② .

❸ Heat a lightly-oiled pan and add egg mixture; rotate pan so that egg spreads evenly to coat pan and forms a thin pancake; cook until lightly brown and flip over to other side; cook a few more seconds until golden and remove; cut into half and trim to a 7 x 3-inch rectangle. Cut each nori sheet in half.

❹ Place an egg sheet flat on counter (long edge on horizontal); spread surface with ¼ of filling; smooth top and place a sheet of nori on top; beginning at each side edge, roll up jelly-roll style to middle (so that rolls will meet in middle); spread a bit of filling between rolls to secure them together; repeat process for other roll. Place rolls on a lightly-oiled heatproof plate; place in steamer and steam 7 minutes; remove and cut each roll into ½-inch sections.

❺ Heat ③ until boiling; add cucumber pieces and cook 3 minutes; remove and place in serving bowl; arrange egg roll sections on top and pour hot ③ mixture over all; serve.

絞肉‥‥‥‥‥‥‥‥‥‥‥‥‥‥‥１２兩
┌ 酒‥‥‥‥‥‥１小匙、麻油‥‥‥１小匙
│ 鹽‥‥‥‥‥¾小匙、炸香紅葱頭‥１大匙
① 味精‥‥‥‥半小匙、葱薑末各‥‥１大匙
│ 糖‥‥‥‥‥半小匙、清水‥‥‥‥６大匙
└ 胡椒‥‥‥‥¼小匙

包心菜‥‥‥‥‥‥２瓣
紫菜‥‥‥‥‥‥‥２張
腐皮‥‥‥‥‥‥‥２張
┌ 高湯‥‥‥‥‥‥半杯
② 鹽‥‥‥‥‥‥‥半小匙
│ 味精‥‥‥‥‥‥¼小匙
└ 酒‥‥‥‥‥‥‥１小匙

┌ 高湯‥‥‥‥‥‥‥４杯
│ 鹽‥‥‥‥‥‥‥１小匙
③ 味精‥‥‥‥‥‥半小匙
│ 胡椒‥‥‥‥‥‥¼小匙
│ 麻油‥‥‥‥‥‥¼小匙
└ 葱(３公分長)６枝

❶ 絞肉調①料拌勻成餡，包心菜（在開水內燙軟），紫菜、腐皮，每張切成四小張。

❷ 將每張包心菜、紫菜、腐皮各抹上餡，包成長５公分之春捲形肉捲（２４個）。

❸ 備中碗一只，將做好肉捲，依順序排好在碗內加②料大火蒸３０分鐘。

❹ 蒸好三色捲上蓋一只盤子，將湯汁濾出加在③料內，隨即將三色捲反扣在大湯碗內並倒入燒開的③料趁熱供食。

■ 捲肉捲時，包心菜須洒少許太白粉，腐皮沾少許水。

清湯三色捲 Three-Colored Rolls with Broth

上海菜　Shanghai
12人份 **12 servings**

	1	lb. chopped pork		
①	1	t. rice wine	• 1	t. sesame oil
	¾	t. salt	• 1	T. minced, sauteed shallots
	½	t. MSG	• 1	T. chopped green onion
	½	t. sugar	• 1	T. chopped ginger root
	¼	t. black pepper	• 6	T. water

	2	outer cabbage leaves
	2	sheets nori*[1]
	2	sheets bean curd skin
②	½	C. stock
	½	t. salt
	¼	t. MSG
	1	t. rice wine

	4	C. stock
	1	t. salt
③	½	t. MSG
	¼	t. black pepper
	¼	t. sesame oil
	6	1-inch sections green onion

❶ Add ① to chopped pork and mix ingredients thoroughly to combine (filling). Cook cabbage leaves briefly in boiling water until soft; remove and drain. Cut each piece of cabbage, nori and bean curd sheet into quarters.

❷ Place 1/24 of filling in center of each piece of nori, bean curd sheet and cabbage*[2], roll up edges to completely enclose filling and form a small roll about 2-inches long.

❸ In a medium-sized soup bowl, arrange the rolls in 3 rows to line bowl; place several rolls in center to form a compact mold; pour ② on top and place in steamer. Steam 30 minutes over high heat; remove.

❹ Drain soup from steaming and add to ③; invert rolls into a soup bowl and demold. Heat ③ until boiling and pour into soup bowl; serve.

*[1] If nori is unavailable, you may use egg sheets, (See P. 184 step ❶).

*[2] Since cabbage leaves may be a little wet for rolling; first sprinkle a little cornstarch on surface, then roll. If bean curd sheet is too dry, first sprinkle surface lightly with water.

■ You may substitute 11b. raw, shelled shrimp for chopped pork to make a shrimp stuffing.

草魚(中段)…1斤	油條……1條	花生粉…半大匙	①⎰鹽………2小匙
豌豆苗………2兩	「炸油」…1杯	葱末……1小匙	味精……1小匙
			高湯………6杯

❶ 草魚對剖兩半，去骨除皮，橫切成極薄片（4兩），放酒1大匙待用。

❷ 豌豆苗取嫩莖部洗淨。油條橫切約1公分片狀，燒開「炸油」，入油條稍炸，即撈起。

❸ 備一湯碗，底擺豌豆苗、再入油條，上面舖好魚肉（一片一片不要重疊），加花生粉，洒上葱末，然後把正在燒滾的①料，倒入沖熟，隨即用筷子攪勻，再洒入胡椒粉、醋，趁熱供食。

■ 取魚片後剩餘之魚骨和魚肉，可做為燉煮高湯用。

草魚肉可改用蝦、雞肉、猪腰
花生粉可改用芝麻粉   ⎰等加以變化
豌豆苗可改用容易煮熟的青菜，如生菜，西洋菜
油條可改用炸冬粉、毛菇、草菇

湯泡魚生 Fresh Fish and Vegetable Broth

湖南菜 Hunan
12人份 12 servings

1⅓ lbs. fillet of flounder or haddock	1 "you tiau" *2	½ T. crushed peanuts *3	①⎰2 t. salt
2 oz. green vegetable *1	1 C. oil for frying	1 t. chopped green onion	1 t. MSG
			6 C. stock

❶ Slice fish meat into paper-thin pieces; mix with 1T. rice wine.

❷ Trim any old leaves and hard stems from vegetable; cut "you tiau" into ⅓-inch slices. Heat oil for deep-frying and deep-fry "you tiau" 1 minute; remove and drain.

❸ In a large soup bowl, place green vegetable and "you tiau" sections; add fish slices, piece by piece; sprinkle crushed peanuts and chopped green onion on top. Heat ① until boiling; pour over fish slices and vegetable; sprinkle black pepper over all and stir; serve immediately.

*1 The pictured vegetable is called "dou miau" and may be purchased at a Chinese grocery store. If unavailable, substitute spinach, watercress, or lettuce.

*2 A "you tiau" is a type of crispy Chinese deep-fried cruller. If unavailable, substitute toasted croutons, or rice noodles and use in step 3 as directed; straw or button mushrooms may also be used.

*3 You may substitute crushed sesame seeds or omit completely.

①			③		④		⑤		⑥	
鯧魚⋯⋯⋯1斤4兩			熟筍絲⋯⋯2大匙		鹽⋯⋯⋯⋯⅓小匙		紅辣椒絲⋯1大匙		熱高湯⋯⋯4杯	
鹽⋯⋯⋯⋯1小匙			紅蘿蔔絲⋯2大匙		味精⋯⋯⋯半小匙		冬菇絲⋯⋯1大匙		鹽⋯⋯⋯⋯1小匙	
味精⋯⋯⋯半小匙			火腿絲⋯⋯1大匙		糖⋯⋯⋯⋯半小匙		榨菜絲⋯⋯2大匙		味精⋯⋯⋯半小匙	
酒⋯⋯⋯⋯1大匙			冬菇絲⋯⋯1大匙		胡椒⋯⋯⋯¼小匙		葱絲⋯⋯⋯1大匙		胡椒⋯⋯⋯¼小匙	
胡椒粉⋯⋯¼小匙			葱絲⋯⋯⋯1大匙		麻油⋯⋯⋯半小匙		薑絲⋯⋯⋯1大匙		麻油⋯⋯⋯半小匙	
太白粉⋯⋯1大匙					太白粉⋯1½大匙					

②	
蝦仁(剁碎)⋯	半杯
絞肉⋯⋯⋯⋯	

❶ 將鯧魚之魚頭、魚尾切下，用油炸熟，擺在盤兩端。

❷ 魚去骨取淨肉，斜切24薄片（4公分×5公分）計24片，攤開在菜板或盤上，調①料備用。

❸ 把②料與③料、④料攪拌成「餡」。

❹ 魚肉1片放上餡半大匙，捲成魚捲，全部做好，置於蒸盤內（盤內需塗油），上洒⑤料，水開大火蒸5分鐘，取出置魚頭及魚尾之中間，淋上⑥料即可。

如意魚捲 Steamed Fish Rolls with Broth

台灣菜 Taiwanese
12人份 **12 servings**

①		③		④		⑤		⑥	
1 whole pomfret* (about 1⅔ lbs.)		2 T. shredded precooked bamboo shoot		⅓ t. salt		1 T. shredded hot red pepper		4 C. hot stock	
1 t. salt		2 T. shredded carrot		½ t. MSG		1 T. shredded pre-softened Chinese black mushroom		1 t. salt	
½ t. MSG		1 T. shredded precooked Chinese ham		½ t. sugar		2 T. shredded Szechuan pickled mustard green		½ t. MSG	
1 T. rice wine		1 T. shredded Chinese black mushroom		¼ t. black pepper		1 T. shredded green onion		¼ t. black pepper	
¼ t. black pepper		1 T. shredded green onion		½ t. sesame oil		1 T. shredded ginger root		½ t. sesame oil	
1 T. cornstarch				1½ T. cornstarch					

②	
chopped raw shrimp	Combined ingredients equal ½C.
chopped pork	

❶ Clean fish and cut off head and tail. Heat oil for deep-frying and deep-fry head and tail until golden brown; remove, drain and place on serving plate.

❷ Cut fillets from mid-section of fish and cut each fillet diagonally into 12 thin slices; lay pieces flat on counter and rub surface of each with ① .

❸ Combine ingredients of ② , ③ and ④ and lightly throw against inside of bowl to mix thoroughly, (filling).

❹ Place ½T. filling in the center of each fish slice and roll up "jelly-roll style". Place each roll on a lightly-oiled heatproof plate and sprinkle ⑤ on top. Place in steamer and steam 5 minutes over high heat; remove and arrange rolls on serving plate between head and tail. Heat ⑥ until boiling and pour over fish rolls; serve.

* If pomfret is unavailable, substitute halibut or haddock.

①	冬瓜	2斤	②	水	4杯
	雞腿	2隻		葱	2枝
	火腿(4公分四方)	12片		薑	2片
	冬菇(泡軟)	6朵		酒	1大匙
	干貝	半兩		鹽	1小匙
				味精	半小匙
				胡椒	¼小匙

❶ 冬瓜去皮切成直徑4公分、厚1.5公分圓型塊狀，雞腿切塊，以熱水燙洗撈起。

❷ 將①料及②料同置燉盅，用玻璃紙封口，放進蒸鍋蒸約40分鐘即可供食。

■ 冬瓜形狀，可由個人喜好決定，圓形較美觀，家庭食用可切成方塊，既省時又不浪費。

原盅三味 Three-Flavor Steamed Soup

上海菜　Shanghai
12人份 12 servings

①	1	portion winter melon (about 2⅔ lbs.)	②	4 C. water	
	2	chicken legs		2 stalks green onion	
	12	thin 1½-inch squares Chinese ham		2 slices ginger root	
	6	pre-softened Chinese black mushrooms		1 T. rice wine	
	2	dried scallops		1 t. salt	
				½ t. MSG	
				¼ t. black pepper	

❶ Remove the skin from the winter melon and cut the meat into wafer-shapes* 1½ inches in diameter and ½ inch thick; cut the chicken legs, through bone, into bite-size pieces; place briefly in boiling water to clean.

❷ Place the ingredients of ① and ② in a pan and steam 40 minutes over medium heat; remove and pour into serving bowl; serve.

* The winter melon may be cut into a variety of "small shapes" according to your preference.

冬瓜·····················1斤半	①料	②	③
瘦火腿（3公分×1公分）24片	鹽·······半小匙	高湯······¼杯	高湯·····4杯
瘦肉·····················3兩	酒·······半大匙	鹽·······半小匙	鹽·······1小匙
	太白粉···1大匙	味精······¼小匙	味精·····半小匙
	冬菇（大）···3朵	酒·······半大匙	胡椒·····⅛小匙
	嫩薑絲···1大匙		麻油·····半小匙

❶ 冬瓜切片，第一刀不斷，第二刀切斷，共切24塊。（中間留縫每塊約6公分×3公分×1公分）。

❷ 瘦肉切片，拌①料燙熟。冬菇泡軟，每朵切4片。

❸ 冬瓜用滾水煮1分鐘取出，火腿夾在冬瓜縫裡，取一中型湯碗，將夾好火腿之冬瓜，整齊排在湯碗內，上置肉片、冬菇及淋上②料，水開蒸10分鐘，取出倒出湯汁於③料內，即反扣於湯碗內，加入燒開③料，上洒嫩薑絲即成。

■ 冬瓜皮勿削過厚，以保留冬瓜之青綠。

冬瓜火腿夾 Winter Melon Sandwiches with Chinese Ham in Broth
廣東菜 Cantonese
12人份 12 servings

- 1 portion winter melon (about 2 lbs.)
- 24 thin sticks precooked Chinese ham (about 1 x ⅓ inch)
- 3 oz. pork loin

① {
- ½ t. salt
- ½ T. rice wine
- 1 T. cornstarch
- 3 big Chinese black mushrooms
}

② {
- ¼ C. stock
- ½ t. salt
- ¼ t. MSG
- ½ T. rice wine
}

③ {
- 4 C. stock
- 1 t. salt
- ½ t. MSG
- ⅛ t. black pepper
- ½ t. sesame oil
- 1 T. shredded ginger root
}

❶ Remove skin from winter melon and cut melon meat into 48 pieces (2x1x⅔-inch). Make a horizontal slit in each piece through thickness to create a "pocket" for ham slices.

❷ Slice pork loin into thin, bite-size pieces and mix with ① ; cook in boiling water until pieces change color; remove and drain. Soften black mushrooms in warm water and drain; remove stems (discard) and cut caps into quarters.

❸ Cook the winter melon pieces in boiling water for 1 minute; remove, drain and insert a slice of ham in "pocket" of each piece of winter melon. Arrange winter melon slices to line a medium-sized soup bowl; add pork loin slices and mushroom quarters on top and pack securely; pour ② over all and place in steamer. Steam 10 minutes over high heat; remove and drain liquid and add to ③ . Invert winter melon into a serving bowl and demold; heat ③ until boiling; pour into soup bowl and sprinkle shredded ginger on top; serve.

■ When removing skin from winter melon, leave a thin layer of green skin to add to attractiveness of mold.

冬瓜半個…(約)5斤	鴨肉(切丁)……1杯	高湯…6杯
干貝…………2個	洋菇(切丁)……半杯	鹽…2小匙
冬菇(泡軟切丁)¼杯	濕蹄筋(切丁)…¼杯	味精1小匙
瘦火腿(切丁)1大匙	鴨肫(除皮切丁)¼杯	
薑…………6片	蓮子…………¼杯	

❶ 冬瓜頭一節（約７～８吋長），在冬瓜切口處刻花，瓜核全部取出洗淨，用開水煮約２０分鐘，再用清水漂涼。

❷ 將干貝加水¼杯蒸爛，撕成絲，②料放入滾水內，川燙約３０秒撈出。

❸ 將①料、②料、③料，倒入冬瓜盅內，（湯加到瓜盅９分滿）中火蒸約１小時以上，即可供食。

■ 此湯適宜夏季宴客，清爽可口、家庭做可將使用材料簡化、濕蹄筋、鴨肫、蓮子免用。

錦繡冬瓜盅 Eight-Treasure Soup in Winter Melon
廣東菜 Cantonese　12人份 12 servings

- ½ winter melon (about 7lbs.)
- 2 dried scallops
- ¼ C. diced pre-softened Chinese black mushrooms
- 1 T. diced precooked Chinese ham
- 6 slices ginger root

(1)

- 1 C. diced duckling meat
- ½ C. diced button mushrooms
- ¼ C. diced pork tendons
- ¼ C. diced duckling gizzards
- ¼ C. pre-softened lotus seeds

(2)

- 6 C. stock
- 2 t. salt
- 1 t. MSG

(3)

❶ Trim winter melon to 7 inches high; cut a design around side as illustrated in picture; remove seeds and clean out inside. Place winter melon in boiling water to cover and cook 20 minutes over medium heat; remove and place in cold water to cool; drain.

❷ Rinse scallops and place in ¼C. water; steam ½ hour until soft; shred. Cook each ingredient of ② separately in boiling water for 30 seconds; remove and drain.

❸ Place ingredients of ① , ② and ③ in winter melon (liquid should fill only 90% of winter melon*); place in steamer and steam 1 hour over medium heat; serve.

■ This is a refreshing summer soup.

* If the hole in the winter melon is too small to hold 6C. stock; reduce the amount of ingredients in ③ to half.

小排骨……12兩

①
醬油………1大匙
鹽…………半小匙
味精………半小匙
糖…………2小匙
五香粉……半小匙
醋…………半大匙
蒜(剁碎)…半大匙
番薯粉……2大匙
(或太白粉)

「炸油」………6杯
葱…………2枝
白蘿蔔………1斤
(或芋頭切片炸香)

②
高湯……4杯
鹽…………1小匙
味精………半小匙
胡椒………¼小匙
麻油………¼小匙
酒…………1小匙
香菜………2大匙

❶ 小排骨剁成3公分長計24塊，以①料拌醃20分鐘，炸時加番薯粉拌勻，白蘿蔔煮熟切塊備用。

❷ 「炸油」燒熱，中火先將排骨炸3分鐘，隨下葱同炸1分鐘至排骨呈金黃色撈出，裝於中碗，水燒開中火蒸30分鐘，上置白蘿蔔反扣於大湯碗內，加入燒開之②料上洒香菜即成。

排骨酥湯 Sparerib Soup

1 lb. spareribs

①
1 T. soy sauce
½ t. salt
½ t. MSG
2 t. sugar
½ t. 5-spice powder
½ T. vinegar
½ T. chopped garlic
2 T. cornstarch

6 C. oil for frying
2 stalks green onion
1⅓ lbs. Chinese turnip*

②
4 C. stock
1 t. salt
½ t. MSG
¼ t. black pepper
¼ t. sesame oil
1 t. rice wine
2 T. chopped coriander

❶ Cut the spareribs into 1-inch sections (about 24); add ① and mix; let soak 20 minutes. Add cornstarch and mix before deep-frying. Cook turnip 10 minutes in boiling water; remove, drain and roll-cut into bite-size pieces.

❷ Heat oil for deep-frying; deep-fry spareribs 3 minutes; add green onion stalks and deep-fry an additional minute (spareribs should be golden brown); remove and drain. Arrange spareribs and onions in a medium-size bowl; place in steamer and steam 30 minutes over medium heat; remove and place turnip pieces on top; invert and demold onto a serving plate. Heat ② until boiling and pour over sparerib mold; sprinkle chopped coriander on top and serve.

* You may substitute 1⅓ lbs. taro root, cut into thin slices and fried until golden for turnip.

	小排骨‥‥‥‥‥4兩		黃豆芽‥‥‥‥‥‥6兩
①	水‥‥‥‥‥‥‥9杯		番茄(小)‥‥‥‥‥1個
	薑‥‥‥‥‥‥‥2片	②	鹽‥‥‥‥‥‥‥2小匙
			味精‥‥‥‥‥‥1小匙

❶ 排骨切小塊，與番茄分別在開水內川燙一下撈起，把番茄去皮去籽，切丁備用。

❷ 油2大匙燒熱，將番茄略炒盛起。

❸ 排骨放入①料內燒沸，改用小火煮40分鐘後，再加黃豆芽，炒好的番茄及②料續煮20分鐘即可。

排骨黃豆芽湯 Bean Sprout and Sparerib Soup

四川菜　Szechuan
12人份　**12 servings**

	4 oz. spareribs	6 oz. bean sprouts	
①	9 C. water	1 small tomato	
	2 slices ginger root	2 t. salt	②
		1 t. MSG	

❶ Cut spareribs into bite-size pieces; blanch tomato in boiling water and remove skin; remove seeds and dice.

❷ Heat pan and 2T. oil; stir-fry diced tomato for about 30 seconds and remove.

❸ In a pan, add spareribs and ① ; heat until boiling and then reduce heat to low and simmer 40 minutes; add bean sprouts, tomato and ② ; cook an additional 20 minutes and remove to serving bowl; serve.

蘿蔔絲	2杯	水	8杯
活鯽魚（約４〜５條）	1斤	① 鹽	2小匙
葱（３公分長）	6枝	味精	1小匙
薑	6片	雞油	1大匙

❶ 猪油６大匙燒熱，把魚煎至兩面金黃色後，將魚鏟開，葱薑炒香，隨即下酒１大匙，加①料及蘿蔔絲，蓋鍋以中火燒煮，約２０分鐘，見魚湯燒至乳白色，澆上熟雞油１大匙即可。

■ 食時先將鯽魚置盤，上洒蒜末、薑末、醬油、醋等，以免魚刺及魚肉混魚湯中。

蘿蔔丝鯽魚湯 Shredded Turnip and Fish Soup　上海菜 Shanghai　12人份 12 servings

2　C. shredded turnip
4–5 small crucian*[1] (about 1⅓ lbs.)
6　1-inch sections green onion
6　slices ginger root

① {
8　C. water
2　t.　salt
1　t.　MSG
}
1　T. melted chicken fat

❶ Heat pan and 6T. oil; fry fish on both sides until golden brown; push fish to the side of the pan and stir-fry green onion and ginger until fragrant; add 1T. rice wine and ① . Add shredded turnip and cook over medium heat for 20 minutes until liquid has turned a white color; add melted chicken fat and remove to serving bowl*[2], serve.

*[1] If crucian is unavailable, substitute pickerel or another small, fresh water fish.

*[2] Before serving this soup, the fish may be removed, placed on a serving plate and topped with a sauce made of chopped garlic, ginger, soy sauce, and vinegar. It may then be served separately with the soup.

①里肌肉…12片
醬油……1小匙
太白粉…1小匙

②水…………3杯
鹽………1小匙
味精……1小匙

③細粉………半把
榨菜……12片
小黃瓜…12片

④葱花……1大匙
胡椒……¼小匙
麻油……半小匙
醬油……半小匙

❶ 里肌肉調①料，細粉用熱水泡軟備用。

❷ 油2大匙燒熱，中火把里肌肉炒熟盛起，將②料燒開，放入肉片及③料即可起鍋倒入置有④料的湯碗內即成。

■ 榨菜及小黃瓜放入湯內，應即離火，否則不脆就不好吃了。

榨菜細粉湯 Szechuan Mustard Green and Bean Thread Soup

四川菜　Szechuan
6人份　6 servings

① 2 oz. pork loin
1 t. soy sauce
1 t. cornstarch

② 3 C. water
1 t. salt
1 t. MSG

③ ½ package bean threads
¼ C. thinly sliced Szechuan pickled mustard green
½ C. thinly sliced cucumbers

④ 1 T. chopped green onion
¼ t. black pepper
½ t. sesame oil
½ t. soy sauce

❶ Slice pork loin into paper-thin pieces; mix with ① . Soften bean threads in warm water and drain; cut in half.

❷ Heat pan and 2T. oil; stir-fry pork slices until color changes; remove. Heat ② until boiling and add pork slices and ③ . Prepare ④ and place in serving bowl; when mixture boils again, pour into prepared serving bowl and serve.

■ Szechuan pickled mustard green and cucumber slices should not be over cooked to retain their crunchiness.

	干貝………2個	紅葱頭…4粒		鹽………半小匙		高湯…………⎫	
	火腿絲……¼杯	蝦仁…2兩		味精………1小匙		蒸干貝餘汁 ⎬6杯	
①	冬菇絲……¼杯	絞肉…6兩	②	胡椒………¼小匙	③	鹽…………1小匙	
	熟筍絲……半杯			麻油………半小匙		味精………1小匙	
	熟紅蘿蔔絲…半杯			太白粉…半大匙		酒…………1小匙	
				蛋2個煎成蛋皮		胡椒………¼小匙	
						麻油………半小匙	

❶ 干貝加水¼杯，蒸軟撕細絲。

❷ 紅葱頭切片小火炸香，連同蝦仁（剁碎）、絞肉及②料攪勻，加①料（½）拌勻即為餡。

❸ 備中碗1只塗油，蛋皮舖上（干貝絲放中間）再將餘½①料順序排列在四週，中間以餡填滿，
大火蒸約４０分鐘取出，反扣在湯碗內，蛋皮用刀劃開成八片（下面3公分處連接），注入燒開
③料，掀開蛋皮成花瓣狀即可供食。

菊花干貝 Stuffed Egg Flower Soup

台灣菜 Taiwanese
12人份 12 servings

	2 dried scallops		1 t. salt		stock
	¼ C. shredded precooked Chinese ham		1 t. MSG		liquid from steaming scallops } 6 C.
①	¼ C. shredded presoftened Chinese black mushrooms	②	¼ t. black pepper	③	1 t. salt
	½ C. shredded precooked bamboo shoot		½ t. sesame oil		1 t. MSG
	½ C. shredded precooked carrot		½ T. cornstarch		1 t. rice wine
	4 shallots		2 eggs		¼ t. black pepper
	2 oz. raw, shelled shrimp				½ t. sesame oil
	6 oz. chopped pork				

❶ Add ¼C. water to scallops and steam ½ hour; remove and shred. (add liquid to ③). Beat eggs lightly;
heat a lightly oiled pan and add beaten eggs; rotate pan so that egg spreads evenly to coat pan and forms
a thin pancake. Cook until lightly brown and flip over to other side; cook a few more seconds until golden
and remove.

❷ Mince shallots and saute in 2T. oil until golden brown; remove and drain. Rinse and devein shrimp;
drain and chop finely, Mix chopped shrimp with chopped pork, ② and minced, sauteed shallots; add
½ of ① and mix together. (filling.)

❸ Lightly oil a medium-sized soup bowl; line the bowl with the egg sheet and sprinkle the shredded scallops
in the middle of sheet. Arrange the other half of ① on egg sheet in a decorative pattern; add filling on
top and pack down lightly; smooth top of filling with a spoon and place in steamer; steam 40 minutes
over high heat; remove. Drain off liquid from steaming (add to ③) and invert into a soup bowl; make
8 light diagonal cuts in egg sheet stopping 1 inch from edge of egg sheet. Heat ③ until boiling and pour
into serving bowl; open egg "petals" and serve.

<table>
<tr><td>猪腦‥‥‥‥‥1 付
冬菇 (泡軟)‥‥2 朵
圓玻璃紙‥‥‥1 張
（直徑２０公分）
雞肉‥‥‥‥‥3 兩
①{鹽‥‥‥‥‥⅛小匙
太白粉‥‥‥1 小匙</td><td>蘆筍丁‥‥‥‥½杯
②{雞蛋‥‥‥‥‥2 個
清水‥‥‥‥‥¾杯
鹽‥‥‥‥‥‥¾小匙
味精‥‥‥‥‥半小匙
酒‥‥‥‥‥‥1 小匙
葱薑末各‥‥1 小匙
芹菜末‥‥‥1 大匙</td><td>高湯‥‥‥‥‥4 杯
鹽‥‥‥‥‥‥1 小匙
③{味精‥‥‥‥半小匙
麻油‥‥‥‥半小匙
酒‥‥‥‥‥‥1 小匙</td></tr>
</table>

❶ 猪腦用火柴棒捲去上面一層筋略洗淨切塊。冬菇 1 朵切小丁，1 朵對切四瓣劃花。雞肉切丁，調①料醃約２０分鐘。

❷ 備 1 只中碗，將玻璃紙沾水舖底，先置四瓣冬菇，再將猪腦置上。

❸ ②料攪勻加入冬菇丁、雞肉丁、蘆筍丁，倒入已置好猪腦等之中碗內，中火蒸３０分鐘，用筷子插入見蛋液不沾筷子即熟，隨即反扣在大湯碗內倒入燒開③料，趁熱供食。

■ 爲求美觀可依個人喜好，排上火腿末、豌豆、紅蘿蔔等。

猪腦蒸蛋 Steamed Pork Brain and Eggs with Broth

台灣菜　Taiwanese
12人份　12 servings

1 pork brain 2 pre-softened Chinese black mushrooms 1 7-inch circle heavy-duty cellophane 3 oz. chicken meat ①{⅛ t. salt 1 t. cornstarch ½ C. diced asparagus	②{2 eggs ¾ C. water ¾ t. salt ½ t. MSG 1 t. rice wine 1 t. chopped green onion 1 t. chopped ginger root 1 T. chopped celery	③{4 C. stock 1 t. salt ½ t. MSG ½ t. seame oil 1 t. rice wine

❶ Using a matchstick, remove the thin outer membrane from the pork's brain; rinse and cut into bite-size pieces. Dice 1 black mushroom and cut the other into quarters; lightly score the tops of the quarters. Dice the chicken meat and mix with ① ; let soak 20 minutes.

❷ Rinse the cellophane in water and use it to line a medium-sized soup bowl; arrange the black mushroom quarters in the bottom of bowl, then add the pork brain pieces on top.

❸ Lightly beat the ingredients of ② ; add the diced mushroom, diced chicken meat and asparagus; mix lightly and pour into the bowl containing the pork brain. Place in steamer and steam 30 minutes over medium heat until egg has set (Test with a chopstick; when chopstick comes out clean, the egg is done); remove and invert into soup serving bowl. Heat ③ until boiling and pour into soup bowl over egg mold; serve.

■ Note: You may sprinkle chopped ham over egg mold and decorate the top with a green pea.

鮑魚⋯⋯⋯⋯半罐	①	高湯⋯⋯⋯⋯半杯	②	高湯⋯⋯⋯⋯4杯
熟豬肚⋯⋯⋯半個		鹽⋯⋯⋯⋯半小匙		鹽⋯⋯⋯⋯1小匙
鹹菜⋯⋯⋯⋯4兩		味精⋯⋯⋯¼小匙		味精⋯⋯⋯半小匙
熟筍⋯⋯⋯⋯1枝		酒⋯⋯⋯⋯1小匙		麻油⋯⋯⋯半小匙
				酒⋯⋯⋯⋯1小匙

❶ 鮑魚、豬肚、鹹菜、筍各切長方片（6公分×2公分）。

❷ 備中碗先將鮑魚片按照順序相疊排在內圈，豬肚片以同樣方式排在外圈，空間處以鹹菜、筍片及剩餘鮑片、肚片填滿，並加①料蒸約15分鐘。

❸ 蒸好鮑魚等，上蓋一只盤子，將湯汁濾出加在②料內，隨即反扣在大湯碗內，倒入燒開之②料趁熱供食。

猪肚處理法：

❶ 將豬肚除去污油洗淨，從邊切開10公分翻面，再以粗鹽1大匙、醋1大匙搓揉至無黏液時，用水冲洗幹淨後，以開水燒煮3分鐘取起，用刀刮下白垢洗淨。

❷ 將水6杯，葱2枝，薑2片，酒1大匙連同洗淨豬肚放入快鍋，水開燒煮20分鐘即可。

鮑魚豬肚湯 Abalone with Pork Stomach in Broth
台灣菜　Taiwanese　12人份　12 servings

½　1-lb. can abalone
½　precooked pork stomach*
4　oz. pickled cabbage
1　precooked medium-sized bamboo shoot

① { ½　C. stock / ½　t. salt / ¼　t. MSG / 1　t. rice wine }

② { 4　C. stock / 1　t. salt / ½　t. MSG / ½　t. sesame oil / 1　t. rice wine }

❶ Slice abalone, pork stomach, pickled cabbage and bamboo shoot into thin slices 2-inches long and ⅔-inch wide.

❷ In a medium-sized soup bowl, arrange the abalone slices to line the center of bowl; arrange the pork stomach slices around the abalone slices. Place the pickled cabbage slices, bamboo shoot and any end pieces in the middle to fill the bowl; pack down securely and add ① . Place bowl in steamer and steam 15 minutes over medium heat; remove.

❸ Drain off liquid from steaming and add to ② ; invert bowl and demold into soup serving bowl. Heat ② until liquid begins to boil and pour into serving bowl; garnish top with a sprig of coriander.

* To pre-condition pork stomach:

❶ Remove any fat from pork stomach; cut the stomach horizontally about 3 inches long and turn inside out; rub exterior and interior surface thoroughly with 1T. salt and 1T. vinegar; rinse both surfaces repeatedly with cold water until both are rid of any slimy residue; drain and cook in boiling water for 3 minutes; remove and use the edge of cleaver to further scrape away any covering; rinse and drain.

❷ Place 6C. water, 2 stalks green onion, 2 slices ginger root, 1T. rice wine and pork stomach in a pressure cooker and cook 20 minutes until stomach is tender. (If no pressure cooker is available, cook ingredients in a covered pot for about 1 hour over medium heat; remove and use as directed).

① 鰱魚頭……1 斤
②{ 里肌肉……2 兩
　醬油……1 小匙
　太白粉…1 小匙
　熟紅蘿蔔片6片
　熟筍片…12片
　青江菜或大白菜1斤

①{ 醬油……1 大匙
　酒………1 小匙
　醋………1 小匙

冬粉………1 把
豆腐………1 塊
冬菇………3 朵
蒜苗………1 枝
③{ 水…………4 杯
　鹽……1½小匙

❶ 魚頭以①料醃約20分鐘，入油鍋兩面煎黃，置砂鍋內。

❷ 里肌肉切片，調②料。

❸ 青菜煮熟撈起，每棵剖開成四半，冬粉燙熟，豆腐切塊冬菇泡軟備用，蒜苗切段分蒜白及蒜葉。

❹ 油2大匙燒熱將蒜白下鍋炒香，加③料蓋鍋待滾，改小火煮30分鐘後，再將豆腐、冬菇、肉片及各料放入砂鍋內調入味精半小匙再煮約10分鐘，最後洒上蒜苗葉即成。

砂鍋魚頭　Stewed Fish Head Casserole

上海菜　Shanghai
6人份　6 servings

1　fish head (about 1⅓ lbs.)
①{ 1　T. soy sauce
　 1　t. rice wine
　 1　t. vinegar

2　oz. pork loin
②{ 1　t. soy sauce
　 1　t. cornstarch

6　slices precooked carrot
12　slices precooked bamboo shoot
1⅓ lbs. green cabbage*

1　package bean threads
1　square bean curd
3　dried Chinese black mushrooms
1　stalk fresh garlic or leek

③{ 4　C. water
　 1½ t.　salt
　 ½　t.　MSG

❶ Clean fish head and mix with ① ; let soak 20 minutes; drain head and retain liquid. Heat pan and 4T. oil; fry fish head on both sides until golden; remove and place in casserole.

❷ Cut pork into paper-thin bite-size slices; mix with ②

❸ Precook green cabbage in boiling water about 1 minute; cut each stalk into 4 sections. Cut bean threads in half and soften in hot water; remove and drain. Cut bean curd into 8 squares; soften black mushrooms in warm water; remove stems (discard) and cut caps into bite-size pieces. Diagonally shred garlic stalk and separate white and green sections.

❹ Heat pan and 2T. oil; stir-fry white garlic shreds until fragrant; add ③ and cover; simmer 30 minutes over low heat. Add bean curd, bean threads, pork loin, vegetables and ½t MSG; cover and cook 10 minutes more. Sprinkle green garlic sections over top and serve.

* Green cabbage ("chin jian tsai") is the pictured Chinese vegetable and may be purchased at a Chinese grocery store. If unavailable, substitute cabbage or broccoli.

嫩豆腐……3塊　　蝦仁…………半杯　　　　高湯…………4杯
冬菇………4朶　　①{酒…………1小匙　②{鹽…………2小匙
筍片………半杯　　太白粉……2小匙　　　味精………半小匙
　　　　　　　　　熟肉片………半杯
　　　　　　　　　蒜苗(切片)…¼杯

❶ 豆腐切塊，冬菇泡軟，蝦仁調上①料。

❷ 取一砂鍋，入②料及豆腐、冬菇、筍，待燒開即改小火，煮約半小時，臨起鍋前，投入蝦仁、肉片、蒜苗及味精半小匙即成。

■ 砂鍋保溫，此爲冬天美食。

砂鍋豆腐 Bean Curd Potage

北平菜　　Peking
6人菜　　6 servings

- 3　squares bean curd
- 4　Chinese black mushrooms
- ½　medium-sized precooked bamboo shoot (approx. ¾C.)
- 2　oz. raw, shelled shrimp

①{ 1　t.　rice wine
　2　t.　cornstarch

- ½　C. precooked slices pork loin
- ¼　C. diagonally shredded fresh garlic or leek

②{ 4　C. stock
　2　t. salt
　½　t. MSG

❶ Cut each bean curd into 8 squares; soften black mushrooms in warm water and cut into bite-size pieces. Cut bamboo shoot to thin, bite-size pieces. Rinse and devein shrimp; drain and mix with ① .

❷ Pour ② into casserole; add bean curd, black mushroom and bamboo shoot. When liquid begins to boil, cover and simmer 30 minutes over low heat. Add shrimp, pork loin, shredded garlic and MSG; cook an additional minute until shrimp change color; remove and serve.

■ This soup is ideal for winter-eating.

白菜……2斤半
絞肉……12兩

① {
鹽…………1小匙
味精………半小匙
麻油………半大匙
酒…………半小匙
胡椒………¼小匙
葱花………1小匙
薑末………1小匙
太白粉……半大匙
}

② {
太白粉……半大匙
醬油………半大匙
水…………半大匙
}

③ {
味精………¼小匙
鹽…………半小匙
醬油………1大匙
}

❶ 白菜洗淨，取4大片留用，其餘切5公分長段，油6大匙燒熱，略炒白菜，加水2杯燒煮5分鐘後置砂鍋內。

❷ 絞肉加①料拌勻，甩打數下後分做成四個肉丸子，沾上②料，放入油鍋兩面煎黃，即可置白菜上，最上面再以四張白菜葉蓋在肉丸上，調入③料慢火煮約1小時，即可供食。

砂鍋獅子頭 Lion's Head Casserole

上海菜　Shanghai
12人份　12 servings

3⅓ lbs. Chinese cabbage
1 lb. chopped pork

① {
1 t. salt
½ t. MSG
½ T. sesame oil
½ t. rice wine
¼ t. black pepper
1 t. chopped green onion
1 t. chopped ginger root
½ T. cornstarch
}

② {
½ T. cornstarch
½ T. soy sauce
½ T. water
}

③ {
¼ t. MSG
½ t. salt
1 T. soy sauce
}

❶ Rinse cabbage lightly and remove 4 outer leaves (retain); tear rest of cabbage into 2-inch squares; drain. Heat pan and 6T. oil; stir-fry cabbage sections until soft and add 2C. water; cook for 5 minutes over medium heat; remove and place in the bottom of a heatproof casserole.

❷ Chop pork finely and mix with ① ; lightly throw mixture against inside of mixing bowl to combine ingredients; separate into 4 portions and shape into balls. Coat each ball with pre-mixed ② . Heat pan and 6T. oil; fry pork balls on all sides until golden brown; remove and place on cabbage in casserole; cover pork balls with 4 outer cabbage leaves and add ③ ; cover and simmer 1 hour over low heat; serve.

海參……… 1 斤		多菇（切片）……6 朶		③	多粉（1 把）3 兩	魷魚（燙熟切花）1 條
①	葱……… 2 枝	熟紅蘿蔔片… 1 2 片			白菜（切塊）2 斤	如意捲……… 1 2 片
	薑……… 2 片	熟筍片……… 1 2 片	②		高湯……… 1 0 杯	
	酒…… 1 大匙	魚丸……… 1 2 個		④	鹽……… 1 大匙	
		蝦丸……… 1 2 個			味精…… 1 小匙	
		叉燒肉（切片）… 3 兩				

❶ 海參切長條，油2大匙燒熱，炒香①料加酒1大匙、水4杯燒開放入海參煮5分鐘撈起備用。

❷ ③料分別燙熟。

❸ 火鍋內先放白菜，上置其他各料（如圖狀）並注入④料至七分滿，煙筒內加炭點燃上桌即可，邊煮邊吃，湯和佐料可隨時補充。

■ 如意捲請參照本書第203頁清湯如意捲做法，火鍋材料可用蝦、雞肉、豬肉、牛肉、蹄筋、鵪蛋、豬肚、豬肝、唐好菜、菠菜、荷蘭豆、白蘿蔔、菜心……等，任意選用。

什錦火鍋 Ten-Flavor Fire-Pot

台灣菜　Taiwanese
12人份　12 servings

	1⅓ lbs.sea cucumbers*1	6	slices pre-softened Chinese black mushrooms	③	1 2oz. package bean threads
①	2 stalks green onion	12	thin slices precooked carrot		2⅔ lbs.Chinese cabbage
	2 slices ginger root	12	thin slices precooked bamboo shoot		10 C. stock
	1 T. rice wine	12	meatballs*2	④	1 T. salt
		12	shrimp balls*3		1 t. MSG
		3	oz. roasted pork or precooked pork, beef or chicken		
		1	squid (about 6oz.)		
		12	½-inch sections "Egg & Shrimp Rolls"		

❶ Cut sea cucumbers into bite-size pieces. Heat pan and 2T. oil; stir-fry ① until fragrant; add rice wine and 4C. water; when liquid boils, add sea cucumber and cook 5 minutes; remove and drain (discard liquid). Prepare squid as directed in steps ❶ and ❷, "Stir-Fried Squid with Dried Red Peppers".

❷ Rinse cabbage and drain; cut leaves into bite-size pieces and cook in boiling water until soft and fragrant. Soften bean threads in hot water; remove and drain.

❸ Using a Mongolian Fire-pot , portion cabbage pieces in the bottom of the pot; portion helpings of each ingredient on cabbage as illustrated; add ④ to fill 70% of pot; heat fire or turn on heat and cook until liquid boils. Each person helps himself by taking ingredients as desired from fire-pot; add ingredients and stock as necessary.

*1 See note on pre-conditioning cucumbers in "Pork Balls and Sea Cucumbers" on P. 128.

*2 Prepare meatballs as directed in "Pork Balls and Sea Cucumbers".

*3 Prepare shrimp balls as directed in "Fried Shrimp Balls" on P. 111.

■ You may also make a make-shift Mongolian Fire-pot by using a shallow soup pot over an electric hot plate.

燕窩……1 兩	酒………半大匙		太白粉……4 大匙
①{ 高湯……1 杯	高湯………6 杯	③{	水………4 大匙
鹽……¼ 小匙	②{ 鹽………2 小匙		蛋白………2 個
	味精……1 小匙	④{	水………2 大匙
	麻油……1 小匙	豆苗(8公分長)2 0 枝	

❶ 燕窩選擇色白無燕毛者爲佳，先放入熱水（6杯）內浸泡3小時瀝乾，如燕毛太多，可加油半大匙，輕輕漂洗，燕窩細毛即隨油漂浮水面，如未漂淨時，反覆用熱水加油，漂洗至色白無黑雜質爲佳。

❷ 將乾淨燕窩加①料蒸3 0分鐘後，倒入②料燒開，以③料勾汁，立即熄火，並把預先打勻之④料徐徐加入，用鍋鏟攪勻，最後放入豆苗及熟油1大匙即可。

一品燕窩 Bird's Nest Soup

廣東菜　Cantonese
12人份　12 servings

1 oz. bird's nest	½ T. rice wine	③{ 4 T. cornstarch
①{ 1 C. chicken stock	6 C. stock	4 T. water
¼ t. salt	②{ 2 t. salt	④{ 2 egg whites
	1 t. MSG	2 T. water
	1 t. sesame oil	20 spinach leaves

❶ Choose a bird's nest with a white color and no feathers; place in 6C. water and let soak 3 hours or longer; drain. If any feathers remain, pour ½T. oil over bird's nest and rinse lightly until clean. (The oil will attract and collect the feathers.)

❷ Place bird's nest in a heatproof pot; add ① and place in steamer, steam 30 minutes over medium heat; add ② and place over fire. Heat until boiling and add ③ to thicken; turn off heat. Lightly beat ④ and slowly add to heated soup; add spinach leaves and 1T. oil; mix lightly and serve.

令您
賞心悦目的叢書

A Series of Books for
Your Pleasure and Enjoyment

中國菜

我們為了要把中國人吃的藝術貢獻給海內外的每一個家庭,特精選代表我國各地口味之佳餚393道編寫成「中國菜」,此本食譜係以16開精裝本彩色印刷,圖片清晰,說明詳細,實用易學。

CHINESE CUISINE Wei-Chuan's Cookbook

In this new edition of "CHINESE CUISINE" we have selected 221 recipes that represent the wide variety of Chinese food. We hope this will give every family the opportunity to better learn the art of Chinese cooking. The recipes are published in full color with clear pictures and detailed directions for practical usage.

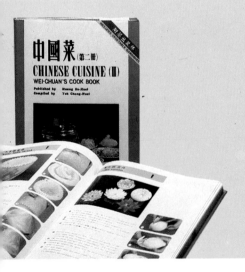

中國菜 (第二册)

黃淑惠女士另一本完美的中國烹飪食譜—"中國菜Ⅱ"又出版了!它是以中英對照版來發行,本書裡有如極富盛名的中國菜和中國餐點一樣,精美的彩色圖片及做法說明,書中附有餐盤裝飾—以各種不同的水果及蔬菜來當盤飾,使您不但可以做出美味可口的中國菜,同時也能擺出如書上所示,既簡單且優雅的盤飾。

CHINESE CUISINE II Wei-Chuan's Cookbook

Ms. Huang Su Huei has published another beautiful Chinese cookbook. CHINESE CUISINE II, published in Chinese-English bilingual has the same excellent quality of full-color photographs and clearly written directions that have made CHINESE CUISINE and CHINESE SNACKS so popular. This book includes an entire section on the preparation of garnishes. A variety of fruits and vegetables are used as garnishes. You will not only be able to prepare delicious Chinese food, but also be able to serve it with the simple yet elegant garnishes shown in this book.

味全 ❀ wei·chuan publishing co.,ltd

出版社有限公司　台北市仁愛路4段28號2樓 2ND FL., 28 JEN AI ROAD, SEC.4, TAIPEI, TAIWAN 106, REP. OF CHINA TEL.(02) 7021148•70211

中國餐點

「中國餐點」一書係搜集我國各省馳名點心及簡餐223道滙編而成，內容包括麵點類、米點類、食品加工類及國外點心等等，每道點心除附有彩色圖片及做法說明外，並配有製作步驟的小圖片說明，文字與圖片相互配合使您一目了然，一學就會。

CHINESE SNACKS Wei-Chuan's Cookbook

CHINESE SNACKS is a collection of 185 kinds of the most famous snacks from every region of China. This edition includes flour and rice products as well as other snack specialities. The recipes are illustrated in full color and give detailed directions. There are also small pictures which show step-by-step procedures to follow in applying specialized cooking techniques. As a whole, the combination of pictures and directions will enable you, as a neophyte or as an expert, to understand easily and to succeed on the first try.

中國菜 實用專輯

"中國菜實用專輯"，係精選89道菜，內附10道點心，道道易學，樣樣可口，平裝精印（ 7¼"×10½"）彩色介紹，附有製作步驟的小圖片解說，深入淺出，是居家宴客不可缺少的良伴。

CHINESE COOKING for Beginners Wei-Chuan's Cookbook

This soft cover "CHINESE COOKING FOR BEGINNERS" (size 7¼" x 10½") is authored by Ms. Huang Su-Huei. There are 79 tasty dishes and 10 delicious snacks in this cookbook, with clear directions and color pictures of illustrations. You can try all these recipes by yourself; you will find that Chinese cooking is easy and enjoyable!

愛與美 插花

這是一本設計新穎，印刷精美，用圖解說明學習簡易的插花參考書，也是一部美化家庭環境，增進生活情趣的寶典。

MEDITATIONS ON NATURE The Art of Flower Arrangement

This book is artistically designed and printed in full color. The sketches and photos in the book will help you to learn this beautiful art more easily. The book is indispensable in adding beauty to your life and daily environment.

wei·chuan's cooking
(COOKING SCHOOL AND BOOK SALES)

1434 South Atlantic Blvd.
Alhambra, CA. 91803 USA
Tel: (213) 289-8288, 289-8289
Effective Jan. 7, 1984 area code will
change from (213) to (818)

烹飪班 Cooking Class

學習內容／

宴席菜、家常菜、中西點心。
油條、燒餅、豆漿、豆腐、春捲皮、北平烤
鴨、鹽水鴨、牛豬肉干、肉鬆、肉脯等。

Subjects:

Banquet Cuisine, Home Cuisine, Chinese and
Western Snacks.
Twisted cruller, baked cake, bean milk, bean
curd, spring roll, Peking roasted duck, spicy
salted duck, dried and seasoned beef and pork
slices, meat fluff, and dried and seasoned meat.

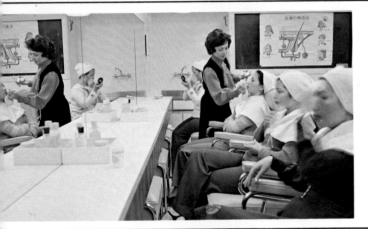

插花班 Flower Arrangement

學習內容／

初級班二個月：基本型的插法
中級班四個月：基本型應用、並列型、小品
花、瓶花、下垂型。
研　究　班：寫景、非寫實、瓶花、應用型。

Subjects:

Basic course: Basic arrangement for two
months.
Middle course: Applied arrangement for four
months.
Advanced course: Comprehensive arrangement
and vase alternation for two months.

美容班 Make-up Class

學習內容／

保　養：皮膚保養　頭髮保養
化　粧：普通化粧　流行化粧

Subjects:
Maintenance:
skin care, nighttime skin care, use of face
beautifier, hair care.
Make-up:
ordinary make-up, fashion make-up.

縫紉班 Sewing Class

學習內容／

初級三個月：裙子、襯衫、長褲、洋裝、童
裝等。
中級三個月：夾裡服裝(裙子、洋裝、套裝等)
高級三個月：自由變化、製作。

Subjects:
Basic course: skirt, shirt, trousers, Western and
children's dresses for three months.
Middle course: Dress with lining (skirt, Western
dress and suit) for three months.
Advanced course: Free alterations and creation
for three months.

味全家政班　　**Dept. of Home Economics Wei-Chuan Foods Corp.**
台北市松江路125號5樓　5th Fl., 125, Sung Kiang Rd., Taipei, Taiwan, Rep. of China
電話：(02)551-3564・521-4331　Tel: (02) 551-3564, 521-4331

中國菜

味全食譜

	著作權執照號碼
版權所有	台內著字第4160號

編　著　黃　淑　惠

出版者　味全食品工業股份有限公司
　　　　　附設家政短期職業補習班

發行者　黃　淑　惠
　　　　　味全出版社有限公司
　　　　　台北市仁愛路四段28號2樓
　　　　　電話／702-1148・702-1149
　　　　　　　　704-2729
　　　　　郵政劃撥18203號

中華民國61年元月初版發行
中華民國63年10月增修發行
中華民國65年 5 月創新發行
中華民國72年 2 月創新發行B9版

中華彩色印刷公司　承印